Nishi Amane
and Modern Japanese Thought

Nishi Amane

AND MODERN JAPANESE

THOUGHT

By Thomas R. H. Havens

Princeton University Press

Princeton, New Jersey

1970

This book has been composed in Linotype Times Roman

Publication of this book has been aided by
a grant from the Whitney Darrow Publication Reserve Fund
of Princeton University Press

Printed in the United States of America
by Princeton University Press
Princeton, New Jersey

For My Parents

Preface

The life of the mind is a subject of historical inquiry that is fraught with evanescent pitfalls, but it is also a fascinating and fruitful area of research. Both the hazards and the rewards are usually increased when a foreigner confronts the intellectual history of Japan. The language, culture, and traditions of Japan loom formidably before the historian, but the dividends which accrue from his investigations can be measured both by the insight into the Japanese mind offered by the non-Japanese writer and by a broadened grasp of the Japanese intellectual tradition in a comparative context. Nineteenth-century Japan, the setting for this book, presents particularly rich opportunities for the historian of thought because the major currents of Chinese philosophy, native Japanese ideology, and Western social theory ran strong during the years treated here.

I am indebted to the editors of the *Journal of Asian Studies* for permission to reprint in Chapters IV and VI portions of my article, "Comte, Mill, and the Thought of Nishi Amane in Meiji Japan," *Journal of Asian Studies*, XXVII, 2 (February 1968), pp. 217-228. The editor of *Modern Asian Studies* has kindly given permission to incorporate portions of my article, "Scholars and Politics in Nineteenth-century Japan: The Case of Nishi Amane," *Modern Asian Studies*, II, 4 (October 1968), pp. 315-324.

The Foreign Area Fellowship Program provided generous financial assistance for my research, and Connecticut College has granted funds to support part of the writing of this book.

It is a pleasant duty to acknowledge my gratitude to many friends for their assistance in preparing this study. I am particularly indebted to Professor Kazue Kyōichi, of Chuo University, Tokyo, whose patient and instructive guidance has helped me greatly. I am also grateful for the cogent comments and wise counsel of the late Professor Joseph R. Levenson. I am very grateful to Professor Delmer M. Brown for supervising my research with insight and care. I have greatly profited from the advice and criticisms of Professors F. Edward

Preface

Cranz, H. D. Harootunian, Marius B. Jansen, Kawahara Hiroshi, Douglas E. Mills, Murakami Toshiharu, Ōkubo Toshiaki, Irwin Scheiner, Donald H. Shively, Umetani Noboru, and V. H. Viglielmo. The following individuals gave me generous assistance with the materials: Mr. D. de Roo van Alderwerelt, Professor Hayashi Takeji, Mr. Nishi Kaneo (Nishi Amane's grandnephew), Mr. Nishi Torioto (Nishi Amane's grandson), Professor Nobuya Bamba, Professor Ōkubo Toshiaki, Professor Tanegashima Tokiyasu, and Mr. Eiji Yutani and Mrs. Kiyoko Koessel of the East Asiatic Library, University of California, Berkeley.

For assistance in preparing the manuscript, I am indebted to Mrs. Grace O'Connell, Miss Lissa K. Vogt, Miss Elizabeth Jolly Heath, and my wife, Betsy F. Havens. I am grateful to Miss R. Miriam Brokaw and the staff of Princeton University Press for expert editorial care. Responsibility for errors of fact, translation, or interpretation rests wholly with the author.

THOMAS R. H. HAVENS

New London, Connecticut
September 1969

Contents

Note

The 1954 edition of *Kenkyusha's New Japanese-English Dictionary* has served as the authority for romanizing Japanese terms. Macrons have been used to indicate long vowels in all words save the most familiar proper nouns. The Wade-Giles system has been followed for Chinese terms. Japanese names are given in the customary Japanese manner, with the family name preceding the personal name, except for cases of Western language publications in which Japanese authors have chosen to place their personal names first. For the sake of consistency, dates have been converted to the Gregorian calendar, except for instances in which reference is made to specific months in the lunar calendar, e.g., "the tenth month of 1857." A section containing brief biographies of the major figures in Nishi's career appears at the end of the main text. A list of works cited is included at the end of the book.

Nishi Amane
and Modern Japanese Thought

one

The Intellectual in Japan's Transition from Feudalism to Modernism

The politicians, journalists, commercial and industrial entrepreneurs, educators, bureaucrats, and scholars who guided the Japanese nation through the first two turbulent decades of the Meiji period (1868-1912) disagreed among themselves on many issues, but one thing to which nearly all assented was the pressing need to root out the "evil customs and absurd usages" of their country's feudal past.

This was no mere academic question in the nineteenth-century context. The mature feudalism of sixteenth-century Japan had developed by 1603 into a more advanced form of feudalism unparalleled in European history: the *bakuhan* system of the Edo period (1603-1868). Japanese politics during this era was characterized by the overlordship of the Tokugawa family military government (*bakufu*), beneath which some 250 domains (*han*) exercised regional hegemony. The elaborate control devised by Tokugawa Ieyasu (1542-1616), the first shogun, and his successors had not remained a frozen institutional apparatus throughout the long Edo period, but Japanese political culture, and to a considerable degree Japanese civilization as a whole, remained staunchly feudal until the arrival of the West in 1853.[1] Once the imperial restoration of 1868 had been safely accomplished and Japan had embarked on her historic path toward modernization, the early Meiji leaders perceived the urgency of putting their feudal tradition squarely behind them. Only by renouncing their historical experience, they were convinced, could Japan hope to catch up with the contemporary

[1] See Toshio G. Tsukahira, *Feudal Control in Tokugawa Japan: The Sankin Kōtai System* (Cambridge, Mass., 1966), and Conrad Totman, *Politics in the Tokugawa Bakufu 1600-1843* (Cambridge, Mass., 1967).

The Intellectual in Japan's Transition

West and share equal footing with the countries of Western Europe as a modern, progressive state.

This rejection of the past included Japan's intellectual heritage, which was mainly Confucian. Fukuzawa Yukichi (1834-1901), the most famous of the Meiji scholars, expressed his abhorrence of the feudal ideology in these words:

"It is not only that I hold little regard for the Chinese teaching, but I have even been endeavoring to drive its degenerate influences from my country. . . .

"The true reason for my opposing the Chinese teaching with such vigor is my belief that in this age of transition, if this retrogressive doctrine remains at all in our young men's minds, the new civilization cannot give its full benefit to this country. In my determination to save our coming generation, I am prepared even to face singlehanded the Chinese scholars of the country as a whole."[2]

In short, thinking men were prepared to do battle with their tradition on many fronts, including the realm of ideas as well as the sphere of institutions.

For very different reasons, the modern determinist historians in Japan have applauded their forebears' eagerness to "struggle against feudalism," believing that in struggle are the germs of inevitable historical process. Marxist historiography suffered grievous vicissitudes before World War II, because of the mercurial record of leftist movements in general and of the Japan Communist Party in particular. A good deal of the Marxist research in the late 1920's and 1930's was intended either to corroborate or attack the ever variable official line of the JCP, which was understandably more concerned with promoting political revolution than historical objectivity. Beginning with Kawakami Hajime's *Keizai taikō* (Principles of Economics), published in 1928, the major Marxist writers became involved in a lengthy and complicated intramural controversy known as the Kōza-Rōnō dispute on the nature of the Meiji restoration and the growth

[2] Fukuzawa Yukichi, *The Autobiography of Fukuzawa Yukichi,* tr. Eiichi Kiyooka (rev. ed., Tokyo, 1960), p. 216.

of Japanese capitalism.[3] The Kōza faction regarded the events of 1868 as a transfer of power from a feudal elite to a monarchist clique which had installed a teen-age emperor at the apex of an "absolutist" political hierarchy. Yet beneath this actuality was a frustrated potentiality: the restoration was also an incipient proletarian uprising, deriving its momentum from the city poor and the landless peasants. These elements, according to the Kōza view, were building a significant urban-agrarian lower-class movement until it was aborted by a counter-revolutionary alliance of former feudal leaders and merchant-capitalists. This development thwarted the proletarian revolution and led directly from feudalism to a new "absolutist" stage, in which the Meiji state not only failed to eradicate the dark stains of the past but also paved the way to imperialism. The Rōnō group, by contrast, interpreted the restoration as a fairly successful bourgeois revolution which initiated the arduous task of democratic reform. Although the job was far from finished in the 1930's, the Rōnō scholars maintained, Japan had now progressed sufficiently from its feudal past to permit a true proletarian socialist revolution.[4]

No matter how tempestuous the debates, however, few men in either camp questioned the Marxist assumption that history was a succession of developmental stages, among which was the stubborn weed, feudalism, that thrived in Japan until at least 1868. It was beyond doubt that the feudal stage had persisted uncommonly long in their country and that the attainment of democracy and socialism was contingent upon a revolt against the past. The issue between Kōza and Rōnō

[3] The Kōza group takes its name from *Nihon shihonshugi hattatsushi kōza*, 7 vols. (Tokyo, 1932-1933). The Rōnō group published a journal, *Rōnō*.

[4] The Rōnō faction denied that absolutism was inevitable and emphasized the external threat to Japan as a primary cause of the Meiji restoration. See Marius B. Jansen, "From Hatoyama to Hatoyama," *Far Eastern Quarterly*, xiv, 1 (November 1954), pp. 65-79; Hugh Borton, "Modern Japanese Economic Historians," *Historians of China and Japan*, ed. W. G. Beasley and E. G. Pulleyblank (London, 1961), pp. 289-295; and the special issue devoted to Japanese intellectuals, *Journal of Social and Political Ideas in Japan*, ii, 1 (April 1964).

was when, or whether, such a revolt had occurred and, if so, what shape it had taken. This assumption about the procession of historical stages still flourishes in postwar Japan, for example, in the works of Tōyama Shigeki, a leading contemporary scholar of the restoration. Tōyama attributes Japan's successful modernization to the purge of feudalism, especially because the catharsis was propelled by massive peasant uprisings in the mid-nineteenth century.[5] Thus, the Meiji reformers were effective in the degree to which they rooted out Japan's feudal vestiges, however ill-defined. (The works of E. H. Norman, who compiled massive evidence of "feudal decay" in late Tokugawa Japan, have lent further support to these views.) To all of this determinist persuasion, 1868 is a monument: sequentially, the restoration was a break with the past; in terms of value, that break was good to the extent that it was a clean one.

Not only was this outlook suspect because of the a priori ideological assumptions of its proponents; it also failed to stand the test of further research. A fresh evaluation of the link between Tokugawa feudalism and Meiji modernization has arisen since World War II, both in Japan and abroad. Simply stated, the new view is that the Tokugawa period was less an age of evil customs or Procrustean repressions than an era in which the foundations for modern nation-building were laid. Such writers as Albert Craig and Marius B. Jansen have not only refuted the Marxist interpretation of restoration politics in the vital domains of Chōshū and Tosa; they have also confirmed the essential political and social continuities during the changeover from feudal to modern Japan.[6] As a leading textbook puts it, "once Japan was launched on the course of modernization, certain underlying conditions made possible rapid progress, though most of these conditions had existed for at least a century without seriously affecting the Tokugawa regime."[7] Among the more

[5] Tōyama Shigeki, *Meiji ishin* (Tokyo, 1951).

[6] Albert Craig, *Chōshū in the Meiji Restoration* (Cambridge, Mass., 1961); Marius B. Jansen, *Sakamoto Ryōma and the Meiji Restoration* (Princeton, 1961).

[7] John K. Fairbank, Edwin O. Reischauer, and Albert M. Craig,

important were nationalist sentiments, a well-developed economy, the network of private and state-sponsored schools, a lessening degree of social hierarchy, strong administrative leadership, and the peculiar strength of the throne. Each constituted an inheritance that made it possible to achieve the Meiji goals of strength and wealth more rapidly and more completely than had Japan in fact been capable of a clean break with the past. In short, it is now commonly accepted that the Tokugawa experience, far from retarding subsequent modernization, was an essential cornerstone for the Meiji reforms.

Lurking behind this view, however, is the danger of rendering too favorable an appraisal of the pre-modern period. This rediscovery of the Edo era may be approaching the limits of its effectiveness, insofar as it tries to credit the success of modernization to feudal strengths. Postwar research has unquestionably yielded a valuable dividend in correcting various deterministic evaluations, and it has certainly begun to do justice to an epoch long ignored by historians. But it should not be forgotten that Tokugawa Japan was overwhelmingly feudal, not modern. Whatever signs of modernism appeared before 1853 did so in a setting vastly different from that of Meiji Japan: they remind us that coming events may cast their shadows before, but they are merely shadows, not substance. Without denying the important historical continuities at play, it should be remembered that Meiji Japan was above all an era of change.

Through the lenses of Fukuzawa and his peers, the degree and speed of this change are distorted; their lack of perspective has filled their works with an exaggerated sense of upheaval, drawing too sharp a line between Tokugawa and Meiji. They were wrong to dismiss their past as useless or irrelevant, but they were right that a fundamental intellectual reorientation and a basic institutional reorganization were necessary. Likewise, the Marxists have been too zealous in

A History of East Asian Civilization, II, *East Asia: The Modern Transformation* (Boston, 1965), p. 288.

labeling the restoration as a nascent proletarian uprising, but their studies have justly assessed the mammoth inhibitions which Tokugawa feudalism placed upon modernization.

This emphasis on change is particularly useful in analyzing the character of social and political thought in the early Meiji period. It is clear that in the case of a leading group of Japanese thinkers, the *keimō* (enlightenment) scholars of the 1870's, the overwhelming experience in their intellectual development was their contact with the novel doctrines of the contemporary West: positivism and utilitarianism. However much these intellectuals owed to their Confucian heritage, they thought of themselves as men of a new age, beholden to new teachings which they deemed requisite for the modern society they hoped to create. As always, both continuities and changes are at work in the history of Meiji thought, but of the two the latter is vastly more important.

This study is an inquiry into the nature of one man's intellectual response to the historical events of his lifetime. Nishi Amane (1829-1897), who was among the earliest Japanese scholars to acknowledge the cultural supremacy of Europe over Japan, was the first man sent abroad by his government to study the Western social sciences. Upon his return he introduced European concepts of natural and international law to Japan, but he is best known as the scholar who first brought positivism and utilitarianism back from abroad. Nishi was not the most eloquent nor the most important of the *keimō* scholars, nor was he typical of literate opinion in Japan as a whole. He was representative of the best thinking in early Meiji Japan, a scholar who was thoroughly familiar with the Confucian tradition but firmly committed to the doctrines of the modern West. It is Nishi as thinker, not philosopher, with whom I am concerned: the man thinking in his historical milieu, not pondering eternal truths. By understanding the logic of his intellectual position and the reasonableness of his attitudes, we may elucidate the dilemma of the man of letters in coming to grips with modernism. Throughout, I shall attempt to speak of significance, not influence, because

The Intellectual in Japan's Transition

Nishi was a man of great foresight rather than lasting impact. I shall try to show that Nishi's mental fibre was largely Western in composition and that, or perhaps therefore, his writings are highly relevant to understanding modern Japan. This is a study of the intellectually significant, not the biographically reconstructible, Nishi.

Before we turn to the issues which preoccupied Nishi and his generation, it will be useful to sketch the dimensions of Japan's intellectual ecumene immediately before Commodore Matthew C. Perry's visit in 1853. From today's perspective, it is the latter half of the nineteenth century in Japan that seems filled with chaos and violent changes, but to the observer of Japan in 1850, the first half of the century hardly appeared quiescent. The later Tokugawa period—especially after 1800—was a time of intense ideological ferment, when older dogmas were frequently subjected to oblique criticisms and occasionally to direct assault. Nishi was obliged to choose his own intellectual values in a climate of sharply contending doctrines and uncertain truths, in an age when time-honored philosophies no longer seemed adequate and newer ones were still untested.

If the political world of Tokugawa Japan was staunchly feudal, its intellectual realm was just as securely Confucian. A Japanese version of Sung period Confucianism supplied the philosophical underpinnings for the *bakufu* and social structure established by the Tokugawa family early in the seventeenth century. This Japanese Neo-Confucianism, known as Shushigaku, was an adaptation of the teachings of Chu Hsi (1130-1200) and of other Chinese scholars who had constructed a complex metaphysical system to supplement the ancient teachings of Confucius. In Shushigaku, great weight was given to "the way of mankind" (*jindō*), a formulation of ethical conduct that was officially sanctioned by the ruling Tokugawa house, in order to restore the social hierarchy that had been disrupted by a century of feudal wars. This conservative ethical schema assigned all members of society to their respective proper stations and insisted on the importance of personal morality to solidify the stratifica-

9

tion. Political leadership, in this system, was exercised by statesmen who were thought to be morally superior—as though selected by heaven rather than because of their personal achievements. The feudal warriors (samurai), functionless after the Tokugawa settlement of 1603, were the primary targets of Shushi teachings: they above all were obliged to uphold the five ethics and five virtues (*gorin gojō*) that were regularly promoted by Tokugawa orthodoxy. But whereas the customary five virtues of Chinese Confucianism had consisted of benevolence, justice, etiquette, wisdom, and fidelity, in Shushigaku they were redefined to comprise loyalty, filiality, duty, service to one's master (*hōkō*) and keeping to one's station (*bugen*).[8] The five Chinese ethics or relationships had normally emphasized loyalties to the family, but in Tokugawa Japan one's principal moral obligation was loyalty to the feudal lord. Hence from the moment it received official sponsorship, Edo period Neo-Confucianism was a different breed from the Sung original.

Formality and custom were the markings of Shushi teachings, resulting in a gradual decline in intellectual flexibility among Japanese Neo-Confucianists after the late seventeenth century. The Tokugawa shoguns, in electing to patronize Shushigaku, showed far more interest in the political and social usefulness of the Chinese ideology than in its metaphysical or philosophical ramifications. Ieyasu and the Hayashi scholars who advised him foreshadowed the fallacious "Eastern morality, Western technology" aphorism of the 1850's when they tried to import the utilitarian aspects of Chu Hsi without also accepting the Confucian culture-centrism prerequisite for that utility. Shushigaku possessed only sterile social theory and rusty moral exhortations: it lacked an examination system, a bureaucratic ethos, a mandate of heaven, and the other trappings of a celestial empire. Because Ieyasu failed to create the mechanisms within which

[8] Maruyama Masao, "Kaikoku—Opening of the Country," tr. Isono Fujiko (mimeo., 1958), p. 13. See also Ishida Ichirō, "Tokugawa Feudal Society and Neo-Confucian Thought," *Philosophical Studies of Japan*, v (1964), pp. 7-17.

The Intellectual in Japan's Transition

Neo-Confucianism could be really useful, and because such mechanisms would themselves have foundered without a firm commitment to the overweening culturalism of Confucianism, it is not surprising that Shushigaku failed to develop a significant tradition of metaphysical speculation or ethical introspection. Its aridity as a mere prescription for social ritual rendered it more and more intellectually vacuous and epistemologically confining as the Tokugawa era wore on.

Because of its hortatory, non-institutional nature, the official doctrine could not be rigidly enforced, and thus it is remarkable how late into the Edo period Shushigaku, for all its limitations, remained the dominant intellectual current.[9] Although Maruyama Masao is certainly right that true Neo-Confucianists considered criticism of the *bakufu* "not so much as a rebellion against their authority as a system leading directly to the collapse of morality and sanctities,"[10] no doubt the continuing preeminence of Shushigaku stemmed mainly from the political prestige of its patrons. So long as feudalism remained intact, Shushi ideologies retained a privileged status as the official rationale.

After the mid-point of the Edo era, nevertheless, Japan's intellectual life began to exhibit a remarkable flexibility that belied the Shushi supremacy. A number of important schools of thought started to challenge orthodox Neo-Confucianism after about 1725, producing an intellectual ferment of major proportions by the early nineteenth century. Out of this ferment emerged two major themes, which together ultimately overshadowed the official ideology and helped to lay the groundwork for the Meiji reforms. One was a consciousness of the nation-state as a unique entity founded on peculiarly Japanese myths and traditions and endowed with distinctive native institutions. The other was a new spirit of rationality and practicality in intellectual investigation. Each of these trends deserves some elaboration because of the

[9] Albert M. Craig has shown that Shushi teachings prevailed in Chōshū well into the Bakumatsu period (1853-1868). Craig, *Chōshū*, passim.

[10] Maruyama, "Kaikoku," p. 9.

11

critical role it played, once it was transformed by the coming of the West, in the restoration process and the creation of the Meiji state.

It is hazardous to speak with conviction about the growth of nationality consciousness in the history of a nation which has long perceived the remarkable distinctiveness of its own civilization. But it was in the later Tokugawa period that a consistent articulation of their awareness of nationality began to appear in the writings of several clusters of Japanese scholars, particularly among the members of the National Learning school (Kokugaku), the Wang Yang-ming school (Yōmeigaku), and the Mito school. National Learning grew up in the eighteenth century, when such writers as Kamo Mabuchi (1697-1769), Motoori Norinaga (1730-1801), and Hirata Atsutane (1776-1843), in reaction to the Chinese scriptural authority of Neo-Confucianism, started to idealize Japan's own ancient myths and traditions. Theirs was essentially an assault on the Chinese doctrine that political and moral truths were uniform throughout the world. What is more, by denouncing the corrupting influences of China, they hoped to clarify the real nature of early Japanese civilization and establish the superiority of Japan over all other lands.[11] Restoring the purity of Japanese culture was their crusade; the pure Japanese heart (*magokoro*) was their holy grail. For the most part, the Kokugaku scholars were content to pursue these atavistic ideals through literary and philological study, but one ideologically significant result of their investigations was the discovery that the shogun, who bore a Chinese-sounding title, was a mere latter-day vassal of the emperor and that it was the historical duty of all Japanese to be absolutely loyal to the throne. No matter how bookish or lacking in political content this assertion may have been, it represented a flouting of the priorities in the Shushi ethical code, implying a monistic pattern of national loyalties rather than the multi-centered labyrinth of *gorin gojō*. The talk of emperor and cultural uniqueness was something that might

[11] David M. Earl, *Emperor and Nation in Japan: Political Thinkers of the Tokugawa Period* (Seattle, 1964), pp. 66-81.

12

in a different season suddenly become vastly more relevant politically.

The Yōmeigaku school condemned Shushigaku not in terms of governmental authority but in the realm of individual ethics. It was one of the many varieties of Confucianism that sprang up in the eighteenth century; its adherents followed the teachings of the Neo-Confucian revisionist Wang Yang-ming (1472-1528), a Chinese military leader and introspective philosopher. Yōmeigaku thinkers such as Kumazawa Banzan (1619-1691) emphasized the inner spirit, not outward forms or principles, and they prided themselves on acting according to their own consciences.[12] This individualistic orientation was an implicit denial of the externally imposed moral codes of the Tokugawa regime, but it must be remembered that until very late in the Edo period Yōmeigaku remained the doctrine of a few isolated scholars and lacked any real corporate basis. Only in the Bakumatsu period (1853-1868) did it intrude upon politics: it was then that the Yōmeigaku spirit of sincerity and action had a great appeal to the samurai loyalists, or *shishi*, who wanted to subvert the feudal regime for which the rival Shushi school was the ideological justification. Both Yoshida Shōin (1830-1859), the martyred revolutionary, and Saigō Takamori (1827-1877), Satsuma leader in the restoration, were trained in Yōmei studies, from which each derived his commitment to the practical application of learning and the unity of knowledge and action.[13] Yōmeigaku fitted the Bakumatsu *shishi* ideology in its emphasis on the purity of purpose and sincerity of one's actions, so that samurai devoted to a lofty cause could defy the Shushi norms of the enfeebled *bakufu*. Yet it must be remembered that Yōmei doctrines contributed to this *shishi* ideology only in the context of an acute diplomatic and political emergency. It was not until 1853 that

---

[12] See *Sources of Japanese Tradition*, ed. Wm. T. de Bary (New York, 1958), pp. 378-392; Galen N. Fisher, "Kumazawa Banzan, His Life and Ideas," *Transactions of the Asiatic Society of Japan*, second series, 16 (1938), pp. 221-258.

[13] Earl, *Emperor and Nation*, p. 139; Jansen, *Sakamoto Ryōma*, p. 188.

The Intellectual in Japan's Transition

Yōmeigaku realistically augmented the nationality consciousness that was coalescing around the imperial throne through the desperate disruptions of the *shishi*.

The third important source of nationality sentiments, the Mito school, was a branch of Neo-Confucianism that concentrated on political and historical studies. Founded by Tokugawa Mitsukuni (1628-1700), the Mito school utilized Chinese historiographical methods to chronicle the dynastic legitimacy of the Japanese imperial system. The net effect of its major publication, the *Dai Nihonshi* (History of Japan), was to underscore the importance of the throne as the central force in Japanese history. Although their studies were confined to the ancient and medieval periods of Japanese history, these scholars found themselves, in effect, rationalizing the symbolic functions of the ceremonial emperor in a political culture dominated by the *de facto* power of the Tokugawa shoguns.[14] By stressing the preeminence of the concepts of loyalty and filiality (*chū* and *kō*) toward the imperial institution, Mito lent Chinese-style academic sanction to the sublimation of the Japanese emperor, implicitly (but not explicitly) denying the dominant Shushi ethics.[15] Although Mito followers had no intention of undermining the political hegemony of the *bakufu*, their historicism ultimately led, in the early nineteenth century, to the growth of "an orthodox attitude"[16] toward the throne—the notion that the emperor should assume real control in Japanese politics. This attitude was formulated as the concept of *kokutai*, most notably in the *Shinron* (New Proposals) of Aizawa Seishisai (1782-1863), written in 1825. The *kokutai* was a theory of state which blended religious, ethical, and historical beliefs in a specifically political ideology, focusing on the supremacy of

[14] Herschel Webb, "What is the *Dai Nihon Shi*?" *Journal of Asian Studies*, XIX, 2 (February 1960), pp. 135-150.

[15] Miyagi Kimiko, " 'Wakon Yōsai'—Nihon no kindaika ni okeru rinriteki shutai no kanōsei to genjitsu," *Nihonshi kenkyū*, 72 (May 1964), pp. 40-45.

[16] Webb's phrase, in "The Development of an Orthodox Attitude Toward the Imperial Institution in the Nineteenth Century," *Changing Japanese Attitudes Toward Modernization*, ed. Marius B. Jansen (Princeton, 1965), pp. 167-191.

the emperor as head of the Japanese polity and society. According to this idea, it was not that the shogun was an outright usurper but rather that the emperor was the historically legitimate ruler whose authority could not be challenged.[17] This was the first overt instance of nationality consciousness expressed in concrete political terms, and its fundamentally Confucian origins remind us of how crucial the Chinese teachings were in developing the loyalist attitudes which erupted so violently after 1853.

These literary, religious, moral, and historical influences of the major schools of thought—National Learning, Wang Yang-ming, and Mito—by the mid-nineteenth century combined in a manner which is typified by the career of the patriot Yoshida Shōin. Not only was this youthful Chōshū samurai indebted to Yōmeigaku; he was also firmly convinced of the superiority of the native tradition vis-à-vis Chinese culture, after the fashion of the Kokugaku scholars. Above all, Shōin was a great propagandist for the Mito ideology of *kokutai*, firmly devoted to anti-foreignism and unquestioningly loyal to the imperial house. The precise articulation of his ideas occurred in the chaotic milieu of 1853 to 1859. His attention during these years shifted from negative considerations of national defense before 1856 to positive affirmation of emperor-loyalty thereafter.[18] He represented that process by which loyalties to clan lords, already grown abstract and impersonal by mid-century, were elevated to the throne itself in the face of national danger.[19] By synthesizing, in a crude but dramatic manner, the principal proto-nationalist theories of the preceding decades, Shōin symbolized both the ferment of later Edo period intellectual life and the grow-

[17] See Earl, *Emperor and Nation*, pp. 88-89, 213-225; Robert N. Bellah, *Tokugawa Religion: The Values of Pre-Industrial Japan* (Glencoe, Ill., 1957), p. 104; Herschel Webb, *The Japanese Imperial Institution in the Tokugawa Period* (New York, 1968), passim.

[18] Earl, *Emperor and Nation*, pp. 176-192. For a collection of documents and commentary on Yoshida Shōin, see *Sekai kyōiku hōten, Nihon kyōikuhen, Yamaga Sokō-Yoshida Shōinshū*, ed. Murakami Toshiharu and Kumura Toshio (Tokyo, 1965), pp. 151-437.

[19] See Marius B. Jansen, "Tokugawa and Modern Japan," *Japan Quarterly*, xii, 1 (January-March 1965), p. 32; Craig, *Chōshū*, pp. 147-149.

15

ing consensus on pan-Japanese specifically political values centering on the monarchic institution.

While an awareness of nationality was essential in the restoration movement and the Meiji nationalism that followed, the spirit of reason and practicality which developed in the later Edo period was a significant forerunner of both the intellectual reorientation and the national reform programs of the 1870's. This sense of rationality in Japanese scholarship flowed partly from the later Yōmeigaku school, which insisted upon the concrete application of book learning, but its Tokugawa origins lie in the writings of the Ancient Learning (Kogaku) school of the early eighteenth century. Ancient Learning was an antiquarian branch of Confucianism which spurned the external metaphysics of Neo-Confucianism in favor of the teachings of the ancient Chinese classics. Its pivotal figures, Itō Jinsai (1627-1705) and Ogyū Sorai (1666-1728), rejected the Shushi world-view in favor of a more empirical approach to knowledge. Whereas Jinsai called for individual moral perfection, following the inclinations of the inner conscience, Sorai concentrated on group-centered institutions to promote improvement in the condition of society.[20] Both agreed, however, that realistic programs for social amelioration were urgently required and that the Shushi goal of sainthood through a search for abstract values was *muyō* (useless).[21] In time their ideas were reflected in the concepts of nature and action (*shizen* and *sakui*) in later Edo period political thought; some would have it that Sorai even anticipated the need for national wealth and power that was later expressed in the Meiji slogan *fukoku kyōhei* (enrich the country, strengthen the army).[22]

The other important locus of practical thought in the

[20] J. J. Spae, *Itō Jinsai, a Philosopher, Educator, and Sinologist of the Tokugawa Period* (Peking, 1948), p. 204; *Sources of Japanese Tradition*, p. 423.

[21] Sagara Tōru, "Kindai shisō juyō no gakumonteki zentei," *Kōza kindai shisō*, ed. Kaneko Musashi and Ōtsuka Hisao (Tokyo, 1959), IX, p. 72.

[22] *Ibid.*, p. 75. On *shizen* and *sakui*, see Maruyama Masao, *Nihon seiji shisōshi kenkyū* (Tokyo, 1952).

The Intellectual in Japan's Transition

Tokugawa period was the cult of Western learning known as Rangaku (Dutch Studies), which flourished in Edo and some of the major clan cities after the mid-eighteenth century. Rangaku was concerned with the study of European medical science, weaponry, astronomy, and technology, as revealed through the medium of Dutch books, since contact with other European countries was proscribed for most of the Edo period. Rangaku was a minor branch of scholarship in the Tokugawa intellectual world and its narrowly technical field of vision precluded any challenge to the Shushi epistemology, let alone subversion of Tokugawa authority (in fact the *bakufu* was its principal patron).[23] Rangaku was the palest of shadows when compared with the massive outburst of Western studies after 1853, called Yōgaku. But these crude beginnings were significant for their practicality: in time the *bakufu* encouraged its administrators to learn the rudiments of European arithmetic for the utilitarian reason that it would make them better bureaucrats. Just as Sorai, however great his capacity for mischief-making in attacking the Shushi world-view, had been protected, not throttled, by the shogun because his social theories were helpful in governing,[24] so the *bakufu* and the clan chieftains favored rather than feared Rangaku. Still, the fact that a handful of educated men in feudal Japan were working with the elementary stuff of Western technology—Arabic numerals, taxonomic paradigms, medical diagrams, and the like—meant that their country was not wholly ignorant of the practical knowledge that had developed in the West.

The collective force of Yōmeigaku, Rangaku, and Sorai and his followers was insufficient to overturn the prevailing Shushi theories of knowledge before the middle of the nineteenth century. But the nascent consciousness of nationality and the spirit of rationalism in the later Tokugawa period were present in two major streams of political ideology that

[23] Numata Jirō, *Yōgaku denrai no rekishi* (Tokyo, 1960), pp. 78-99.
[24] Wm. T. de Bary, "Some Common Tendencies in Neo-Confucianism," *Confucianism in Action*, ed. David S. Nivison and Arthur F. Wright (Stanford, 1959), pp. 31ff.

The Intellectual in Japan's Transition

surfaced in the second quarter of the nineteenth century under the impetus of sporadic incidents with foreign vessels along the Japanese coast in the early 1800's and the repercussions of the Opium War of 1839-1842. One was an internationalist school that was known by its slogan, "open the country" (Kaikoku); the other was exclusionist, advocating "expel the barbarians" (Jōi). Each sought to advance Japan's national aspirations and sincerely imagined that it was acting in the best interests of the nation. Each employed the growing spirit of rationality in analyzing the foreign threat: Carmen Blacker has made it clear that both Kaikoku and Jōi acknowledged the need for Western armaments.[25] However, a leading Jōi spokesman, Aizawa Seishisai, warned against the dangers of adopting Western morality and called for a new emphasis on Japan's traditional, native ethics. Kaikoku representatives, such as Sakuma Shōzan (1811-1864),[26] agreed that Eastern morality was superior but believed that it was compatible with the spirit of science: their slogan was "Eastern morality, Western technology" (*tōyō no dōtoku, seiyō no geijutsu*). The Jōi school held that the chief problem was the internal, moral one, and therefore it denounced all foreign contacts. Kaikoku followers, however, said that Japan's most pressing need was to adopt Western techniques as quickly as possible, and for that purpose limited foreign intercourse was essential.[27]

Events, in short, were leading Japan in the direction of greater nationalism and rationalism. Political debate on exclusion intensified after the West arrived in full force, and the intellectual drift toward practicality was confirmed in the Jitsugaku (Practical Studies) scholarship of the Bakumatsu period.[28] Functionally the Yōmeigaku-Sorai-Rangaku

[25] Carmen Blacker, *The Japanese Enlightenment: A Study of the Writings of Fukuzawa Yukichi* (Cambridge, Eng., 1964), pp. 18-22.

[26] Richard T. Chang has written a dissertation at the University of Michigan on "Fujita Tōko and Sakuma Shōzan: Bakumatsu Intellectuals and the West" (Ann Arbor, 1964).

[27] See also W. G. Beasley's excellent introduction to *Select Documents on Japanese Foreign Policy, 1853-1868* (London, 1955).

[28] See Minamoto Ryōen, "Meiji ishin to jitsugaku shisō," *Meiji ishinshi no mondaiten*, ed. Sakata Yoshio (Tokyo, 1962), pp. 41-50;

The Intellectual in Japan's Transition

tradition paralleled the rise of nationalist consciousness in Kokugaku, Yōmeigaku, and Mito thought: the latter helped to create the political dialogue that foreshadowed the restoration, and the former anticipated the new vogue of liberal, practical inquiry about the contemporary West that occurred in the Bakumatsu era and thereafter.

But the ideological ferment of Tokugawa Japan, for all its diversity, became intellectual chaos only after 1853. Only when American naval vessels were anchored off Uraga Beach was it evident that what was needed was more than an overhaul of the ancient military system. The versatility and originality of pre-modern Japanese thought is quite apparent in the existence of these sentiments of nationality and practicality, sentiments which were no less real for being confined to theoretical dispute. But they remained theory until Perry's expedition arrived. This event forced Japan's intellectuals, as well as her politicians, into a fundamental reconsideration of their national heritage, a reevaluation that was colored at every vital juncture by the inescapable physical superiority of the West. Whether men such as Nishi Amane would ever have undertaken a thorough review of their tradition without the Western stimulus cannot be known. What is known is that the character of their intellectual response to their environment in the next three decades was of an utterly different nature from that of the most utilitarian Rangaku scholar before 1853.

Japanese Thought in the Meiji Era, ed. Kōsaka Masaaki, tr. David Abosch (Tokyo, 1958), pp. 3-17; Setsuko Miyoshi, "The Role of Kokugaku and Yogaku During the Tokugawa Period," Ph.D. dissertation in history, Georgetown University (Washington, 1965).

19

two

The Early Development of
Nishi's Thought

Ordinarily biography is written by the humble about the great, but now and again a Plutarch records the life of an Alcibiades and thereby rescues him from the obscurity which failing memory imposes on the dead. In a sense this was the case with Nishi Amane, whose fame has been enhanced by association with the name of his biographer, the eminent late Meiji novelist Mori Ōgai (1862-1922). A fellow clansman from Tsuwano and briefly a pupil of Nishi's, Ōgai wrote the biography at the family's request soon after Nishi died in 1897.[1] As an authorized biographer, he was obliged to observe the injunction *de mortuis nil nisi bonum,* but happily he eschewed the stylized conventions of Japanese biography. As a result, Ōgai's work constitutes a reliable and reasonably detailed source for understanding the process by which Nishi shifted his convictions from Neo-Confucianism to the teachings of Ogyū Sorai, and ultimately to European thought.

FROM NEO-CONFUCIANISM TO THE
THOUGHT OF SORAI

Nishi was born on March 8, 1829, in the mountain village of Tsuwano, near the western extremity of Honshu in the ancient region known as Iwami, now Shimane Prefecture. Nishi's father Tokiyoshi, a minor warrior,[2] held the hereditary position of personal physician to Lord Kamei of Tsuwano. The family was typical of the small band of scholar-aristocrats whose sketchy knowledge of European science and medicine, laboriously gained via the Dutch language, was

[1] Mori Ōgai, *Nishi Amane den, Ōgai zenshū* (Tokyo, 1923-1927), VII, pp. 125-197.
[2] In 1713 the Nishi family stipend was 80 koku of rice, in 1789 it was 90 koku, and in 1817 it was 100 koku. Ōgai, *Nishi Amane den,* pp. 127-128.

promoted for expedient purposes by their domain chieftains. Originally from the region of Tōtōmi, Nishi's ancestors moved successively to Higo and Hizen (Kumamoto and Nagasaki, respectively). In Nagasaki, members of the family became translators, presumably of Dutch, and in 1700 a Nishi first swore allegiance to the Kamei family and became court physician by virtue of his access to Western medical knowledge in Dutch textbooks.[3] Since Western books were generally banned by the military government before 1720,[4] the Nishi case was one of the first instances of official patronage of Western knowledge in Japan.

Tsuwano was the isolated castle town of a small domain in the mountains north of Chōshū. The ruling family, Kamei, received the fief in 1617 in belated recognition of the services of Kamei Korenori (1557-1612) to Oda Nobunaga, the first of the great sixteenth-century generals.[5] The Tokugawa settlement of the early seventeenth century had designated Tsuwano as an outer, or *tozama,* fief, a status it retained until the Meiji restoration. In 1813 it was rated at 43,000 koku of rice, a figure which was unchanged in 1869.[6] Kamei Korekane (1822-1884), the last daimyo of Tsuwano, inherited his position in 1839 and became a fervent advocate of restoring Japan's classical institutions and ancient ways of life. Korekane was a leading official in the early Meiji Department of Religious Ceremonies (Jingikan) and plotted the separation of Shinto and Buddhism that signaled the latter's

---

[3] Ōkubo Toshiaki, "Kaisetsu," *Nishi Amane zenshū,* ed. Ōkubo Toshiaki (Tokyo, 1945), p. 36. This volume was the only one published in a projected multi-volume series. In 1960 Ōkubo edited the first volume in a new series, also entitled *Nishi Amane zenshū.* Vol. 2 appeared in 1961 and vol. 3 in 1966. Hereafter these will be cited as *NAZS* 1945, *NAZS* 1960, *NAZS* 1961, and *NAZS* 1966.

[4] The ban was never complete, since hardly anyone could read European languages in the earlier Edo period, and only Christian books were absolutely forbidden before the shogun Yoshimune lifted the ban in 1720. See C. R. Boxer, *Jan Compagnie in Japan* (The Hague, 1936), p. 61.

[5] *Sekai jinmei jiten, tōyōhen* (Tokyo, 1952), p. 210.

[6] *Nihonshi jiten,* ed. Kyōto Daigaku Bungakubu Kokushi Kenkyūshitsu (rev. ed., Tokyo, 1963), p. 676; *Nihon kindaishi jiten,* ed. Kyōto Daigaku Bungakubu Kokushi Kenkyūshitsu (Tokyo, 1958), p. 652.

discredit after 1868. He was made a viscount in accordance with the Peerage Act of 1884 and became a count posthumously in 1891.[7]

Although it was a small *han,* Tsuwano had a rich tradition of scholarship. The Confucianism taught in its schools was the orthodox Shushi brand, but among its scholars Tsuwano also counted a number of National Learning advocates, including Okakuma Shin, Ōkuni Takamasa, and Fukuba Yoshishizu. Ōkuni, sixty years old in 1853, wrote clamorous polemics in protest when Perry's expedition reached Japan. Fukuba was a disciple of Ōkuni and also of Hirata Kanetane, the adopted son of the famous Atsutane. Both Ōkuni and Fukuba served with Kamei in the early Meiji Jingikan. Shortly after the restoration, Nishi had occasion to criticize Ōkuni's school of thought in an essay prepared for Lord Kamei, but his rebuttal of National Learning fell on deaf ears.[8]

Despite the family calling, there is no evidence that Nishi's early education included Western studies. Ōgai bows to convention by citing Nishi's childhood precocity: his grandfather, Tokiyasu, started him on the scholarly path at age four with readings from the *Canon of Filial Piety* and, at six, the four Confucian books.[9] Apparently Tokiyasu was the scholar in the family, and as a child Nishi spent a great deal of time at his side learning to read the difficult Chinese texts out loud. The death of his grandfather in 1837 seems to have affected Nishi profoundly for a child of eight. Perhaps it was his penchant for study which earned Nishi the childhood nickname of Rojin, "fool," for as the eldest of four children

[7] *Nihonshi jiten,* p. 270; *Nihon kindaishi jiten,* p. 503. See the biographical section at the end of the main text.

[8] Ōkubo, "Kaisetsu," *NAZS* 1945, p. 36; Ōkubo, "Kaisetsu," *NAZS* 1960, p. 637; *Nihon kindaishi jiten,* pp. 51, 532. Nishi's essay is entitled *Fukubōshisho* and appears in *NAZS* 1960, pp. 291-308. Ōgai, claiming that the essay is mistitled, explains that Nishi "discusses three types of learning, Japanese, Chinese, and Western, but concludes that there is but a single truth." Quoted in Ōkubo, "Kaisetsu," *NAZS* 1960, p. 637.

[9] Ōgai, *Nishi Amane den,* p. 129. The four books were the *Great Learning, Analects, Doctrine of the Mean,* and *Mencius.*

Early Development of Nishi's Thought

(two boys and two girls) he is thought to have been outwardly gentle but inwardly serious and rather dour.[10] Mencius was the main emphasis at the *han* school, the Yōrōkan, when Nishi entered at age eleven. His teen-age education apparently encompassed the orthodox Neo-Confucian teachings which prevailed in most *han* schools up to 1868. Nishi later dismissed this period in his life with the remark: "we had stressed Sung studies for generations. I, Amane, did not want to go against this alone."[11]

The first of several turning points in Nishi's career occurred in 1845 or 1846 when he began to read the works of Ogyū Sorai.[12] He first encountered Sorai's *Commentary on the Analects* out of curiosity: "in fact, when I was about seventeen or eighteen, I was ill for several days, and while I was recuperating I fabricated the rationalization that although this was a heretical book, it would not be blasphemous to read it in bed, so I spread open this *Commentary on the Analects* and read it."[13] Sorai's writings were hard to understand for one who had previously "thought that I would be able to attain a position close to enlightenment through Sung studies." Concentrating so completely on Neo-Confucianism, Nishi had "embraced the notion that the Jinsai and Sorai schools were my bitter enemies." Once he read Sorai, however, he began to understand the inadequacies of Sung

[10] Ōgai, *Nishi Amane den*, pp. 128-129; Kazue Kyōichi, "Nishi Amane no shūgyō jidai," *Nihon oyobi Nihonjin* 1428 (April 1964), pp. 46-47; "Nishi Amane," *Kindai bungaku kenkyū sōsho*, ed. Shōwa Joshi Daigaku (Tokyo, 1956), III, p. 108.

[11] Quoted in Kazue Kyōichi, "Nishi Amane no shōgai to sono shisō," *Tetsugaku kaishi*, 9 (1958), p. 3.

[12] For a study of Sorai's writings, see J. R. McEwan, "Some Aspects of the Confucianism of Ogyū Sorai," *Asia Major*, new series, VIII, part 2 (1961), pp. 199-214. Sorai's political writings are partially translated in McEwan, *The Political Writings of Ogyū Sorai* (Cambridge, Eng., 1962). See also *Sources of Japanese Tradition*, pp. 422-433, and, in Japanese, Maruyama Masao, *Nihon seiji shisōshi kenkyū* (Tokyo, 1952), on Sorai's attitude toward political reform. An English translation of this work by Mikiso Hane is to be published by Princeton University Press in 1970.

[13] *Soraigaku ni taisuru shikō o nobeta bun* (1848), quoted in Kazue Kyōichi, "Nishi Amane no shūgyō jidai," *Nihon oyobi Nihonjin*, 1428 (April 1964), p. 46.

studies and their irrelevance to the problems of this world: "Guided by the *Commentary on the Analects,* I realized that the Sung Confucianism which up to then I had thought to be perfect was in fact not so. I then obtained a collection of Sorai's works and read them, and my previous illusions were entirely dispelled. Thus I reached the conclusion that Sung metaphysics served no purpose for people's daily lives. My mental state was truly like that of a man awakened from a long dream."[14]

Nishi never elaborated on this arid profession of faith in the Sorai school (Soraigaku), nor is there any evidence that as a youth he paid much attention to the numerous other ideologies which claimed samurai allegiances in the 1840's. The record of his teen-age thinking is permanently closed to the biographer, but it is quite apparent that Nishi's adult scholarship was consistently hostile to Sung Confucianism and much more congenial with the teachings of Sorai. We may doubt whether Nishi, as a seventeen-year-old, understood the subtleties of Soraigaku or the implications of his apostasy, but the conversion, however facile, was unquestionably a watershed in his intellectual growth. He did not spell out his criticism of Neo-Confucianism until he wrote *Hyakuichi shinron* (The New Theory of the Hundred and One) twenty-five years later, by which time he had gone far beyond Sorai and planted both feet solidly in the Western world.

While these new ideas occupied his thoughts, Nishi turned briefly in his late teens to the family profession, medical studies. In 1848 his mother died, and his father took a second wife shortly thereafter. It had been taken for granted that Nishi would one day inherit his father's position as the daimyo's physician, but a few months after his mother's death he was precipitately ordered by Lord Kamei to abandon medicine and devote himself to Neo-Confucianism. Nishi's younger brother Tokihisa accordingly replaced him as the successor to the family calling. Nishi's notes show his puzzlement at this turn of events:

[14] *Ibid.,* p. 46.

24

Early Development of Nishi's Thought

"When I had been liberated from the tight bonds of Sung metaphysics and arrived at the positivism of Sorai studies, I by no means refused to continue my family's surgical profession which I had hitherto scorned as a low calling. Rather, positively speaking, I thought it admirable to master the mysteries of the Chinese medicinal arts and Dutch medicine and to spend one's life as a doctor, and I thought that there was value in a son's spending his lifetime at such work. However, suddenly orders were handed down by my clan chief, and I lapsed into the predicament of being obliged to study Sung Confucianism. I was bewildered, and my mental state at this time was one of not knowing what to do.

"Thus, unavoidably, I outwardly engaged in studying Sung Confucianism, obeying my lord's orders, but I did not stop adhering to Sorai studies, which I believed to be true."[15]

These remarks show that Nishi's conversion to the teachings of Sorai had the practical effect of interesting him in medicine for the first time. Since Dutch medicine was an essential part of Japanese medical training, Sorai's philosophy served as a medium for Nishi's first sketchy contacts with Western learning. This encounter was soon foiled by Kamei's order to concentrate on Sung Confucianism, but Soraigaku continued to function for Nishi as a link to the Confucian tradition long after he had committed himself intellectually to the West. That Nishi preserved this link with the past throughout his career does not indicate any compromise or ambiguity in the depth of his allegiance to Western ideas. Instead, it suggests that he used Sorai studies as a channel of communication to Confucian-trained colleagues and as a source of Japanese precedents for many of the Western concepts which he introduced. Those who have identified a strong influence from Confucian thought in Nishi's philosophy have failed to recognize that Soraigaku was the most practical

---

[15] *Ibid.*, p. 46. Murakami Toshiharu has outlined the similarities between Nishi and Sorai, "Nishi Amane no shisō ni taisuru Soraigaku no eikyō," *Kyōto Gakugei Daigaku kiyō*, series A, 25 (October 1964), pp. 111-117. See also Murakami, "Meiji no seishinteki shichū," *Dōtoku to kyōiku*, 125 (October 1968), pp. 14-20.

of the various Confucian schools in Tokugawa Japan and that Nishi ultimately far surpassed Sorai in the degree of his modernism and pragmatism.

It is uncertain precisely why Nishi was commanded to study Shushigaku. There is no evidence that Lord Kamei was aware of Nishi's attraction to the teachings of Sorai; probably the daimyo simply recognized Nishi's scholarly talent and chose to use him as a Confucian teacher in the *han* school system. The professional Confucian teacher was a familiar member of a daimyo's intellectual retinue, although by the mid-nineteenth century he had no corner on knowledge or virtue in the *han*.[16] When Nishi became converted to Sorai's school of thought, he joined those whose rejection of the Confucian world-view had made the Confucian teacher passé by 1850.

Nishi was nonetheless obliged to obey his lord's order. Outwardly he devoted the next four years to Confucianism. In late 1849 he enrolled in the Shōinjuku, an academy in Osaka operated by Gotō Ki, who was a pupil of the famous historian Rai San'yō. Apparently conditions for study were not propitious at Gotō's school, but in his brief time there Nishi met several young samurai who became fellow students of the West in the 1850's. Among his acquaintances, for example, was Matsuoka Rinjirō (1820-1908), a Bizen warrior who also turned to European studies in the middle 1850's and remained a lifelong friend and correspondent.[17] In the autumn of 1850, Nishi transferred to Lord Ikeda's school in Okayama because it contained an extensive library collection.[18] After little more than a year's work in Neo-Confucian texts in Okayama, Nishi's prescribed period of study expired, and he was obliged to return in early 1852 to Tsuwano, which was still recovering from a great flood the preceding

[16] See J. W. Hall, "The Confucian Teacher in Tokugawa Japan," *Confucianism in Action*, ed. David S. Nivison and Arthur F. Wright (Stanford, 1959), pp. 269-301; R. P. Dore, *Education in Tokugawa Japan* (Berkeley and Los Angeles, 1965).

[17] See Ōkubo, "Kaisetsu," *NAZS* 1960, p. 608.

[18] Ōgai, *Nishi Amane den*, pp. 132-134; Kazue, "Nishi Amane no shōgai to sono shisō," pp. 5-6.

year. Lord Kamei immediately summoned Nishi to lecture him on Mencius, and soon thereafter he received a position in the *han* bureaucracy as a reading instructor and supervisor in the domain school. Thus, at twenty-three, Nishi began his teaching career in circumstances which could hardly have been more traditional.

His confining life as a professional Confucian teacher changed abruptly in 1853, however, when Lord Kamei ordered him to lecture at the Tsuwano domain school in Edo, the Jishūdō. From the moment he entered the military capital in the fall of 1853, Nishi was involved in the process of change that at length obliterated his *han,* made his family profession obsolete, and elevated him to positions of power and respect that would have been inconceivable in premodern Japan.

TRANSITION TO WESTERN STUDIES

Perry's squadron reached Uraga on July 8, 1853, and Edo was soon overwhelmed by the uproar of agonizing crises and untoward events that resounded throughout Japan. Despite the immediate clamor to "expel the barbarians," there was general agreement that, *inter alia,* Japan must assimilate the military arts of the West. Because her government was a federation of more than two hundred fifty fiefs dominated by the Tokugawa family, the principal burden of defense fell on the aging *bakufu.* It is significant, however, that many *tozama* fiefs, while berating the shogun for not ousting the foreigners at once, simultaneously realized their own vulnerability and began to make defense preparations.

Regardless of the ideological position they took, virtually all of the *tozama* domains had long understood the urgent requirement for modern weapons and military techniques. If strategy is a system of makeshifts, the daimyo proved to be master strategists. The chief purveyors of Western knowledge in 1853 were "Dutch doctors," the Japanese court and clan physicians who could read Dutch. For a fearful daimyo, the quickest access to Western military science lay in dispatching young retainers to Nagasaki, Osaka, and especially Edo to study the Dutch language, and ultimately the arts of war, in the libraries of these doctors. The typical daimyo, gripped with defense worries and beleaguered with gratuitous advice, improvised by entrusting a handful of young clansmen with the stiff task of obtaining this knowledge. Samurai were sent on dangerous roads to distant cities where they might find a doctor to teach them Dutch in his spare time. Even more formidable was the job of laying hands on Dutch books which explained European military science. Knowledge of the West, so long a matter of curiosity, had suddenly become a requisite of the highest priority. The confrontation with Perry elevated Western studies from a restricted luxury in limited areas to a necessity of ever-broadening scope.

Nishi received his orders to teach Confucian subjects at the domain estate in Edo on March 10, 1853, nearly four months before Perry's first expedition arrived. It was thus quite by accident that he was on hand in Edo during the early months of the diplomatic crisis. He was soon joined there by several future Western studies colleagues who had been sent by their respective lords to learn European military science. Tsuda Mamichi (1829-1903) was a fellow pioneer of Western scholarship who studied military history in Edo in the 1850's.[19] Katō Hiroyuki (1836-1916), like Tsuda, had begun studying the West at a school run by the Kaikoku advocate, Sakuma Shōzan. Katō had been far-sighted enough to realize that knowledge of the West would promote his career; when Perry arrived he too was ordered by his *han* to study military subjects.[20] Fukuzawa Yukichi (1834-1901) began learning Dutch privately in Nagasaki in the spring of 1854, because "all those who wanted to study gunnery had to do

---

[19] Ōgai, *Nishi Amane den*, p. 138; *Nihon kindaishi jiten*, p. 393. The sources variously give Mamichi and Masamichi as the reading for Tsuda's personal name, but Mamichi seems to be the one he preferred. See biographical notes.

[20] David Abosch, "Katō Hiroyuki and the Introduction of German Political Thought in Japan: 1868-1883," Ph.D. dissertation in history, University of California (Berkeley, 1964), pp. 308, 314.

Early Development of Nishi's Thought

so according to the instruction of the Dutch. . . ."[21] Nishi's stated duties in Edo were at first more traditional, but after a few months he likewise was commanded to study coastal defense.[22]

The routine job of teaching Confucian subjects at the Jishūdō led almost immediately to an exciting encounter with Western studies, an experience which became the second major turning point in Nishi's intellectual development. Very soon after he took up his post at the *han* school, he began learning Dutch in his spare time from a doctor at the Kamei estate in Edo, Nomura Shuntai,[23] and he also started to study arithmetic during the winter of 1853-1854. At the same time he began to renew acquaintances with Matsuoka Rinjirō and others from Gotō's Osaka school who were also now engaged in Western scholarship in Edo. Somewhere in the interaction of his new studies, his contacts with old friends, and the brouhaha of politics in the military capital, Nishi derived the inspiration and courage to rush straightaway into full-time investigation of the West. He revealed, in discussions with these men in early 1854, that he was growing impatient with his status as a feudal retainer; he realized that he could not continue as a *han* official and hope to perfect his understanding of the West. Nishi is said to have told his friends: "From now on, if I want to succeed in life and follow the right path, I cannot after all neglect Western learning. Accordingly, if I serve my small fief and must deal with petty matters, I cannot expect to become proficient, even if I steal moments for study. Once I cut myself off from my lord, I shall give it my undivided attention."[24]

Renouncing one's lord was a perilous course of action in feudal Japan, and Nishi's decision to break all ties with Tsuwano shows the strength of his determination. *Dappan,*

[21] Fukuzawa Yukichi, *The Autobiography of Fukuzawa Yukichi,* tr. Eiichi Kiyooka (Tokyo, 1960), p. 21. See biographical notes.
[22] Ōgai, *Nishi Amane den,* pp. 134-135; Kazue, "Nishi Amane no shōgai to sono shisō," p. 6.
[23] Ōgai, *Nishi Amane den,* p. 135.
[24] Quoted *ibid.,* p. 135.

as this crime was known, was a capital offense in the early Edo era, and as late as 1850 it was punishable by exile.[25] In practice only an aristocrat could renounce his *han* registry, but by doing so he became a masterless warrior (*rōnin*). As daimyo lineages were interrupted during the Tokugawa period, increasingly large numbers of samurai automatically became *rōnin*. Since they represented a source of considerable instability, both local and national governments discouraged voluntary additions to the vagrant warrior class by penalizing all renegade clansmen severely. *Dappan* was a rare phenomenon before 1800 because it was not normally possible to gain employment with another daimyo. Without an alternate object of loyalty to replace the fief lord, few samurai were willing voluntarily to exchange their positions in the intra-*han* structure for the *rōnin*'s life of insecurity in a society which permitted no misfits. To transfer one's allegiances to another daimyo was theoretically possible, but lord-retainer loyalties were extremely strong, and personal bonds could not be renounced with impunity.[26] By the nineteenth century, however, more and more warriors were fleeing their domains, usually renouncing their impoverished economic status as samurai in favor of gainful employment in the broad commoner class. In Tosa, only one samurai who committed *dappan* in the late Edo period was fully punished, while numerous others escaped with a lighter penalty.[27] Nevertheless, Nishi's decision to cut himself free was a bold step with enduring consequences. Lord Kamei was powerless to punish him, both because the chaotic events of the era had weakened feudal prerogatives and because Nishi enjoyed *bakufu* protection from 1856 onward. Nonetheless, Kamei refused to forgive Nishi until 1870, when

[25] *Ibid.*, p. 135.

[26] On various aspects of Japanese feudal relationships, see E. O. Reischauer, "Japanese Feudalism," *Feudalism in History*, ed. Rushton Coulborn (Princeton, 1956), pp. 26-48; John W. Hall, "Feudalism in Japan—A Reassessment," *Comparative Studies in Society and History, an International Quarterly*, v, 1 (October 1962), pp. 15-51.

[27] Marius B. Jansen, *Sakamoto Ryōma and the Meiji Restoration* (Princeton, 1961), pp. 100-101.

both men were officials of the new state and Tsuwano *han* was about to be abolished.

Intellectual rather than economic considerations prompted Nishi's fateful choice. His decision was not so much a rejection of his *han* as a positive desire to study questions of national concern. He made it clear in a letter to Lord Kamei that he bore no grudge against his feudal superiors and was grateful for their favors.[28] It is not certain how he reached his decision, nor did he state exactly why he believed he could not neglect Western learning. Inasmuch as Nishi received an official *bakufu* position only after two years of independence in Edo following his *dappan,* his break with the domain did not signify a transfer of political loyalties from *tozama* fief to the central state. Indeed, the historian Miyagawa Tōru denies that Nishi ever felt much loyalty to the *bakufu,* even when he was materially dependent upon it.[29] Rather, it seems that Nishi wanted to concentrate on the broad questions facing the country. Moreover, it is important to bear in mind that he formally renounced his *han* during the ten-day period after April 18, 1854, barely four months after he commenced studying Dutch.[30] This was hardly enough time to master the principles of Dutch syntax, let alone put it to scholarly use. While his boldness was thus not a product of a detailed understanding of the West, somehow Nishi had acquired a taste for the life of a Western studies scholar. Equally important was the fact that Edo was an exciting and dangerous city in the 1850's, an atmosphere any adventuresome young man would relish, and it is easy to imagine that service in Tsuwano seemed a dull alternative. By 1853 Edo had become Japan's brightest window to the West, a focus of national aspirations like Kyoto in the 1860's.

[28] Ōgai, *Nishi Amane den,* pp. 135-136.

[29] Miyagawa Tōru, *Kindai Nihon no tetsugaku* (supplemental ed., Tokyo, 1962), p. 30. Elsewhere Miyagawa asserts that Nishi's choice of Western studies at this time shows his consciousness of nationality, in common with most Japanese scholars of the West during the Bakumatsu period. Miyagawa, "Nihon no keimō shisō," *Kōza kindai shisō,* ed. Kaneko Musashi and Ōtsuka Hisao (Tokyo, 1959), IX, pp. 127-128.

[30] Kazue, "Nishi Amane no shōgai to sono shisō," p. 6.

Early Development of Nishi's Thought

Nishi had no assurance of livelihood in Edo when he quit the *han* registry, but he was quite sure that "if I serve my small fief and must deal with petty matters," there would be no challenge for him in the *han* bureaucracy.

Nishi, at twenty-five, had thus elected to cast off all ties which would hinder his scholarship.[31] It was an extremely significant turning point in his career; it represented a victory for boldness and curiosity, but not yet a conviction that Western ideas were superior. This event is unmistakable evidence that Nishi's intellectual interests had surpassed narrow fief or national bounds and that he was searching for the meaning of Western culture. That he violated the feudal code of loyalty meant that he had permanently rejected its ideological underpinning, Shushi Confucianism.

Nishi's case most clearly illustrates the phenomenon of *dappan* for intellectual reasons, but there were other young samurai-scholars who risked their feudal careers in order to study the West. Takano Nagahide's life exemplified the futility of Western scholarship before 1853. The author of an outline of Western philosophy, he committed suicide in 1844 to avoid persecution for his attempts to expose Japan to Western thought.[32] More fortunate was Tsuda Mamichi, who began studying the West as early as 1850 from Sakuma Shōzan and Mitsukuri Genpo.[33] Shortly after Perry's arrival Tsuda started to quarrel with his lord in the Tsuyama domain, and at length he renounced his *han*.[34] His career during the Bakumatsu period closely paralleled Nishi's, and his break with Tsuyama was similarly a product of intellectual conviction. Katō Hiroyuki was barely seventeen when Perry's ships reached Japan, but he had already begun study under Shōzan's direction in Edo. Katō was never forced to

---

[31] Kazue Kyōichi reasons that Nishi's *dappan* was motivated entirely by intellectual conviction: "Ignoring self-sacrifice, he blindly dashed forward, and his passion for scholarship is most forcefully illustrated by this incident." Kazue, "Nishi Amane no shūgyō jidai," p. 47.

[32] Kuwaki Gen'yoku, *Meiji no tetsugakkai* (Tokyo, 1943), pp. 10-12.

[33] *Nihon kindaishi jiten*, p. 393. See biographical notes.

[34] Minamoto Ryōen, "Meiji ishin to jitsugaku shisō," *Meiji ishinshi no mondaiten*, ed. Sakata Yoshio (Tokyo, 1962), p. 98.

sever all connections with his fief, Izushi, but like Nishi and Tsuda he soon increased the scope of his study of the West beyond military science.[35] Fukuzawa Yukichi also managed to avoid a showdown with his lord. In September 1855, he was called home to succeed his dead brother as family head, a requirement of the feudal code, and it was only with great difficulty and considerable maneuvering that he managed to obtain permission to leave Nakatsu permanently for the sake of Dutch learning. He was fortunate that his fief at least recognized the importance of studying Western gunnery: "this was my one way of escape to study the civilization of the West."[36] For all these men, official service in the feudal fief was incompatible with Western studies. Whether or not they formally renounced their *han,* they rejected the ideological justifications for Japanese feudalism and rushed headlong toward an understanding of the West. Each doubtless knew that there would be some personal advantage in this type of study. Nishi stated no explicit intention to serve his country when he left the *han,* but this was an unspoken premise of virtually all intellectual activity in Japan after 1853.

FULL ATTENTION TO WESTERN SCHOLARSHIP

The great foreign policy dialogue between the Kaikoku and Jōi schools took place mainly in the interval between Perry's first visit in 1853 and the emergence of Ii Naosuke (1815-1860) as the most powerful councilor within the *bakufu* in June 1858. During these five years Japan's political leaders, both in Edo and the domains, groped for an effective way to preserve national independence and yet avoid a war which they knew Japan could not win. The search for a workable policy was pressed most vigorously in Edo, which

---

[35] See Abosch, "Katō Hiroyuki," p. 314.
[36] Fukuzawa, *Autobiography,* p. 50. Probably the most dramatic, although irrelevant, instance of *dappan* was that of Yoshida Shōin. When he was twenty-one, Yoshida took a trip to Edo and Mito against the wishes of his lord in Chōshū. Later he meekly surrendered to Lord Mōri and received only token punishment. See H. van Straelen, *Yoshida Shōin, Forerunner of the Meiji Restoration, a Biographical Study* (Leiden, 1952), p. 22.

remained the locus of political power; control of the *bakufu* still included the right to set the course of external affairs. Centuries of diplomatic isolation and Confucian ethics had encouraged the habit of hyperbole in Japanese political discourse, in the sense that the great majority of clan and court leaders now used such unequivocal terms as "internationalism" and "exclusionism" to promote or attack a course of action.

This same tendency to speak in black-and-white categories plagued many of Japan's young scholars of the West as they pondered the problem of how to confront Europe. Like most samurai, Nishi had been trained to think in monolithic terms, because most traditional thought systems—especially Neo-Confucianism—were unified schemes with all-inclusive world-views. This helps to explain why Nishi, who spent these five stormy years in Edo, decided at length that the master key to Western culture could be precisely identified as a single discipline, philosophy, which he first defined as "the clarification of wisdom and virtue."[37] The training in European studies that led him to this conclusion was typical of the resources for dealing with the West that were available to even the most powerful Japanese leaders in the 1850's: his studies were narrow in scope and meager in facilities. Nevertheless, he made the most of his opportunities, and by the end of the decade he was one of the country's best informed scholars of the West.

Nishi gleaned his education in these years from a variety of fascinating sources, including physicians, a refugee from an exclusionist domain, and an itinerant fisherman. He studied Dutch grammar privately from a number of doctors during 1854-1855, including Sugita Seikei and Ikeda Tachū, a fellow clansman.[38] His most important teacher was Tezuka Ritsuzō (1807-1865), whose school in Hongō Motomachi he entered in late 1855. As a Chōshū retainer, Tezuka had been the object of obscurantist attacks, since he had dared to teach foreign languages in a domain where exclusionist senti-

[37] *Seiyō tetsugakushi no kōan danpen, NAZS* 1960, p. 16.
[38] Ōgai, *Nishi Amane den*, p. 138.

34

ment ran strong, and he had fled to Sakura *han* under an assumed name and later opened a school in Edo.[39] Tezuka's counsel played a major part in Nishi's intellectual development, and the two remained close friends throughout Nishi's student days. Tezuka placed Nishi in charge of the school's lectures on Dutch books late in 1855, exactly two years after he had begun studying the language. He also urged Nishi to start learning English; accordingly, in early 1856 Nishi began to learn a few words with the aid of a Dutch-English dictionary. He started lessons in English conversation with the colorful Nakahama Manjirō, another friend from Gotō's school in Osaka, who at age thirteen had escaped on an American fishing vessel and spent ten years in the United States.[40] Nishi was thus one of the first students of the West to turn his attention to English as well as Dutch. As serious study of the West increased in the 1850's, other scholars realized that Dutch books were inadequate and that English was a much more useful language. Fukuzawa Yukichi, for example, discovered in 1859 that his hard-earned knowledge of Dutch was useless in talking with foreign traders in Yokohama: "I realized that a man would have to be able to read and converse in English to be recognized as a scholar in Western subjects in the coming time."[41] Nishi was very fortunate that Tezuka had prodded him into starting English as early as 1856.

The Tokugawa government, meanwhile, decided under the pressure of events to patronize Western studies. Since 1811 there had been a *bakufu* facility for studying astronomy, one part of which was an office for translating foreign technical books. It is remarkable how quickly the military government reacted to the cultural confrontation after Perry arrived: by

[39] Osatake Takeshi, "Nishi Amane no jiseki ni oite," *Kokushi kaikokai kiyō*, 44 (Feb. 15, 1944), p. 5.
[40] This adventurer was also known as John Man and John Mung. See Kaneko Hisakazu, *Manjirō, the Man Who Discovered America* (Boston, 1956); Emily V. Warinner, *Voyager to Destiny: The Amazing Adventures of Manjirō, the Man Who Changed Worlds Twice* (Indianapolis, 1956).
[41] Fukuzawa, *Autobiography*, p. 98.

Early Development of Nishi's Thought

the spring of 1855 the translation office had been expanded into the Foreign Studies Institute, and a year later it was further enlarged and renamed the Foreign Books Research Institute (Bansho Shirabesho). This unit became the training ground for the intellectual elite which dominated Japanese scholarship in the 1870's. The institute was both a school and a research group in Western studies, and its purpose was to study the Dutch language and Western culture in general.[42] In reality the content was restricted to languages and technology until the 1860's, but it was nonetheless the most significant Japanese center for Western studies. Probably its most practical function on behalf of the *bakufu* was diplomatic. Representatives of the institute met various foreign envoys, including Townsend Harris (1804-1878), and translated numerous diplomatic messages.[43] The research institute also published a number of dictionaries, grammars, and texts. Although the *bakufu* regarded it primarily as a training school for skilled technicians, the fact that an institute of such broad scope and activity existed under the aegis of the state indicates how important Western studies were to the Tokugawa government.

The research institute formally opened its Kudanshita school in early 1857 under the direction of two main teachers, Mitsukuri Genpo and Sugita Seikei. Both were leading Dutch doctors, and Sugita had been Nishi's tutor two years before. There were one hundred ninety-one pupils on opening day.[44] Nishi's close friend and teacher, Tezuka Ritsuzō, was soon added to the staff as the head English instructor, and on his recommendation Nishi was made an assistant instructor of Dutch on May 26, 1857. Tsuda Mamichi re-

[42] Asō Yoshiteru, *Kinsei Nihon tetsugakushi* (Tokyo, 1942), pp. 21-22. On the Bansho Shirabesho, see Marius B. Jansen, "New Materials for the Intellectual History of Nineteenth-century Japan," *Harvard Journal of Asiatic Studies*, xx, 3-4 (December 1957), pp. 569-594.

[43] "Nishi Amane," *Kindai bungaku kenkyū sōsho*, ed. Shōwa Joshi Daigaku (Tokyo, 1956), III, p. 123. David Abosch has described the Bansho Shirabesho in "Katō Hiroyuki," pp. 163-197, 322.

[44] Asō, *Kinsei Nihon tetsugakushi*, p. 22.

ceived a similar position on the same day.[45] Each of them was expected to carry out various assignments for the *bakufu* as well.

Nishi's appointment was the start of a career in national service that lasted nearly thirty years. One of his first duties was to investigate Russian encroachment in the unsettled northern island, Hokkaido. In the tenth month of 1857 he presented a memorial to Hitotsubashi Keiki (1837-1913), the future shogun, in which he summarized his proposals for dealing with the West. The gist of his petition was that while the solution to defense problems lay in perfecting Japan's military capabilities, it was more important to make certain internal political changes. "Indeed, although we may despise the Western barbarians and their various lands, we must rely not upon the advantages of large weapons and the size of our ships but upon reforms in our government and the selection of talented men."[46] Arms alone could not remove the threat; Japan's "evil customs of hierarchy"[47] must also be eliminated. Nishi called for a reform of samurai morality, in which each warrior individually would have the proper spirit to face the foreign problem. By this he did not mean that there should be absolute social equality but rather that hierarchical relationships within the samurai class should be abandoned so that all warriors could equally take more individual initiative in political and diplomatic affairs. Rather than seeking complete reform of the feudal structure, Nishi held that the evils of bureaucratic red tape should be purged

---

[45] *Ibid.*, p. 22; Kazue, "Nishi Amane no shōgai to sono shisō," p. 7; Ōgai, *Nishi Amane den*, pp. 138-139. In addition to Asō's pioneering work, three writings by Numata Jirō are relevant to the Bansho Shirabesho: "Yōgaku to sono henshitsu," *Meiji ishinshi kenkyū kōza* (Tokyo, 1958), II, pp. 249-261, is an excellent review of the literature on the subject; *Yōgaku denrai no rekishi* (Tokyo, 1960) covers the topic throughout the Edo period; and *Bakumatsu yōgakushi* (Tokyo, 1952) concentrates on the years 1853-1868. See also Satō Masanosuke, *Yōgakushi kenkyū josetsu* (Tokyo, 1964).

[46] *Tōshi jūgatsu sōkō*, quoted in Furuta Hikaru, "Nishi Amane, keimōki no tetsugakusha," *Asahi jyānaru*, IV, 16 (Apr. 22, 1962), p. 94. *Tōshi jūgatsu sōkō* also appears in *NAZS* 1966, pp. 180-192.

[47] *Ibid.*, p. 94.

and that capable men should run the government in a business-like manner.[48]

This memorial is the first tangible evidence that Nishi consciously identified himself with the national interest. That he was concerned with the problem of samurai morality shows the continuing effect of Confucian ideas upon his thought. Like Sorai, he was interested in moral rejuvenation within the framework of strong political institutions,[49] although Nishi later broke with Sorai's analyses by emphasizing individual ethics to the exclusion of institutions and forms of government. Nishi shared with all responsible writers the basic assumption that above all Japan must not become the colony of another power. His interest in the rehabilitation of warrior ethics accorded well with the Jōi school's insistence on moral regeneration for warding off the West. In common with both Jōi adherents and their Kaikoku rivals, he readily admitted Japan's need to adopt Western weapons and military techniques as rapidly as possible. Yet Nishi did not denounce all foreign intercourse outright, as had the Jōi school, and his intense interest in Western studies led him to take a stand on external contacts which was in reality much closer to the Kaikoku position. His modest call for governmental reforms could hardly have offended either exclusionists or internationalists. Nishi's outlook was thus one that cannot be clearly labeled "Kaikoku" or "Jōi," but it appears to have been a reasonable attitude for a Japanese student of the West to take in the late 1850's.

It is curious to note that Nishi's proposals in the Hokkaido petition were in keeping with the demands that were being put forth at exactly the same time by other samurai whose thought owed much to the Yōmei school. Yokoi Shōnan (1810-1869) and Yoshida Shōin sought to free the samurai for individual action by eliminating needless bureaucratic formalism and archaic feudal ranks.[50] Internal reform was a basic demand of the *shishi* whose Yōmeigaku training led

---

[48] Kazue, "Nishi Amane no shōgai to sono shisō," pp. 7-8.

[49] See *Sources of Japanese Tradition*, ed. Wm. T. de Bary (New York, 1958), p. 423.

[50] See *ibid.*, p. 617.

them to stress sincerity and individual purpose. To this extent the ideas in Nishi's memorial were in harmony with much of the *shishi* thought at the time, but it is significant that he did not couple his request for reform with an attack on the Tokugawa *bakufu* itself. Although his petition failed to indicate what his concept of nation was, the document was concerned entirely with a problem facing the whole country, one that Nishi believed could be resolved without overturning the Tokugawa family or the whole feudal structure.

The emphasis on internal reform as well as outward military strength in the Hokkaido petition shows that Nishi's thinking was as progressive as any in Japan in 1857, but it does not necessarily reflect the results of his four years' training in Western studies. Furuta Hikaru has argued that the Hokkaido memorial demonstrates that Nishi recognized the superiority of certain non-material aspects of Western culture: "against the background of the 'black ships' of the West, he noticed their 'civilization and institutions' and frankly acknowledged those points which were superior. This is clearly different from the existing 'Eastern morality, Western technology' way of thinking."[51] In fact, however, Nishi did not clearly admit Western cultural supremacy until five years later. His ideas in 1857 were not sufficiently distinct from those of other scholars who never acknowledged that Western civilization was superior to let us say that he had yet bridged the morality-technology fault. During the next five years Nishi made his full conversion to Western philosophy. He spent this period working at the research institute, continuing his study of the West in preparation for the next major phase in his career, which began with his trip to Holland in 1862.

[51] Furuta, "Nishi Amane," p. 94.

three

Study Abroad and Service
at Home

The year 1860 was probably one of the half-dozen most important in the history of modern Japan. Not only was it a critical turning point in the process of restoration, but it was also a landmark in Japan's unfolding perception of the West. The months since Ii Naosuke's rise to power in June 1858 were characterized on the one hand by a growing agreement within the *bakufu* on the need for a moderate foreign policy and on the other by spreading resentment and hostility toward the Western powers, especially among the *tozama* clans. This intensifying ideological polarization began to reflect itself from about 1860 onward in the two capital cities: Edo became a magnet for diverse internationalists and Kyoto for various exclusionists, so that Kaikoku sympathies increasingly came to be identified with the *bakufu,* while Jōi sentiments grew more firmly aligned with the throne. It is against this background of *de facto* moderation vis-à-vis Europe and simultaneous isolationism on the part of the Jōi school that the assassination of Ii, the last effective *bakufu* councilor, bore such grave consequences in the months that followed. The anti-foreign movement reached a climax on March 24, 1860, when Ii was murdered by retainers of the various major daimyo whose influence at court he had recently purged. The death in September 1860 of Tokugawa Nariaki, Lord of Mito, removed a leading critic of the military government, but it also withdrew the yoke of restraint from less responsible opponents of the state and opened the way for further reckless anti-foreign incidents by headstrong samurai. Henceforth the shogun found his power slipping through his fingers like sand; more and more Kyoto was becoming the site of struggles for political control.

Study Abroad and Service at Home

The year 1860 also represented the start of a new phase in Japan's investigations of Western knowledge. Whereas Sakuma Shōzan's generation had responded to the Opium War with the "Eastern morality, Western technology" equation, Nishi and his associates at the Bansho Shirabesho derived their first concrete awareness of the West from Perry's arrival in 1853 and accordingly concentrated on languages and military studies.[1] In 1860, however, the focus of these efforts to understand European culture began to shift from the Edo research institute to the West itself. The first Japanese mission to the United States departed from Edo in January of that year, and among those aboard was Fukuzawa Yukichi, as the personal steward of Captain Kimura.[2] The wide gap in understanding that still divided Japan and the West was evident in the fact that the envoys on this historic voyage—far from being swept off their feet with admiration for Western culture—were at first disillusioned with what they saw. The initial reaction of Fukuzawa and Murazaki Awajinokami to America, for example, was one of dismay at its barbarousness.[3] Nevertheless, the 1860 mission was a great advance in contacts between the two civilizations; as Fukuzawa observed, there was much more to the West than simple military superiority.[4] Nishi too had hoped to be included in the voyage, for he was aware that it would be an unexampled chance to observe Western life at first hand, but he lacked the necessary contacts to gain a place aboard. His opportunity came two years later, when the *bakufu* elected to broaden the scope of Western studies under its aegis by dispatching scholars to Europe to study something much more elaborate than languages and weaponry, namely the contemporary Western social sciences. In 1862, therefore,

[1] See Minamoto Ryōen, "Meiji ishin to jitsugaku shisō," *Meiji ishinshi no mondaiten*, ed. Sakata Yoshio (Tokyo, 1962), p. 98.

[2] See Fukuzawa's account of this trip in *The Autobiography of Fukuzawa Yukichi*, tr. Eiichi Kiyooka (Tokyo, 1960), pp. 104-120, and Muragaki Tanso, *Kokai Nikki: The Diary of the First Japanese Embassy to the United States of America* (Tokyo, 1958).

[3] Maruyama Masao, "Kaikoku—Opening of the Country," tr. Isono Fujiko (mimeo., 1958), pp. 29-30.

[4] Fukuzawa, *Autobiography*, pp. 112-118.

41

Study Abroad and Service at Home

Nishi and Tsuda Mamichi became the first of a small flow of Japanese students sent abroad by the state when they received government orders to spend the next two years studying in Holland.

THE LEIDEN YEARS

Nishi and Tsuda had begun plotting a trip abroad as early as March 1858, but sickness, marriage, and warfare conspired to delay the fulfillment of their dreams. Nishi became ill with cholera in the autumn of that year, and plans for study abroad were further disrupted by Nishi's marriage in 1859 to Ishikawa Masuko.[5] Unable to join the first trade mission in 1860, they repeatedly petitioned the *bakufu* for permission to study in the United States and managed to gain tentative approval in 1861, just as the American Civil War erupted to postpone the venture indefinitely.[6] According to Nishi's notes, Townsend Harris, the American consul, personally informed him that the trip would be impossible owing to the conflict in the U.S.[7] But finally, in 1862, their efforts bore fruit. Japan had contracted with Holland to have a number of ships built, and several Japanese naval officers and civilian technicians were being dispatched to Rotterdam as observers. In addition to roughly fifteen naval officers, there was room in the party for a few government bureaucrats, and at length the application of the Foreign Books Research Institute for space on the sailing was approved.

[5] The daughter of an Echigo samurai, Masuko married Nishi at eighteen and kept a desultory diary between the years 1854 and 1875. She was a minor poetess. Masuko had no children, but in 1869 she and Nishi adopted Hayashi Shinrokurō (1860-1933) as Nishi's *yōshi*. Shinrokurō spent his career in the navy, rising to vice-admiral and serving from 1918 onward in the upper house of the diet. See *Nishi Masuko kankei shiryō* (Tokyo, 1966), issued as a supplement to *NAZS*. Pp. 1-48 contain the diary.

[6] Mori Ōgai, *Nishi Amane den, Ōgai zenshū* (Tokyo, 1923-1927), VII, pp. 148-152; Hayashi Takeji, "Bakumatsu no kaigai ryūgakusei—sono ni—Nihonjin no sokuseki o tazunete," *Nichibei fuōramu*, x, 2 (February 1964), p. 82. See also Hayashi, "Bakumatsu no kaigai ryūgakusei no seikaku," *Rekishi kyōiku*, xv, 1 (January 1967), pp. 8-17.

[7] *Oran kikō, NAZS* 1966, p. 343.

Study Abroad and Service at Home

Once arrangements had been made with the Dutch government for looking after the institute representatives while they were in Holland, the *bakufu* chose Nishi and Tsuda for the trip, with the explicit purpose of studying subjects as yet untaught in Japan: Western economics, law, and political science. Since the seventh century, Japanese scholars had crossed the Yellow Sea to drink at the fountain of Chinese civilization; now Nishi and Tsuda became the first to study in Europe under official sponsorship.

Before investigating the reasons why the Tokugawa government wanted to learn about European social science, let us inquire about the level of Nishi's perception of the West. What elements of European civilization did he consider important as he set out for Leiden? In what ways had his thinking matured in the five years since the Hokkaido memorial? Some of the answers are contained in a letter that Nishi wrote to his old friend Matsuoka Rinjirō about Japan's internal problems and the nature of the West as he was preparing to leave his professorship at the research institute:

"Although I would say that Western studies are exceedingly popular throughout the capital, the Mito school theory of 'revere the emperor, expel the barbarians' has penetrated very deeply. Every day there are disturbances by the *rōnin*, as they are obstinate and hard to change. I think that there are also difficulties within the government. Recently the minister of the daimyo of Chōshū came to Kyoto, and I am sure that Lord Shimazu [of Satsuma] agreed with him point by point about the Osaka incident and the troubles in his neighborhood. In any case, at present I think that we shall suffer more from the riots of conservatives than from incidents with foreign countries. It seems, I fear, that we are duplicating the mistakes of the Ch'ing emperor. . . . I venture to say that this arises from the conceit of our empire, the land of the gods, and our great contempt of other countries. The portions of Western philosophy and economics that I have read have contained truly surprising theories of justice and fairness. I have learned how greatly they differ in mean-

43

ing from existing studies, particularly Chinese studies. Christianity is very widespread in the West; however, I understand that it has not adopted the extremely vulgar practices of our archaic Buddhism. The explanations of life's principles in the science 'philosophia' are superior even to Sung Confucianism, and the way in which the West has established the basic principles of economics, based on nature and public order, is superior to monarchical government. The civilization and institutions of the United States and England, I believe, surpass Yao and Shun, who ruled by popular will, and the Chou system. . . ."[8]

This letter is indeed a revealing document, telling us much about the mind of the thirty-three-year-old Nishi. In the sphere of diplomacy, it indicates that Nishi was acutely concerned lest Japan's self-pride deceive her into emulating the disastrous mistakes of the Chinese in dealing with the West. The lessons of the Opium War were plain enough; Japan must do much more than merely turn her back on the world. He seems to be saying that still waters run no mills, that in the long run a domestic policy which resisted change would be more harmful than the actual effects of contact with the West, however menacing it seemed to be. Intellectually, furthermore, the letter shows that Nishi compared "philosophia" with Confucianism and found the latter lacking, further evidence of his tendency at this time to think in terms of broad, unitary thought systems. He did not indicate what he meant by "philosophia," nor is it clear which Western books served as sources for his conclusions, although we know that George Henry Lewes' *Biographical History of Philosophy* (1843) was among the first books on Western philosophy, if not the first, to enter Japan and that it had a great effect on Nishi's generation.[9] Lewes, author of *Life of Goethe* and the lover of novelist George Eliot, was one of

[8] Nishi to Matsuoka Rinjirō, June 12, 1862, quoted in Ōgai, *Nishi Amane den*, p. 152. This letter also appears in *NAZS* 1960, pp. 7-10, under the title *Seiyō tetsugaku ni taisuru kanshin o nobeta Matsuoka Rinjirōate no shokan.*

[9] Asō Yoshiteru, *Kinsei Nihon tetsugakushi* (Tokyo, 1942), pp. 124-127.

Study Abroad and Service at Home

England's most outspoken positivists, and it is safe to assume that Nishi used "philosophia" to mean the European social and political philosophy of the earlier nineteenth century that is generally known as classical positivism. Although Nishi certainly exaggerated the importance of philosophy in his letter to Matsuoka, ranking it above even Christianity as the well-spring of Western culture, his interest in it was important not only because he was the first Japanese to pay real homage to European philosophy but also because he clearly identified an intangible, intellectual factor as the keystone of Western civilization, not some item of hardware or accident of physiology. Moreover, in this letter he embraced certain European virtues which were not central to traditional Japanese thought, justice (*kōhei*) and fairness (*seidai*),[10] and used them to assess the merits of the Western intellectual sciences, indicating that his standard of judgment had begun to drift from Confucian to European norms. Finally, and perhaps most significantly, he acknowledged that Anglo-American civilization and institutions (*seido bunbutsu*) were superior to the ancient ideal Confucian societies, the regimes of Yao and Shun and the Chou dynasty.

This letter forms a recognizable pattern with Nishi's Hokkaido memorial of 1857 and demonstrates how far his thinking had developed during the eight years since his decision to concentrate on Western studies. Like many Japanese intellectuals in 1857, Nishi had acknowledged that the values of the feudal state and society could not be defended with "great rifles and huge warships." By 1862 he admitted not only that Western philosophy, however ill-defined, was "superior even to Sung Confucianism" but also that the civilization of a European country surpassed the archetype of Con-

[10] *Seidai* (fairness) was based on the ancient term *seidai kōmei*, which was used in the *Analects* to describe the heart of a great sage. *Kōhei* (justice) has no classical antecedents. This example is indicative of Nishi's creative use of ancient Chinese terms to indicate modern concepts. He also used *seiri no gaku* alternately with "philosophia" at this time. *Seiri* means "natural endowments" in modern Japanese, but Nishi later used the term *seirigaku* to mean "psychology."

45

fucian society.[11] Nishi no longer thought in terms of Sakuma Shōzan's distinction between "Eastern morality" and "Western technology": he was now attracted to Western studies for the values they taught as well as the technical information they contained. He had reached these convictions through his limited reading in the isolated research institute in Edo, and his letter to Matsuoka indicates that, despite some distorted notions, he was reasonably well prepared for studying Western civilization before leaving for Holland.

Nishi was not alone in denying Shōzan's assumption that Eastern morality was necessarily superior. Katō Hiroyuki, who had deciphered the morality-technology problem by the time he joined the research institute, eagerly searched for the secret of European cultural brilliance in Christianity.[12] Fukuzawa Yukichi concluded that Western superiority lay in the concepts of freedom and equal rights.[13] How had these young scholars managed to overcome the problem of morals and skills that proved such a millstone to the Kaikoku school, as well as to a future generation of Chinese? For one thing, they shared an obvious faith in rationalism and practicality, a product of that curiosity about the West manifested by earlier scholars of Dutch learning. In Nishi's case the teachings of Ogyū Sorai strengthened his belief in pragmatic approaches and concrete solutions. The practical man could certainly see that obscurantist cries for total exclusion

[11] Miyagawa Tōru, who overlooks the Hokkaido petition, attaches great importance to the Matsuoka letter: "Nishi Amane's awakening [to Western philosophy] constituted not merely an important event in the formation of his own thought; we may also say that it was an important turning point for Western studies in Japan, because it was the first step in fundamentally revising the universally accepted idea among Bakumatsu period Western scholars of 'Eastern morality, Western technology.'" Miyagawa, *Kindai Nihon no tetsugaku* (supplemental ed., Tokyo, 1962), p. 25.

[12] David Abosch, "Katō Hiroyuki and the Introduction of German Political Thought in Japan: 1868-1883," Ph.D. dissertation in history, University of California (Berkeley, 1964), p. 322.

[13] See Carmen Blacker, *The Japanese Enlightenment: A Study of the Writings of Fukuzawa Yukichi* (Cambridge, Eng., 1964), p. 29; Furuta Hikaru, "Nishi Amane, keimōki no tetsugakusha," *Asahi jyānaru*, IV, 16 (Apr. 22, 1962), p. 94; Kazue Kyōichi, "Nishi Amane no shōgai to sono shisō," *Tetsugaku kaishi*, 9 (1958), pp. 7-8.

were worse than useless: they prevented a reasoned, expedient solution, which to Nishi meant a measure of internal reform.

What is more, Nishi and his colleagues seem to have shared with nearly all contending schools a keen sense of nationality and national purpose. Rather than using the crisis for partisan advantage, they perceived that the national interests of all concerned could best be served by accommodating in some degree the Western culture of which military superiority was merely one obvious manifestation. Once their pragmatism and sense of nationality led them to believe that the West was superior in some respects, Nishi and his group earnestly investigated the whole realm of Western civilization for the key to its brilliance. The Kaikoku and Jōi schools, while seeking to exclude Western morals, had each managed to fit bits of Western culture into its system. But to both the indivisible cultural unit was Japanese, whereas Nishi and his colleagues accepted the idea of Western cultural superiority. Later Nishi's group fortuitously overcame monistic patterns of thought, thanks again, in some respects, to their rationality and nationality consciousness, and they devised a workable mixture of East and West that served the objective of national strengthening. But already, by the early 1860's, this small band of scholars had become convinced that certain nonmaterial aspects of this superior Western culture were essential for Japanese development. They spent the next fifteen years determining precisely which aspects these were, propagating their ideas among government leaders and the literate public. It is from this point that the study of modern, academic philosophy begins in Japan. Nishi was the first in his country systematically to study European philosophic systems; we should remember that he was a scholar of philosophic thought rather than a formal philosopher.

Such was the degree of Nishi's understanding of the West when his ship left Shinagawa on July 14, 1862. At Nagasaki some young medical students joined the group, and all were transferred to a Dutch ship, the *Kallipus,* for the voyage to

Europe. Their vessel floundered in the Straits of Gaspar, however, and the crew and passengers were taken to Batavia for a lengthy stopover until passage could be secured on another ship, the *Ternate*. The entire trip lasted eight months. En route Nishi prepared a short speech on the history of Western philosophy, which he modestly acknowledged to be the first ever given by a Japanese. In his remarks, he made no effort to conceal his admiration of Socrates and Plato, the former of whom "is comparable to our Confucius." It was here that he explained philosophy (*kitetsugaku*)[14] as the "clarification of wisdom and virtue."[15] This fragmentary speech would seem to confirm that philosophy was the most important of Nishi's many interests and that he considered himself a pioneer in the field, even before reaching Holland.

At length the day of arrival came in April 1863, when the ship finally reached Marseilles. Nishi and Tsuda immediately entrained for Rotterdam and then transferred to Leiden, where they spent the next two and one-half years. The Dutch government assigned Nishi and Tsuda to the care of J. J. Hoffmann, a professor of Chinese and Japanese studies at the University of Leiden.[16] Eight days after arriving in Holland, Nishi wrote Hoffmann about the purpose of his studies:

"We know nothing at all of the requisite knowledge for carrying on relations with the various states of Europe and

[14] In this document Nishi alternately uses *huirosohuia* in phonetic script and *kitetsugaku* to mean "philosophy." *Kitetsugaku* means "to seek clarity." In creating this term, Nishi based it on the word *kiken*, "to seek wisdom," which appears in the *Ta-chi t'u-shuo* of the Confucianist Chou Lien-yin (1017-1073). Not until he wrote *Hyakuichi shinron* (1874) did Nishi use the modern term for "philosophy," *tetsugaku*. See Asō, *Kinsei Nihon tetsugakushi*, pp. 225-226; Miyagawa, *Kindai Nihon no tetsugaku*, pp. 21-22.

[15] *Seiyō tetsugakushi no kōan danpen*, *NAZS* 1960, pp. 16-17. This fragment also appears in Asō, *Kinsei Nihon tetsugakushi*, pp. 40-41. Asō argued that the lecture had been prepared for the research institute shortly before Nishi left for Holland, but Ōkubo Toshiaki has established that it was written on shipboard. Ōkubo, "Kaisetsu," *NAZS* 1960, pp. 611-613.

[16] Kazue Kyōichi, "Nishi Amane no shūgyō jidai," *Nihon oyobi Nihonjin*, 1,428 (April 1964), p. 48. For Hoffmann, see biographical notes.

for reforming our domestic administration and institutions, nor of such subjects as statistics, law, economics, politics, and diplomacy. For this reason our aim is to study all these subjects. Since it is really impossible in such a short stay to study all of these many important matters, I have decided to make a list of various subjects to be studied successively, and to give it to the young students sent the next time. This is an outline of what I plan to study. What I expect of you, given the above facts, is that you select a good teacher for me. French plays an extraordinarily large role in all branches of learning, but speaking it is exceedingly difficult for us. Those who speak it fluently are extremely rare. I hope to study this too as time permits. I have already studied English and can read and understand it, but I cannot converse."[17]

Their mission, in other words, was to absorb and carry home knowledge of the contemporary European social sciences because they were useful—they would both help Japan become fit for "carrying on relations with the various states of Europe" and also enable her to lay plans for "reforming our domestic administration and institutions." The feebleness of actual attempts at reform notwithstanding, clearly the Tokugawa government now regarded Europe as the model not only for technical matters such as diplomatic practice but also for basic institutional change. As an official *bakufu* emissary, Nishi acknowledged that Japan had to learn the secrets of domestic and international politics through the medium of European academic disciplines, an extraordinarily frank admission of European supremacy in this realm.

Nishi's intentions, however, were not so unimaginative as to be confined to his orders from Edo. After stating the official purpose of the trip, he informed Hoffmann that he had a personal objective as well:

"In addition to the above, I hope to learn those subjects

[17] Nishi to Hoffmann, 1863, in Vissering family archive, quoted in Itazawa Takeo, *Nihon to Oranda* (Tokyo, 1956), pp. 166-167. Itazawa's version is a Japanese translation of the original Dutch.

within the realm of philosophy. The religious thought that is prohibited by our national law differs, I believe, from those things advocated by Descartes, Locke, Hegel, and Kant, so I hope to study them too. This work is probably difficult, but, in my opinion, there are not a few points in the study of these subjects which will serve to advance our civilization, so I hope to study at least a part, although in such a short time it may be difficult. Because I know nothing of European practice, I acknowledge that without your friendly advice I would be able to decide nothing on my own."[18]

It is not clear what Nishi meant by "the religious thought that is prohibited by our national laws," although there is a strong likelihood that this refers to Christianity. Nishi reemphasized his utilitarian approach to his studies in this letter, asserting that learning secular philosophy had merit because it could "serve to advance our civilization."

Hoffmann replied by wisely suggesting that Nishi and Tsuda, before getting into social science or philosophy, spend the first few months perfecting their Dutch. Accordingly they studied the language six hours weekly under the direction of J. A. Van Dyck, a local high-school principal.[19] Hoffmann then introduced them to Simon Vissering (1818-1888), a leading professor of economics at Leiden. Vissering eagerly accepted the challenge of force-feeding the elements of social science to the Japanese. He worked out a crash program of instruction in five areas: natural law, international law, constitutional law, economics, and statistics. His choice of these five topics demonstrates the practical, scientific character of contemporary academic thinking in Europe, especially by contrast with Japan, where none of these subjects was then taught.[20] That the Japanese requested such courses indicates how much a part they were of the practical spirit of the times.

[18] *Ibid.*, pp. 166-167.
[19] Hayashi, "Bakumatsu no kaigai ryūgakusei—sono ni," p. 87; Asō, *Kinsei Nihon tetsugakushi*, p. 53.
[20] Nishi's notes of Vissering's lectures confirm this point. They are entitled *Goka gakushū kankei bunsho, NAZS* 1961, pp. 134-135. See Asō, *Kinsei Nihon tetsugakushi*, pp. 53-55.

Study Abroad and Service at Home

Vissering lectured to Nishi and Tsuda every Thursday and Friday night for nearly two years. Their notes reveal that they took their work seriously, and they carefully copied down Vissering's words for transmission to Japan.

It is interesting to observe what efforts Nishi and Tsuda subsequently made to diffuse their new knowledge in Japan.

(1) Natural law (*natuurregt*). Nishi's term for natural law was *seihō no gaku*, which has become *shizenhō* in modern Japanese.[21] Nishi gave lectures at his private school in Kyoto in 1867 based on Vissering's teachings about natural law, and he prepared a revised version of his notes on this subject under the title *Seihōsetsu yaku* (Outline of Natural Law Theories), also in 1867. This manuscript was never published, but Kanda Takahira (1830-1898), later a charter member of the Meiji Six Society, edited a revised version, based on Nishi's lecture notes and *Seihōsetsu yaku*, which was published in 1871 as *Seihō ryaku* (Outline of Natural Law).[22] Yoshino Sakuzō included *Seihō ryaku* in the *Meiji bunka zenshū* volume of representative Meiji period works on law.[23]

(2) International law (*volkenregt*). Nishi translated this as *bankoku kōhō no gaku*, which in modern Japanese is *kokusai kōhō*.[24] The *bakufu* ordered Nishi to translate his notes of Vissering's lectures on international law shortly after he returned to Edo in 1866. The result was a book, *Bankoku kōhō*, published in 1868.[25] Two versions were published, an official one for government use and another for popular dissemination, the latter of which apparently no longer exists. *Bankoku kōhō* is little more than a lecture outline, with some criticism, and it is important mainly as one of the first

[21] This term dropped out of common usage after the early Meiji period.
[22] Nishi's version was called *Seihōsetsu yaku*; Kanda's was known as *Seihō ryaku* and appears in *NAZS* 1961, pp. 103-133.
[23] *Meiji bunka zenshū*, ed. Yoshino Sakuzō (Tokyo, 1927-1930), VIII (Law volume).
[24] *Bankoku kōhō no gaku* was commonly used for "international law" or "the law of nations" during the Bakumatsu period.
[25] *Bankoku kōhō*, *NAZS* 1961, pp. 3-102.

commentaries on international law in Japan. It supplemented William Martin's Chinese translation of Wheaton's *Elements of International Law,* which was published in Peking in 1864 and introduced to Japan a year later.[26]

(3) Constitutional law (*staatsregt*). This was known as *kokuhō no gaku,* or *kokuhōgaku* in modern Japanese. Tsuda took charge of translating Vissering's lectures on this topic, on orders from the *bakufu,* and published *Taisei kokuhōron* (Discussion of Western Constitutional Law) under official auspices in 1868.[27] This book was the most polished translation of the group, receiving wide acclaim as the pioneering Japanese work on Western law, and with its publication Tsuda began a successful legal career.

(4) Economics (*staatshuishoudkunde*). No translation of the lectures on this topic was ever prepared.

(5) Statistics (*statistiek*). Nishi's term for this was *seihyō no gaku,* which is *tōkeigaku* in modern Japanese. Tsuda was given the responsibility of translating material on this topic also. The result was a book called *Hyōki teikō* (Charts and Classifications), which appeared in 1874. This was likewise the first such book to appear in Japan.[28]

In sum, of the five courses that Vissering devised, four led to published works in precisely those areas of knowledge which Nishi and Tsuda had been charged with studying. These books constituted the beginnings of social science in Japan.[29]

Hence, Simon Vissering had considerable influence on the development of these new disciplines in Meiji Japan. A grad-

[26] Blacker, *The Japanese Enlightenment,* p. 126. Cf. the chapter on "The Introduction of International Law, 1862-1874" in I.C.Y. Hsü, *China's Entrance into the Family of Nations: The Diplomatic Phase, 1858-1880* (Cambridge, Mass., 1960), pp. 121-148.

[27] The book was entitled *Taisei kokuhōron.* See Ōkubo, "Kaisetsu," *NAZS* 1961, pp. 691-698.

[28] See *ibid.,* p. 704.

[29] Hayase Toshio considers Nishi the founder of Japanese sociology, on the strength of these translations of Vissering's lectures. Hayase, "Meiji shoki ni okeru Nihon shakaigaku zenshi—shakaigakusha to shite no Nishi Amane to Konto no jisshōshugi," *Ōkurayama ronshū,* 1 (June 1952), p. 85.

uate of Leiden, he had practiced law before returning to the university as an assistant to Professor Thorbecke, the future prime minister of Holland. Vissering himself later went into politics and served as finance minister. He was strongly opposed to the German historical school and was a positivist in epistemology and a utilitarian in ethics.[30] As an economics professor at Leiden, he advocated the teachings of Adam Smith and classic liberalism. The emphasis on free markets and free trade thus directed Nishi's and Tsuda's attention to orthodox English economics, which they later informally transmitted to Japan, apparently with some effect on early Meiji trade policies.[31] The predominantly British orientation of Dutch scholarship at this time contributed to the great admiration of English ideas felt by Nishi, Tsuda, and most of the early Meiji advocates of "civilization and enlightenment."

England, the mother of colonialism and the world's greatest imperial power, was seemingly an improbable choice as a model for nation-building, at least in Asia. It was the English merchant marine that had precipitated the humiliation of China by running opium from India to Canton. Indeed, of all the European powers, none was more resented in East Asia than Britain. But precisely because she was the world's richest and most powerful nation, England was a natural object of Japanese respect and emulation, if not outright admiration. Her government and institutions appeared to broadminded Japanese to be a proper blend of monarchism and modernism. As an island nation, she resembled Japan geographically, economically, and in her detached outlook on diplomatic affairs. Nishi and Tsuda had become pioneers in carrying back English thought to Japan, and their cases are added evidence that England was quite as important a source as France or Prussia for Japan's cultural growth in the early Meiji period.[32]

[30] *Ibid.*, pp. 94-95.
[31] "Nishi Amane," *Kindai bungaku kenkyū sōsho*, ed. Shōwa Joshi Daigaku (Tokyo, 1956), III, p. 112; Ōkubo, "Kaisetsu," *NAZS* 1961, pp. 702-703.
[32] Professor Mikiso Hane has written an excellent dissertation on the impact of English thought on early Meiji Japan. His evidence

Study Abroad and Service at Home

Not only did the two scholars fulfill their official *bakufu* mission, but Nishi also managed to satisfy his private ambition to learn more about Western philosophy. In addition to their formal work with Vissering, both Nishi and Tsuda attended occasional lectures by C. W. Opzoomer (1812-1892), the leading historian of philosophy in Holland at the time. Although no notes exist from these lectures, Nishi later remarked in *Jinsei sanpōsetsu* (Theory of the Three Human Treasures): "When I was studying in Holland ten years ago, a famous philosopher of that period in Holland was Opzoomer. This man seems to have respected Comte . . . and Mill."[33] Philosophy clearly interested Nishi most among his various subjects, and he devoted many of his later essays to expounding contemporary European positivism and utilitarianism. Opzoomer was probably the chief inspiration to Nishi during his study abroad, and Nishi brought back a number of his books, as well as some by Vissering, when he returned to Japan.[34] Opzoomer intro-

---

demonstrates that England was the chief model for many Japanese reforms and was the predominant source for "enlightened" thought in the early Meiji era. His thesis places German and French influence on modern Japan in proper perspective. Hane, "English Liberalism and the Japanese Enlightenment, 1868-1890," Ph.D. dissertation in history, Yale University (New Haven, 1957). See also his "Nationalism and the Decline of Liberalism in Meiji Japan," *Studies on Asia*, ed. Robert K. Sakai, IV (1963), pp. 69-80.

[33] *Jinsei sanpōsetsu*, NAZS 1960, p. 514.

[34] Unfortunately, Nishi's essays are undocumented, and it is impossible to know precisely which books he brought home and which he later ordered. However, a catalogue of the Western language books in Nishi's library was compiled by his illegitimate son Boppei upon Nishi's death, under the title *Kodanshaku Nishi Amanekun isho mokuroku*. This longhand list, on faded legal paper, shows that four books by Opzoomer (items 169-172) and three by Vissering (items 247-249), all dealing with law, remained in Nishi's library in 1897. Apparently the list is incomplete, and doubtless Nishi at one time owned other Western books. This bibliography survived the 1923 Kanto district earthquake and fire, which destroyed many of Nishi's books and manuscripts. It was presented to the Tokyo Imperial University Branch Library sometime before 1923 and was acquired by the National Diet Library in 1953. No significant Western language books of Nishi's remain in the family library. I am indebted to Professor Ōkubo Toshiaki for lending me this bibliography and to Nishi's

duced Nishi and Tsuda to Anglo-French positivism, especially the works of Auguste Comte (1798-1857) and John Stuart Mill (1806-1873). He also apparently lectured them on Kant, as Tsuda indicated in an introduction to Ōgai's biography:

"Later, when we studied abroad in Holland, we both lived in Leiden. We learned about the essentials of European political science from Dr. Vissering, professor of law at Leiden University. At our leisure [Nishi and I] used to argue together. But he was fond of the Kantian school of philosophy, whereas I preferred Comte's positivism. Therefore we could not but regret that our disagreement was like a round hole and a square peg."[35]

Despite Tsuda's testimony, however, Nishi had little interest in Kant. There are occasional references to Kant's ideas about eternal peace in Nishi's *Bankoku kōhō,* which was basically a translation, and in *Heifūron* (Discussion of Military Service), but there is little resemblance between Kant's thought and Nishi's, and it is doubtful that Nishi ever read Kant at all.[36] Comte and Mill, on the other hand, were crucial to the development of Nishi's mature thought, in that their empiricism, logic, and economic doctrines contributed heavily to his theories of state and society, as well as his ethical thought. However, because there are no records of substance concerning Nishi's work with Opzoomer, it is impossible to determine what plan of study he followed in learning philosophy. It is known, nonetheless, that Opzoomer, Vissering, and Hoffmann all belonged to the Anglo-French positivistic movement, that Nishi introduced this school of thought to Japan after he returned home, and that such ideas had a definite appeal in early Meiji Japan. Hence Opzoomer and

---

grandson, Mr. Nishi Torioto, for showing me the contents of the family library in Odawara.

[35] Quoted in Asō, *Kinsei Nihon tetsugakushi,* p. 66.

[36] *Heifūron* appears in *NAZS* 1966, pp. 18-96. On Nishi's understanding of Kant, see Asō, *Kinsei Nihon tetsugakushi,* pp. 66-68.

his colleagues were important middlemen in transmitting this philosophy to Japan.

Nishi and Tsuda lived a frugal and studious life in Leiden, and they did almost no traveling outside Holland. When their two and one-half years in Leiden ended on December 1, 1865, they went to Paris to meet some Japanese associates before returning home via Suez. Their ship reached Shinagawa on February 13, 1866, bringing them back in time to make a futile effort, under orders from the *bakufu,* to use their new knowledge to solve Japan's growing political problems.

FRUSTRATING SERVICE IN A TOTTERING REGIME

Japanese politics had undergone remarkable gyrations during the three-year absence of Nishi and Tsuda. Political power and initiative gradually slipped from the hands of helpless *bakufu* officials into the grasp of certain major daimyo in Western Japan. Economic difficulties resulting from trade with the West helped give birth to the peasant revolts and other forms of social unrest that have engrossed some latter-day Marxist historians.[37] The larger *tozama* domains were meanwhile busily pursuing modern industrial and military policies that strengthened their own local economies as well as their national political influence. The continuing diplomatic debacle vis-à-vis the West increasingly reinforced the demand that direct imperial rule replace shogunal sovereignty. In the summer following Nishi's return from abroad, the fourteenth shogun, Iemochi (ruled 1858-1866), died at age twenty while his troops were vainly trying to subdue the Chōshū restorationists. Hitotsubashi Keiki (Tokugawa Yoshinobu, 1837-1913), son of Nariaki, the late lord of Mito, was made the new shogun once the *bakufu* troops had been withdrawn from the engagement. Keiki's boldness and ingenuity briefly revived the *bakufu's* fortunes, but the death of the Kōmei Emperor in February 1867 gave great emotional impetus to the spirited movement to restore his teen-age son,

[37] See Hugh Borton, *Japan's Modern Century* (New York, 1955), pp. 56-60.

later known as the Meiji Emperor, to a position of real authority in political affairs. A series of intricate negotiations among representatives of the court, *bakufu,* and western clans resulted in a steady pruning of the shogun's authority. Keiki's resignation in November 1867 was soon followed by the imperial announcement of January 3, 1868, that all power had reverted to the throne.[38]

Nishi divided his time during these two turbulent years between Edo and Kyoto, the latter of which was the center of the political and ideological storm. After he and Tsuda had returned from Holland, both were instructed to rejoin the Foreign Books Research Institute, now known as the Institute of Development (Kaiseijo), and on March 2, 1866, Nishi was made an assistant professor.[39] The scope of the research institute had been considerably broadened during their absence, and a new school had been opened at Ogawamachi near the present Chuo University. Nishi's and Tsuda's return led to further curriculum growth: "Moreover, various sciences such as law, economics, and philosophy were imported by Nishi Amane, Tsuda Mamichi, and others, and the academic style of the research institute also underwent a great change."[40] The work of the institute, although increasingly useless to the desperate *bakufu,* continued undisturbed through the scramble for power in Kyoto and the early years of the new state, until it was taken over by the fledgling Ministry of Education. It later served as the principal base upon which Tokyo University was created in 1878.

Nishi did not share the placid scholarly life of his colleagues at the institute during these topsy-turvy years. Instead, on April 27, 1866, he was made an official *bakufu* adviser on European affairs. He was expected to be an intellectual factotum who could use the new knowledge from Holland to counsel the floundering military government in

---

[38] For an excellent summary of these events, see W. G. Beasley, "Introduction," *Select Documents on Japanese Foreign Policy, 1853-1868,* ed. Beasley (London, 1955), pp. 86-91.

[39] Ōgai, *Nishi Amane den,* p. 163.

[40] Numata Jirō, *Yōgaku denrai no rekishi* (Tokyo, 1960), p. 167. See also Asō, *Kinsei Nihon tetsugakushi,* p. 26.

the negotiations for political control that were taking place in Kyoto. With this appointment he was made a full professor at the institute and given an allowance of one hundred *hyō* and an office salary of twenty *kō*.[41] One of his first duties was to translate Vissering's lectures on international law, which he completed as *Bankoku kōhō* the next autumn. Tsuda was meanwhile busy translating his notes from Vissering's lectures on constitutional law. Such work was, of course, extremely bookish and not likely to be very useful to its beleaguered patrons; having made the two scholars advisers, the *bakufu* seems not to have known quite how to utilize them.

A chance to be of tangible service came on October 27, when the new shogun, Keiki, ordered Nishi and Tsuda to drop their other projects and join him in Kyoto, where he was maneuvering to retain *bakufu* initiative in the political crisis.[42] The ostensible purpose of the summons was to provide Keiki with cogent advice on European constitutional practice during the frantic search for a plan to conserve the *bakufu*'s deteriorating authority. Instead, Nishi found himself in the background when he got to Kyoto, consigned to passing the days and weeks idly without being consulted by anyone. His notes indicate the anguish he felt:

"Both [Tsuda] and I returned from Holland and we soon received an emergency summons from the present shogun for questioning on our views of the world, including national political affairs. However, this [interrogation] never took place, and in the end we never knew why we had been summoned. Speaking confidentially, the fact that the shogun patronized scholars did not mean that he utilized them. Isn't he like the ancient lords who were fond of dragons? This evil custom is apt to lead to decadence."[43]

Tsuda, declaring that he had nothing to do, gave up and returned to the Institute of Development at Edo, but Nishi was obliged to stay on in Kyoto. His biographer noted that,

[41] Ōgai, *Nishi Amane den*, p. 163.   [42] *Ibid.*, p. 164.
[43] From Nishi's *Shiki*, quoted *ibid.*, p. 165.

"bored and lonely, he blotted out the days in carousing. When he had time, he simply made revisions in his translation of *Bankoku kōhō*."[44] He submitted the corrected manuscript to the *bakufu* on February 2, 1867, but it had understandably slight effect on the course of political events.[45]

One way to dispel the boredom was to teach. Since he could not return to the institute in Edo, Nishi decided in March 1867 to start a private school where he would instruct young samurai in the fundamentals of Western studies. Among the courses were lectures on international and national law. Such a venture had little prospect of popularity in the capital, where anti-foreign sentiments were strong, but shortly after Nishi opened the school at Sūjakuji, the temple near Shijō where he lived, he had nearly five hundred pupils.[46] A great number of the students who came to learn English were recommended by Kimura Shūsaburō, who had just returned from a trip abroad for the *bakufu*. Nishi thus found himself operating a school for the sons of Tokugawa partisans in the hostile environment of Kyoto, since most of his students came from the domains of Kuwana, Tsu, Fukui, and Matsuyama;[47] all but Tsu were *bakufu* allies, and Tsu's status was semi-*fudai*. Few persons imagined in the spring and summer of 1867 that the *bakufu* would soon disappear completely; most expected it to persist, however emasculated, and hence there seemed to be some utility in educating the sons of its allies. In this way Nishi indirectly used his recently acquired knowledge to benefit his government. Ōgai, however, later noted that Nishi's heart was not in his work:

"The work of the private academy slowly flourished, and his *bakufu* job gradually grew more leisurely. Amane, his heart stymied in daily events, chatted with his doctor friends and neither participated in nor listened to a single secret

---

[44] Ōgai, *Nishi Amane den*, p. 165.

[45] *Ibid.*, p. 166.

[46] Kazue, "Nishi Amane no shōgai to sono shisō," p. 15. See also Ōgai, *Nishi Amane den*, p. 166; Ōkubo, "Kaisetsu," *NAZS* 1961, pp. 685-687.

[47] Hayashi, "Bakumatsu no kaigai ryūgakusei—sono ni," p. 90.

scheme. Despondently, without pleasure, he drank aimlessly and conserved his energies."[48]

Another urgent command to counsel Keiki came on April 18, 1867. The job was to teach the shogun French as well as to lecture him on representative government in the West. Keiki was reportedly a good student with a prodigious memory, but he was far too busy dealing with foreign officials and contenders for his power to devote much time to study. Furthermore, Keiki was addicted to the new gadgets and inventions that the foreigners were bringing in, so he diverted Nishi by having him translate the manuals of instructions for such items as electric lightbulbs and sewing machines. Nishi wrote Katō Hiroyuki during the summer of 1867, mentioning the shogun's fascination with a telegraph transmitter which someone had given him and adding that Nishi was working on a translation of a Dutch almanac.[49] Later that summer Nishi received a promotion in rank and accompanied the shogun on several trips to Mito, Edo, and Osaka, lodging for a time with an Uemachi liquor dealer in the latter city. But there was no sign that Keiki would find him more challenging assignments than these desultory translation projects. Such trivial work prompted Nishi to write Tsuda in despair: "I do not know about the future. Just now I am nothing but a functionary. I have nothing to do with politics. Of what benefit is this for the people?"[50] It is interesting that Nishi used a curious term for "functionary," the compound *kangan,* which is an inversion of the word for "eunuch" (also *kangan*). The implication is that he felt like a useless supernumerary, without any voice in political decisions. This is an indication of the uses to which the country's most advanced scholars were being put.

On one question, however, Nishi's erudition proved of

[48] Ōgai, *Nishi Amane den,* p. 166.
[49] Nishi to Katō, summer 1867, quoted in Kazue, "Nishi Amane no shōgai to sono shisō," p. 14. See also Hayashi, "Bakumatsu no kaigai ryūgakusei—sono ni," p. 89.
[50] Nishi to Tsuda, May 29, 1867, quoted in Tsuda Dōji, *Tsuda Mamichi* (Tokyo, 1940), p. 101.

great value to the shogun: drafting a constitution that would meet the demands for an imperial restoration and yet preserve real power in Edo. As early as 1843 Sugita Seikei had translated the Dutch constitution, and European constitutional government was widely admired in Bakumatsu Japan.[51] As the political crisis deepened in the 1860's, many plans arose to replace the shogunate with a conciliar government in which the daimyo would gain political initiative, acting in the name of a resuscitated imperial institution. Sakamoto Ryōma and Nagaoka Kenkichi devised the most famous of these in 1867, which Yamauchi Yōdō presented with some changes to the *bakufu* in October 1867 as the Tosa Memorial. This scheme provided that the shogun would resign without prejudice and that a bicameral legislature would be formed. The upper house would be composed of the major feudal lords, while the lower chamber would represent the samurai and perhaps even commoners.[52] Osatake Takeshi has identified the antecedents of certain aspects of the Tosa plan in two minor memos which Nishi presented to the *bakufu* in the spring of 1867.[53] Some would have it that the theory of the separation of powers in Japan originated with Nishi Amane,[54] but in fact such ideas were well-known in Japan by the time he returned from Holland. Nishi's role before October 1867 was a more modest one, limited to occasional lectures to Keiki on the threefold division of powers in English constitutional theory.

The eight-point Tosa Memorial was handed to the *bakufu* on October 28, 1867. Keiki and his advisers vacillated for ten days, unsure whether to accept the plan or risk war with Satsuma and Chōshū, the leading restorationist domains. Fi-

[51] Osatake Takeshi, "Ishinmae ni okeru kenpō sōan," *Teikoku Gakushiin kiji* (July 25, 1942), p. 327.
[52] See Marius B. Jansen, *Sakamoto Ryōma and the Meiji Restoration* (Princeton, 1961), pp. 294-295, 312-313, for an authoritative account of the genesis of the Tosa plan.
[53] Osatake Takeshi, "Nishi Amane no jiseki ni oite," *Kokushi Kaikokai kiyō*, 47 (Feb. 15, 1944), p. 9; Osatake, "Ishinmae ni okeru kenpō sōan," pp. 349-350. These memos have evidently been lost.
[54] See, for example, Tōyama Shigeki, *Meiji ishin* (Tokyo, 1951), pp. 245-246.

Study Abroad and Service at Home

nally Keiki called a meeting on November 8 at the Nijō Palace, at which he announced to all the daimyo present in Kyoto his decision to resign as shogun and transfer his powers to the throne. Nishi was present at this meeting. Later in the day, according to Ōgai, Keiki questioned Nishi anew "about the three-part division of state powers and the English parliamentary system. Accordingly, he stated a brief outline and withdrew. He then wrote a detailed account beneath his lamp and titled it *Seiyō kansei ryakukō* [Outline of Western Governmental Systems]. The following morning he presented it."[55]

This outline was little more than a set of observations about European parliamentary practice. It mainly concerned the procedures of a collective assembly, apparently in an effort to brief Keiki on contemporary Western practice in light of the eight-point plan which he had just been forced to accept. This short-order outline served as a kind of preamble to a more weighty document which Nishi immediately set about writing, *Gidai sōan* (Parliamentary Draft), which he handed to Keiki in early December.[56] Intended as the *bakufu* answer to the Tosa plan, *Gidai sōan* was a detailed constitution for a revised Japanese polity in which the shogun would continue to hold most executive powers. It divided political authority among the court, the *bakufu,* and the various *han,* in a pattern much like a monarchic federation. Its chief provisions were given as "rights":

(1) The rights of the imperial court. It is highly significant that Nishi proposed strict limits on the court's powers. While acceding to the inevitability of a stronger throne (he granted the emperor the "rights of legal sanction"), Nishi restricted

---

[55] Ōgai, *Nishi Amane den,* pp. 167-168. Ōgai gives the title of Nishi's outline as *Seiyō kansei ryakukō.* Although Osatake, "Nishi Amane no jiseki," p. 9, says that this manuscript has been lost, Ōkubo reasons that it is the same as *Taisei kansei setsuryaku,* which appears in *NAZS* 1961, pp. 184-196. See Ōkubo, "Kaisetsu," *NAZS* 1961, p. 717. Osatake states that Nishi prepared the draft the night before the November 8 announcement, but Ōgai dates it as the night of November 8.

[56] *Gidai sōan, NAZS* 1961, pp. 167-183.

the court's rights to determining reign names, authority over weights and measures, titular headship of Shinto and Buddhism, and the rights of conferring titles, conscripting a new army, and demanding service from the daimyo.

(2) The rights of the *bakufu*. The *bakufu* would retain the general powers of administration, right of direct control over the land (as opposed to *han* rule), the right to use the title *taikun* (a variant for shogun), the right to establish an administrative office in Osaka, the right to establish cabinet officers, the right of appointment and dismissal, the right of the shogun to preside over the proposed upper house and to have superior voting rights, the right to disband the lower house, and the right to institute a new bureaucracy.

(3) The rights of the daimyo. These consisted of the right to participate in a parliamentary assembly, in which the upper house would be composed of daimyo and the lower of samurai. No provision was made for commoners, and representation would be based on the domains rather than population. Laws passed by the assembly would be forwarded to the *bakufu*, which would secure court approval.[57]

This tendentious document was little more than an imposing legal charter, embellished with the sanction of a European format, for preserving *bakufu* power. The strict circumscription of imperial authority was transparently an attempt to confine the emperor to the ceremonial role he played under the Tokugawa. The rights enumerated for the *bakufu* included many old prerogatives and some new ones that would increase its control, while the jurisdiction and representation of the assembly would be narrower than those in the Tosa plan. Hence, through the numerical preponderance of his friends among the daimyo, Keiki could hope to control the western *han* via simple majoritarianism.

Nishi's constitutional draft was, of course, written for the *bakufu* and thus does not fully reflect his personal ideas about parliamentary government. The reforms that it would institute had already become acceptable to all but the most

[57] *Ibid.*, pp. 175-183.

reactionary *bakufu* leaders. The draft was merely a feeble counter-proposal that came far too late to be of the slightest effect, since it was clear to all that it was a device to perpetuate *bakufu* hegemony. Moreover it had the defects of the Tosa plan without its advantages. Both would establish parliaments with substantial powers, representing more persons. Both plans assumed that compromise among *bakufu,* court, and clans was possible, but Nishi's draft yielded too little of the *bakufu*'s power. Finally, by preserving the *bakufu* and shogun virtually intact, Nishi's proposal purposely skirted the basic demand for a new locus of political power. Tosa's program made much more of the transfer of authority from *bakufu* to court and embodied a genuine imperial restoration. Although it seemed far more likely of acceptance than Nishi's scheme, the Tosa plan failed as a workable solution because it was offensive to the western clans of Satsuma and Chōshū. Hence, Nishi's plan had no chance of success, both because it appeared long after the *bakufu* had lost its bargaining position and because it was far too biased and compromised too few of the shogun's prerogatives.

Nishi's draft was nonetheless the earliest detailed constitutional proposal in Japan.[58] Katō Hiroyuki had written the first systematic Japanese critique of Western constitutional practice in 1864, and in 1867 Tsuda had proposed a number of reforms in the political structure, including constitutional government, in his *Nihon kokusō seido* (General Structure of Japan).[59] Nishi's plan, however, was the first written constitution with articles, clauses, and paragraphs specifying the responsibilities and limits of the various organs of govern-

[58] The Tosa Memorial was a sketchy outline compared with Nishi's plan. Osatake is very generous in assessing Nishi's importance in introducing constitutionalism to Japan. See "Nishi Amane no jiseki," pp. 9-16, and "Ishinmae ni okeru kenpō sōan," pp. 327-350. For other views, see Tōyama, *Meiji ishin,* pp. 245-246, and Asai Kiyoshi, *Meiji rikken shisō ni okeru Eikoku gikai seido no eikyō* (Tokyo, 1935), pp. 195-205.

[59] Katō's book was called *Tonarigusa,* while Tsuda's was *Nihon kokusō seido.* See Abosch, "Katō Hiroyuki," pp. 324-325; Minamoto, "Meiji ishin to jitsugaku shisō," pp. 100-103.

ment. It applied the concept of written law to power relationships in the state, with the expectation that the provisions would be regarded as basic law. Furthermore, Nishi's constitution was predicated on a concept that was quite new and unintelligible to most Japanese, the idea of political rights. He defined the governmental functions of the throne, *bakufu,* and daimyo in terms of specified rights, with the implication that anything not granted as a right was prohibited. He used the term *ken* for "rights," although *ken* traditionally conveyed the clear connotation of might. Mitsukuri Rinshō (1844-1897) is ordinarily credited with first using the concept of rights in Japan in the accepted Western sense of political rights,[60] but this draft shows that Nishi based his constitution on this idea nearly two years before Rinshō's translation of the French Civil Code in 1869. Unfortunately, however, he did not discuss the concept in detail until he published *Hyakuichi shinron* in 1874. In short, as an abstract document Nishi's *Gidai sōan* set several precedents in Japan, but as a pragmatic solution of the contemporary political crisis it was an egregious failure.

The winter of 1867-1868 was a quiet moment in Nishi's career. Two years before he had returned home confident that at last he could put his knowledge to the service of his country, but instead he had been thrust aside, waiting in an obscure temple for infrequent consultations about the entangled events outside. He was never in a position to influence policy; not until it was too late was he able to make concrete constitutional proposals. Apparently he felt sufficiently kindly toward the *bakufu* that he was willing to put his knowledge to its partisan advantage. The demise of the *bakufu* in late 1867 meant the beginning of a protracted period of indecision for Nishi, during which he had to reconsider his allegiances and choose a new career.

[60] See Blacker, *The Japanese Enlightenment,* pp. 104-105. Rinshō first used the present term for "rights," *kenri,* but he took it from the Chinese to translate a French word, so that his contribution to transmitting the basic concept of rights was a limited one.

Study Abroad and Service at Home

THE WESTERN-ORIENTED INTELLECTUAL
IN THE RESTORATION

If, as modern social science has it, it takes intellectuals to make a revolution, Nishi Amane and his fellow scholars of the West were conspicuously absent from the drama that culminated with the restoration of the teenaged Emperor Mutsuhito in January 1868. Indeed, it is quite proper to question whether the events of 1853-1868 constituted a revolution at all, judged against the revolutionary experiences of other nations both before and since. If the twentieth-century Japanese ideologue Kita Ikki (1884-1937) is correct in stating that a revolution is merely a battle unless it involves a war of ideas,[61] it seems prudent to call the Meiji Restoration, as of 1868, merely a power struggle and not a full-dress revolution. While not denying the critical role played by intellectuals of Kaikoku and Jōi persuasions in the process of restoration, three stubborn facts about the tussle for political control in Bakumatsu Japan militate against the view that the restoration was a true revolution. The first is that there was no significant social or economic class conflict; as Thomas C. Smith puts it, Meiji was an "aristocratic revolution"[62] if one at all. The second is that the foreign policy debate between exclusionists and internationalists was greatly overshadowed by a fundamental national consensus on value, centering on the imperial throne. No real clash of ideas took place because there was basic agreement among nearly all politically involved Japanese on the ultimate sovereignty of the emperor and the need for national strengthening. The third is that those intellectuals who most keenly perceived the gap between the cultures of pre-modern Japan and modern Europe—the men most susceptible to "psychic mobility"[63] and alienation from their past—withdrew from the internal conflict and remained neutralists in the restora-

---

[61] George M. Wilson, "Kita Ikki's Theory of Revolution," *Journal of Asian Studies*, xxvi, 1 (November 1966), p. 91.

[62] Thomas C. Smith, "Japan's Aristocratic Revolution," *Yale Review*, L, 3 (Spring 1961), pp. 370-383.

[63] F. W. Mote's phrase.

tion. It is to these Western-oriented scholars that we shall now direct our attention.

Nishi Amane belonged to a group of Bakumatsu-Meiji scholars who may be loosely described as bureaucratic intellectuals. Like earlier generations of Japanese students of the West, they served the *bakufu* as advisers and translators, but in their understanding of Western culture they far surpassed their predecessors, who had been mere technicians. In common with nearly all Japanese intellectuals, they understood the need for "enriching the country and strengthening the army," watchwords of the revolution that followed the restoration. Their training and talents were preeminent credentials for leading the reform movements that would bring the country on a par with the West. Yet these *bakufu* intellectuals did not become particularly estranged from the old regime, nor did they seize the initiative in the restoration movement. Like Nishi, most of them floated idly through the crucial years 1866 and 1867, almost completely cut off from political events. Nishi's experiences shed some light on this problem of why the most liberally educated intellectuals in the country did not take part in the political revolution until the new state was solidly established.

Herbert Passin and others have suggested that these bureaucratic intellectuals felt "committed by feudal or personal bonds to the Tokugawa" and accordingly could not fully participate in the restoration movement before 1870.[64] This was not the case with Nishi, however. He was not a hereditary Tokugawa vassal, and he hardly felt much personal loyalty to the shogun, who kept him, like a dragon, for decoration. His *dappan* had clearly been motivated by intellectual choice: the best opportunity for studying the West in 1854 lay with the *bakufu*. His job with the shogunate was a source of material subsistence but not a cause for unflagging loyalty to the Tokugawa. Furthermore, although it was the *bakufu* which had sent him abroad, Nishi's personal purpose

[64] Herbert Passin's phrase, from "Modernization and the Japanese Intellectual: Some Comparative Observations," *Changing Japanese Attitudes Toward Modernization*, ed. Marius B. Jansen (Princeton, 1965), p. 463.

was to learn subjects which would "serve to advance our civilization." His thinking clearly transcended the scope of the Tokugawa government, and it is therefore difficult to maintain that Nishi was personally bound to the *bakufu.* Tsuda, Katō, and Fukuzawa similarly had no feudal or personal ties to the Tokugawa family. Like all Japanese, these scholars were committed to retrieving Japan's honor vis-à-vis the West. Their vision encompassed an educated and sophisticated public rebuilt according to the superior blueprint of civilized European society. While they did not reject the *bakufu* outright, they certainly did not equate it with the nation; to them the question of who held power was distinctly secondary.

The diary of Koyama Masataka, one of Nishi's pupils at the Sūjakuji private school in 1867, supplies valuable information about his teacher's attitude during the political crisis:

"Amane could not help being bored during the events at this time. Realizing in light of the Kagoshima battle that it was wrong to adhere to the closed-port theories of the enthusiasts, I visited Amane each time I went to Kyoto and sounded out his views. Amane said that the pressing need of the times was to diminish samurai pensions, abolish lineages, and reform the army."[65]

Rather than feeling strongly about the form of government, Nishi wanted to create a modern army and institute certain changes in the social system. Far from being committed to the old regime or the feudal system, he now understood the necessity of remaking Japanese society at large, not just the samurai class, as he had advocated ten years before in the Hokkaido memorial. To seek the diminution of samurai pensions, the abolition of lineages, and military reform was far more than a demand for partially reorganizing feudalism:

[65] Quoted in Ōgai, *Nishi Amane den*, p. 165. Presumably the Kagoshima battle to which Koyama refers was the August 1863 shelling of Kagoshima by the British after the Richardson incident. See W. G. Beasley, *The Modern History of Japan* (London, 1963), pp. 84-85.

it pointed toward the denial of feudalism itself. However, an intellectual convinced of the need to renovate Japanese society could by no means be sure before 1868 that the restoration movement was the wisest depository of his allegiances. Indeed, the *bakufu* remained to the very end the most pro-Western of the contending elements. Nishi was a scholar first and a bureaucrat second, but he elected to stay with the *bakufu* until the end because it appeared to be the best vehicle for his scholarly ambitions and the surest route to reforming Japanese society along European lines. Restorationist thought before 1868 bristled with too much antiforeign emotionalism to earn the support of rational scholars who admitted Western cultural superiority. As Nishi's remarks to Koyama implied, he apparently did not care whether direct imperial rule or revitalized Tokugawa leadership succeeded feudalism, so long as a modern government utilizing certain European concepts would create a new society and army. This position resembled Katō Hiroyuki's subsequent distinction between *kokutai* (national essence) and *seitai* (political body),[66] although Nishi did not formulate the differentiation in these terms in 1868 and in fact rarely concerned himself with political theory. Both men, however, regarded the state as a reasonably interchangeable unit, whereas society (in Nishi's case) and the *kokutai* based on society (in Katō's case) were inviolable entities.[67]

Others in the group of *bakufu* intellectuals took various postures that indicated a diverse response to the restoration movement. Tsuda Mamichi, for example, sided with the *bakufu* simply because he wanted to continue his studies.[68] Yanagawa Shunzō (1832-1870), a professor at the Institute of Development and publisher of Japan's first magazine in 1867, supported the *bakufu* and denounced the Satsuma-Chōshū army.[69] Kanda Takahira served the new government

---

[66] Abosch, "Katō Hiroyuki," p. 366.
[67] For Katō's formulation of *kokutai*, see *ibid.*, p. 373.
[68] Kazue, "Nishi Amane no shōgai to sono shisō," p. 17; Minamoto, "Meiji ishin to jitsugaku shisō," p. 104.
[69] Minamoto, "Meiji ishin to jitsugaku shisō," p. 103. For Yanagawa, see biographical notes.

Study Abroad and Service at Home

from the beginning but was sympathetic to Keiki's position, whereas Katō Hiroyuki resisted as hopeless the shogun's efforts to create a daimyo council after the restoration.[70] Fukuzawa Yukichi, who deserves to be grouped with these men, remained neutral during the restoration because he could not abide either side.[71] In short, the bureaucratic intellectuals showed no common pattern of loyalty to the *bakufu* or throne but rather based their attitudes toward the restoration movement mainly on self-interest, which for all of them included the desire to continue studying and disseminating Western culture.

Nishi's example shows the perplexity that faced the bureaucratic intellectuals when the *bakufu* collapsed. In the political confusion during the winter of 1867-1868, Nishi feared going out alone from his Kyoto lodgings; he noted that one ought to carry pistols at all times for self-defense.[72] Once Keiki had been forced to resign, Nishi grew afraid that he would be arrested by the Satsuma-Chōshū armies as a Tokugawa supporter, and he fled to Wakayama barely three days after the restoration had been formally proclaimed. During this brief self-exile, Nishi hit upon the notion of masquerading as a doctor, presumably in order to escape capture by the new government. He lived (and practiced) under this guise in Wakayama for a few weeks, but soon he decided to return to Edo to settle his fate as a Tokugawa retainer. Traveling as a physician under an assumed name, he sailed to Edo on the freighter *Herman* in April 1868.[73]

As soon as he reached the Tokugawa capital, Nishi was ordered to join Katō, Tsuda, and Udono Nijirō in a final desperate effort at constitutionalism. The *bakufu*, although clearly defeated in Kyoto the preceding winter, was still vainly trying to construct a daimyo council that would create the appearance of government by public opinion. These attempts came to nothing, however, and shortly thereafter the

[70] *Ibid.*, pp. 103-104.
[71] See Blacker, *The Japanese Enlightenment*, p. 9.
[72] Nishi's *Shiki*, quoted in Kazue, "Nishi Amane no shōgai to sono shisō," p. 17.
[73] *Ibid.*, p. 17.

shogun was placed under house arrest in Mito and the remnants of the *bakufu* army were routed.

Nishi, who had accompanied Keiki on his unlucky journey to Mito, now faced a set of disheartening choices. He remained a nominal adviser to the Tokugawa family, but in fact he spent the next several months fleeing the imperial armies and searching for a job. He confided to his friend Asano Jirō: "If I wanted to go out and serve the court, I am afraid I would not be used for anything important. No, I shall stay and follow my lord and the old government. While of course I have no reason to expect anything, my lord has never dismissed me."[74] Nishi had no desire to associate himself in the summer of 1868 with the samurai of the dominant *han* alliance; why, he asked, "should my honor suddenly be diminished or my stipend attached, and why should I be made to rank with the warriors of the victorious western domains?"[75] He also soon realized that it would be impossible to remain attached to the shogun, once the Tokugawa family had been pensioned off in June 1868.[76] He considered returning to Tsuwano, after fifteen years' absence, but this was impossible because "my domain chief's anger has not yet receded."[77] Still a titular adviser to Keiki, he was not free to rejoin the Institute of Development, which was now responsible to the new state. Confronted with these frustrating circumstances, Nishi drifted throughout most of the restoration year, relying on friends such as Tezuka Ritsuzō for money and shelter, trapped by a landslide of events that he had seen coming but could not flee.

By autumn, events had changed considerably. After members of the Tokugawa family had finally withdrawn from their ancient lands and gathered in exile near Shizuoka during the late summer of 1868, most of the three thousand *bakufu* officials remaining in Edo also moved to the shoreline

---

[74] Quoted in Ōgai, *Nishi Amane den*, p. 178.
[75] *Ibid.*, p. 178.
[76] *Ibid.*, p. 178; Kazue, "Nishi Amane no shōgai to sono shisō," pp. 17-18.
[77] Quoted in Ōgai, *Nishi Amane den*, p. 178.

Study Abroad and Service at Home

region on Suruga Bay between Shizuoka and Numazu.[78] Although their armies were shattered, their treasury impoverished, and their political prestige at an unprecedented low, the proud Tokugawa chieftains were as yet quite unreconciled to peaceful retirement at the foot of Mt. Fuji and acquiescence to the supremacy of the western domains. The *han* system remained in existence for more than three years after the restoration, and the exiled Tokugawa family began plotting a counterattack on the new regime almost as soon as its faithful corps of officials had moved to the shoreline region. The Tokugawa leaders reasoned that by reorganizing the alliance of various *han* they could mount an effective challenge to the Satsuma-Chōshū alliance. So long as the feudal domains remained intact, the Tokugawa family could hope to replace the western *han* as the dominant force within the political system through an overt military counterassault.[79] For this purpose the family created the Numazu Military Academy (Numazu Heigakkō) in the autumn of 1868, with the express intention of training officers to lead the offensive against the new Meiji government.

Nishi Amane became the first headmaster of the Numazu Military Academy on November 1, 1868. While still in Edo, Nishi had learned from Ōtsuki Shōshi, an old friend, that the Tokugawa family was eager to found a military school in Numazu. Ōtsuki wrote Nishi that "they do not yet have a person to be superintendent and chief instructor. If you request it, I shall recommend you."[80] As a *tozama* official for the shogunate, Nishi had not expected to be asked back for further service, but when he received a formal offer to head the Numazu academy, he was delighted at the prospect of material support and a chance to continue in the academic milieu. Accordingly, he accepted.

The Numazu Heigakkō was a high-school-level institution for training future army officers, although *heigakkō* now means "naval academy." Nishi's first duty was to establish

[78] Ōkubo, "Kaisetsu," *NAZS* 1961, p. 746.
[79] *Ibid.*, pp. 745-746.
[80] Ōtsuki to Nishi, autumn 1868, quoted in Ōgai, *Nishi Amane den,* p. 179.

72

the martial and academic regulations,[81] a task he undertook singlehandedly. He divided the curriculum into the two categories of physical and mental training, with such items as marching, riding, and artillery included in the former. Within a year Nishi also added a riding school, an infirmary, and an elementary school to the main academy.[82]

The Numazu school was no ordinary military academy; its curriculum included courses in such contemporary Western subjects as logic, English, French, European ethics, mathematics, physics, astronomy, and natural history. The school was probably the most progressive institution of its kind at the time. Nishi is thought to have paid considerable attention to implementing standardized teaching methods in the various classes, and he created a sound administrative apparatus for the school. It is not surprising that the Numazu academy included far more than the usual martial arts. For one thing, the custom of combining military with civil learning was firmly established in traditional samurai education. Since the *bakufu* had been the most active patron of Western studies during the Bakumatsu period, it is not surprising that the Tokugawa family continued to encourage knowledge of Europe. What is more, the sizeable teaching staff, which included twenty-one persons in regular instructional positions plus numerous assistants,[83] permitted a breath and flexibility in subject matter that was most unusual for the period. Many of the faculty members at the Numazu Military Academy had been recruited from the Institute of Development in Edo, as was the case at the School of Literature which Tsuda Mamichi administered for the Tokugawa family in Shizuoka.[84] The Numazu academy was thus a modern form of Tokugawa *han* school, with a radically altered pattern of studies supervised by a number of Japan's leading scholars of the West.

[81] They are contained in his *Tokugawake heigakkō chōsho, NAZS* 1961, pp. 445-469, and *Tokugawake Numazu gakkō tsuika chōsho, NAZS* 1961, pp. 470-476.

[82] Ōgai, *Nishi Amane den*, p. 180; "Nishi Amane," *Kindai bungaku kenkyū sōsho*, III, p. 113.

[83] Ōgai, *Nishi Amane den*, p. 180.

[84] Kazue, "Nishi Amane no shōgai to sono shisō," p. 18.

Study Abroad and Service at Home

It is difficult to determine Nishi's outlook on his work in Numazu. He lectured on philosophy and ethics in addition to his administrative duties. He seems to have plunged headlong into his work and to have done almost no writing during his two years as headmaster. Among his many able students was Hayashi Shinrokurō, whom Nishi and Masuko adopted as their heir in March 1869.[85] Others included Kiyono Tsutomu, "who received the mantle of Nishi Amane in logic studies,"[86] Shimada Saburō, later a foremost journalist and leader of the *jiyū minken* (Freedom and Popular Rights) movement, and Taguchi Ukichi, a famous financier and advocate of free trade in Japan.

Nishi's success as headmaster of the school earned him an appointment to the Meiji Military Department (Hyōbushō) on October 22, 1870, upon his resignation from the Numazu post.[87] This was fortuitous timing, because the ministry absorbed the academy barely a year after Nishi departed and liquidated it entirely in the summer of 1872.[88] Although Nishi left no record explaining why he gave up the Numazu position to become a Meiji bureaucrat, it is understandable that he made the change at this juncture. In the fall of 1868 the new state was still in its formative stage, and the military academy of the Tokugawa family offered an attractive opportunity for a scholar of the West to continue his study. Two years later, however, the Meiji government was infinitely stronger, and the hopelessness of the Tokugawa plans for a counter-coup was apparent to all. As headmaster of the academy, Nishi was doubtless aware that the school was in imminent danger of seizure by the Military Ministry and that the entire feudal clan system had a limited future. Furthermore, he had spent the first three months of 1870 on leave from the academy, visiting in Tsuwano as a counselor to his

---

[85] Ōgai, *Nishi Amane den*, p. 181.
[86] Asō, *Kinsei Nihon tetsugakushi*, p. 201.
[87] Ōgai, *Nishi Amane den*, p. 182.
[88] See Ōkubo, "Kaisetsu," *NAZS* 1945, pp. 25-26, and Ōkubo, "Kaisetsu," *NAZS* 1961, pp. 745-756; Ōgai, *Nishi Amane den*, pp. 179-181; and two books by Ōno Torao, *Numazu heigakkō to sono jinsai* (Shizuoka, 1939), and *Numazu heigakkō fuzoku shōgakkō* (Numazu, 1943).

Study Abroad and Service at Home

former lord, Kamei Korekane, who by then had pardoned Nishi's *dappan*.[89] Kamei was already a leading official of the new Department of Religious Ceremonies, and he no doubt helped persuade Nishi that the Numazu venture was useless. A man with Nishi's vision and practical way of thinking must have realized that his future lay with the strong new government. This constituted not merely materialistic opportunism but also a realistic decision to bend with the revolutionary changes and to opt for the future. Nishi's constant motive was to apply his scholarship to his country's service, and by 1870 the path of bringing Western culture to bear on reforming Japanese society led unmistakably to Tokyo.

If emotional ideologies had scant appeal to the pragmatic *bakufu* intellectuals before 1868, these scholars had little difficulty in joining the new state once it was well established. The shattered *bakufu* was simply no longer a meaningful alternative for the pro-Western scholar. Once the obscurantist anti-foreignism of the restorationists had been supplanted by creative efforts to construct a new polity, *bakufu* bureaucrats became Meiji bureaucrats and contributed far more to their country than had been possible under the Tokugawa regime. But theirs was not a dilemma of material subsistence; teaching was always open to them as a career, and they did not have to take government jobs to earn a living. They were practical men who by 1870 could see that the most efficacious route to national service was the new government. Such concrete considerations led them to accept the new state with little hesitancy and almost no psychological trauma. Far from being dull bureaucrats who worshipped power,[90] they resembled the English utilitarians who welcomed the state as a

[89] Ōgai, *Nishi Amane den*, p. 181.

[90] Funayama Shin'ichi criticizes their bureaucratic mentalities and excessive respect for power in *Meiji tetsugakushi kenkyū* (Tokyo, 1959), p. 67. For a detailed study of the early Meiji leaders, see two works by Bernard S. Silberman, *Ministers of Modernization: Elite Mobility in the Meiji Restoration, 1868-1873* (Tucson, 1964), and "Elite Transformation in the Meiji Restoration: The Upper Civil Service, 1868-1873," *Modern Japanese Leadership: Transition and Change*, ed. Bernard S. Silberman and Harry D. Harootunian (Tucson, 1966), pp. 233-259.

powerful ally in their campaign to civilize the public. They felt the appeal of emperor-loyalty less keenly than most other Japanese, but very soon after 1868 they joined the movement which had restored the emperor and worked toward the goal shared by nearly all parties: national strengthening to become equal to the West.

four

A Leader in Enlightening Japan

Perhaps the primary responsibility of the intellectual in a modern, non-totalitarian society is to identify crucial issues and offer perceptive criticism of the events and forces that shape public life. The greater the degree of social and political change in a modern nation, the more urgent it is that its intellectuals not only express their opinions but also bend every effort to parlay them into action, since a country without reasonable policy alternatives is not likely to retain an open society. During the past century Japan's intelligentsia has often been outspoken but rarely influential in political decision making. This tradition of free criticism is nonetheless an outgrowth of the first Meiji years. Possibly the infant Meiji state was "absolutist" at certain points, but it certainly tolerated, and often encouraged, public discussion of the major national questions in the 1870's. Indeed, in these years Japan experienced a major intellectual upheaval that was characterized by both quixotic optimism and hardheaded realism. So great was the change that novel theories of state and society were suddenly elevated from their feudal status of dissent to that of creative public criticism.

Political events weighed heavily in this process of ideological reorientation. The collapse of the feudal government meant that its ethical rationale, Shushi Confucianism, was now discredited as a functioning system of public behavior. The attack upon Buddhism in the first years of the new regime[1] further weakened the authority of time-honored intellectual categories and created a paradoxical ideological environment: to some the early Meiji period seemed to be blemished by an ethical vacuum; to others it presented an

[1] See William M. Osuga, "The Establishment of State Shintō and the Buddhist Opposition," M.A. thesis in history, University of California (Berkeley, 1949), pp. 1-8.

77

unprecedented opportunity for innovation and creative public debate about assumptions that had too long remained unquestioned. Except for the most reactionary victims of intellectual sterility, all observers devoted themselves to developing new approaches—some monistic, some pluralistic— to the problems raised by the irreversible chain of political events that accelerated after 1868.

Easily the most dramatic and probably the most significant aspect of this intellectual revolution was the phenomenon of *bunmei kaika*, or "civilization and enlightenment," which reached its greatest proportions in the mid-1870's. The first ten Meiji years, it must be remembered, were unique in Japan's history for the staccato pace of institutional change and adjustment to new ideas. Such catchwords as "civilization," "enlightenment," and "liberalism" abruptly replaced Japan-centered theories of restoration as the dominant ideological motif. During most of this period the government actively sponsored the import and distribution of European knowledge, and the intellectual climate was one of great receptivity to the precepts of Western thought. Europe became the object of considerable adulation; what she thought of Japan became a matter for national concern. In no area of Japanese life did peregrine influences predominate more completely than in scholarly circles, especially among the proponents of *bunmei kaika*. However, it is easy to let the articulate and persuasive writings of such early Meiji intellectuals as Nishi Amane distort our perspective. The wit and brilliance of their arguments have caused many persons to overestimate the depth of the Western penetration. It is important to understand the nature of this period of "civilization and enlightenment" in considering Nishi's part in the effort to build a strong, modern Japan.

THE JAPANESE ENLIGHTENMENT

The historical concept of *bunmei kaika* has several connotations.[2] In the most general sense it designates a time cate-

2 This analysis has been suggested in part by Ōkubo Toshiaki,

A Leader in Enlightening Japan

gory in early Meiji history, the period following the establishment of the new state and preceding the strong nationalist and constitutional movements of the 1880's. This era was characterized by heavy borrowing from European political, economic, military, and cultural traditions, in order to construct a powerful and modern nation. In recent years scholars have begun to identify greater indigenous influences in the reforms of the 1870's, and the term *bunmei kaika* has somewhat lost favor as a general label for the period.

Second, the term refers to the early Meiji craze for Western foods, clothing, architecture, and manners. This aspect of *bunmei kaika* has been amply documented by Japanese writers ever since Western trappings first entered the country in large volume.[3] Fads for Western material culture have proved to be an interesting but superficial source of historical inquiry, since such vogues during the 1870's were limited to the principal cities, especially the downtown sections of Tokyo. Western items were always used side-by-side with traditional goods during this period, and the mania reached no greater proportions than did other popular crazes in other centuries of Japanese history. Furthermore, even within the urban areas, European styles and goods appealed mainly to ordinary city dwellers, to the residents of *shitamachi* (low-lying, mid-town areas), rather than to those in the *Yama no te* (well-to-do) sections of Tokyo.[4] Today it amuses us to read of this craze for foreign wares, but at the time Japan's students of the West ridiculed those who felt civilized because they used Western things without appreciating their underlying spirit of rationality.[5] These qualifications notwithstanding, to ordinary urban residents *bunmei kaika* meant a new spirit of modernity and crude sophistication; it signified an

---

"Bunmei kaika," *Iwanami kōza Nihon rekishi* (Tokyo, 1961-1963), xv, pp. 251-286.

[3] See, for instance, *Japanese Thought in the Meiji Era*, ed. Kōsaka Masaaki, tr. David Abosch (Tokyo, 1958), pp. 50-60.

[4] Ōkubo, "Bunmei kaika," pp. 274-275.

[5] See Carmen Blacker, *The Japanese Enlightenment: A Study of the Writings of Fukuzawa Yukichi* (Cambridge, Eng., 1964), p. 38.

optimistic exchange of feudal habits for the trivia of modern industrial society.

Third, *bunmei kaika* denotes a conscious government policy to create a modern, educated class of citizens. This policy accompanied the sudden official shift in 1870-1871 from reviving elements of the native tradition to building a new nation with generous help from abroad. Soon after the Ministry of Education (Monbushō) was created in 1871, the state injected huge sums of money into the new national school system to encourage the teaching of Western languages, science, history, literature, law, and other representative European subjects. The fundamental purpose was to unify the political power of the new state via a single national curriculum. Massive appropriations were used to translate and distribute European textbooks and to hire Western scholars as educational advisers, because the new government believed that Western knowledge was essential to "enriching the country and strengthening the army" (*fukoku kyōhei*). It was a tutelary program thrust upon the public from above, but there was undoubtedly a progressive popular base upon which the efforts were founded. Many scholars have questioned the effectiveness of this policy,[6] but it is important to bear in mind that when the ministry abandoned its overt attempts to promote Western learning in 1877, it did so not because they were producing poor results. Instead, the principal reason for dropping this program was the growing pressure from the popular *jiyū minken* (Freedom and Popular Rights) movement, which was itself a product in some respects of the Western values that the official *bunmei kaika* policy sought to engender.[7] When Western studies were diminished in favor of a greater emphasis on Confucianism after

[6] David Abosch, for example, has found that there was little public responsiveness to the *bunmei kaika* policy and that the new learning won out mainly at the governmental level. Abosch, "Katō Hiroyuki and the Introduction of German Political Thought in Japan: 1868-1883," Ph.D. dissertation in history, University of California (Berkeley, 1964), pp. 185-187.

[7] For further evidence of the effectiveness of the official policy, see Ōkubo, "Bunmei kaika," pp. 280-285.

A Leader in Enlightening Japan

1877, it represented merely a shift in tactics in order to achieve the paramount Monbushō objective of creating broad national unity through education. *Bunmei kaika* as an official policy was far more than an urban phenomenon; it had a strong impact on rural areas as well, through the new unified school system.[8]

The fourth and most significant aspect of *bunmei kaika* was the phase of Japanese intellectual history known as enlightened, or *keimō,* thought. It was in this realm that Nishi Amane was a pioneer and leading spokesman. He and a handful of other scholars of the Bakumatsu period entered the Meiji era already convinced of the superiority of Western culture, and it was during the 1870's that they used their convictions in the nation's service by popularizing broad segments of Western learning. Enlightenment in the early Meiji context meant infusing the literate public with certain political, social, economic, and intellectual values of contemporary European civilization. Although there was no complete agreement among *keimō* scholars on exactly which European values should be inculcated, the consensus was that the European spirit of rationality, practical experience, personal profit, and self-awareness of individual rights must accompany the technological and institutional revolution that was taking place. Traditional customs and ways of thought, the *keimō* scholars believed, must be destroyed together with feudal forms of economic and political organization. These new values were essential, they taught, for creating a strong and rich nation. In this respect intellectuals like Nishi Amane participated in the mainstream of the national effort, and their goals were consistent with the national purpose envisaged by the central government.

Although it may be attractive to think of the early Meiji years as a Japanese *siècle des lumières,* it is significant that these scholars were not necessarily trying to duplicate the European enlightenment of the eighteenth century. They derived their main inspiration from such contemporaneous

[8] See Kano Masanao, "Bunmei kaikaron e no ichishikaku," *Nihon rekishi,* 228 (May 1967), pp. 54-57.

A Leader in Enlightening Japan

Western social philosophies as positivism and utilitarianism. They wanted to expose their country to those urbane modes of thought from abroad that would bring Japan to the "civilized" stage of social development, to the highest level of progress envisaged by European social thought. The means to be employed consisted not of abstract reasoning but of empiricism. "What we should call the truly enlightened world," Tsuda Mamichi wrote in 1874, "is when practical studies become popular in our country and each person attains an understanding of truth."[9] Similarly, Fukuzawa Yukichi took nineteenth-century England, not eighteenth-century France, as his model for Japan's "enlightenment."[10] In his first article in the *Meiroku zasshi,* the journal of the Meiji Six Society, Nishi expressed both the prevalent scholarly dismay with popular ignorance and the general feeling that internal values must be reformed:

"In making many comparisons with European countries, we envy their civilization and lament our own lack of enlightenment, and in the end we conclude that nothing can immediately be done about the folly of our people. We cannot help sighing deeply! Since the great restoration, men of wisdom and ability have emerged, and there have been numerous reforms, from the government offices to the sixty-odd prefectures. . . . It has not been long since the restoration, and while these [reforms] flourish in outward structure, their inner spirit has not as yet spread."[11]

It is important to bear in mind that because the public was, as Nishi thought, so deplorably lethargic and mired in ignorance, the ordinary people had not taken sides in the ideological disputes of the pre-restoration years. Most people had no opinion of exclusionism or internationalism, and there-

[9] Tsuda, "Kaika o susumeru hōhō o ronzu," *Meiroku zasshi,* 3 (February 1874), in *Meiji bunka zenshū,* ed. Yoshino Sakuzō (Tokyo, 1927-1930), xviii, p. 65. Hereafter *Meiroku zasshi* will be cited as *MRZS* and *Meiji bunka zenshū* as *MBZ.*
[10] Blacker, *The Japanese Enlightenment,* p. 33.
[11] "Yōgaku o motte kokugo o shosuru no ron," *NAZS* 1961, p. 579. The article first appeared in *MRZS,* 1 (January 1874) and is included in *MBZ,* xviii, pp. 51-56.

A Leader in Enlightening Japan

fore there was no fund of popular anti-foreign resistance to the civilizing efforts of the *keimō* philosophers. Furthermore, since most commoners had not been ensnared by the "two-headed snake" of *fukko* (return to antiquity) versus *ishin* (renovation),[12] the major problem for the scholars was to change popular feudal habits and traditional values.[13] Nishi-mura Shigeki (1828-1902) and Mori Arinori (1847-1889) supplied a further indication of the purposes of *keimō* scholarship when they outlined the aims of the Meiji Six Society in 1873: "one is to raise the level of scholarship, and the second is to establish standards of morality."[14] All of these statements show that the Western-oriented scholars were quite conscious of their role of didactic leadership in early Meiji society and that they considered enlightenment a tangible objective capable of attainment.

What did these writers mean by "enlightenment"? The terms *bunmei* and *kaika* were new, but like many other words used to convey Western ideas they had roots in Confucian literature.[15] Kanda Takahira first used *bunmei* to translate the English word "civilization" in his *Keizai shōgaku* (Short Study of Economics) in 1867.[16] Fukuzawa popularized the term in his *Seiyō jijō* (Conditions in the West) in 1868, in which he also first employed the words *bunmei kaika* to translate the English phrase "civilization and enlightenment."[17] By enlightenment, however, the Japanese did not mean sim-ply the philosophy of the European enlightenment; they

---

[12] Tokutomi Sohō's phrase, in *Kokumin no tomo*, xx, quoted in Ienaga Saburō and Ino Kenji, "Kindai shisō no tanjō to zasetsu," *Kindai Nihon shisōshi kōza* (Tokyo, 1959), I, p. 43.

[13] See Kazue Kyōichi, "Meiji jidai no shisō," *Nihon no rinri shisō-shi*, ed. Kazue Kyōichi (Tokyo, 1963), p. 277.

[14] Nishimura, *Ōjiroku*, quoted in Tōyama Shigeki, "Meiroku zas-shi," *Shisō*, 447 (September 1961), p. 117.

[15] *Bunmei* is used in the *Shu ching* and *I ching* in a moral sense, with the implication of personal cultivation. *Kaika* was used in the *Ting ming lun* of Ku K'ai-chih (A.D. fourth-fifth centuries) to mean "to plan for progress in world events." Ōkubo, "Bunmei kaika," p. 253.

[16] See *Nihon shisōshi gairon*, ed. Ishida Ichirō (Tokyo, 1963), p. 235.

[17] See *ibid.*, p. 235; Ōkubo, "Bunmei kaika," p. 253.

intended a semi-scientific developmental process whereby ignorance would be progressively transformed into cosmopolitan understanding of this world through rational, empirical investigation. The earliest *keimō* thought owed far more to nineteenth-century European positivism and utilitarianism than to the French enlightenment: Mill was synonymous with enlightened thought well before Rousseau was introduced in Japan.[18] However, the early Meiji scholars generally failed to understand that nineteenth-century empiricism and social ethics had developed from eighteenth-century roots,[19] and therefore at first they often misunderstood the importance of the individual in European thought. The *keimō* scholars were generalists who fancied that they were importing all that was of great significance in European thought, but in fact their overwhelming emphasis was on mid-nineteenth-century systems and ideas. This was quite natural, since it was the civilization of imperial Europe, not that of revolutionary Europe, that Japan was trying to match. A broader understanding of the whole compass of Western philosophy awaited the research of later specialists who dug more deeply into the sources of contemporary European civilization.

In origin, timing, scope, and purpose the Japanese *keimō* period differed considerably from the European enlightenment. Unquestionably the rational, practical ideology of the *keimō* scholars had legitimate antecedents in the Japanese tradition, but it was largely a foreign import imposed upon the country by a small group of intellectuals. The *keimō* movement, unlike its European counterpart, occurred after the political changeover and contributed nothing in the way of ideological justification for the new state until the Meiji

[18] For all practical purposes Rousseau was not introduced to Japan until 1877. See Miyagawa Tōru, "Nihon no keimō shisō," *Kōza kindai shisō*, ed. Kaneko Musashi and Ōtsuka Hisao (Tokyo, 1959), IX, p. 141.
[19] Kazue Kyōichi, "Nihon kindai shisō no shodankai," *Kōza kindai shisō*, ed. Kaneko Musashi and Ōtsuka Hisao (Tokyo, 1959), IX, pp. 103-104.

government was reasonably well established. (It is quite understandable that the *keimō* ideology possessed this ex-postfacto quality, since it was the West as the successful model that Japan was emulating. The enlighteners were introducing and adapting the ideology that had long ago sanctioned the overthrow of the *ancien régime* and smoothed the way for the growth of powerful modern states.) Furthermore, *keimō* thought limited itself to certain practical facets of the Western intellectual world and made no effort to deal with many of the basic philosophical problems that occupied the European philosophers. Finally, the intellectual phenomenon of *bunmei kaika* consistently pursued the specific goal of strengthening the country by replacing feudal habits and attitudes with modern, cosmopolitan ideas, often at the expense of genuinely perceptive inquiry into the nature of truth and knowledge.

Nishi Amane contributed to this movement from beginning to end. At the same time he successfully pursued a busy and responsible bureaucratic career in several departments of the Meiji government. He never permitted his personal commitment to scholarship and Western values to interfere with the ultimate objective of national strengthening. This attitude held true for almost all of the *keimō* leaders and suggests that there were some limits to their effectiveness as objective scholars. However they were not mere apologists for the state, since they often disagreed with the tactics used by the Meiji government to achieve commonly shared goals. Nishi was of course merely one of many intellectuals responsible for the enlightenment of the Japanese people, and his role was chiefly limited to breathing fresh air into the early Meiji academic world. While other *keimō* scholars took charge of the important task of popularizing the new learning in the press, the government, and the schools, Nishi concentrated on the more purely academic matter of introducing and adapting Western philosophical thought to meet Japanese needs.

A Leader in Enlightening Japan

THE TRANSMISSION OF EUROPEAN PHILOSOPHY

Nishi's return to Tokyo in the autumn of 1870 as a newly appointed civil servant in the Meiji bureaucracy brought him the opportunity to hold a responsible governmental position and also a chance to resume his scholarly career. His investiture as head of the translation section of the Hyōbushō (Military Department) was arranged by Vice-Minister Yamagata Aritomo (1838-1922) on the recommendation of Katsu Awa and other mutual acquaintances.[20] Nishi served the ministry for the next seventeen years, obtaining regular promotions in rank and salary, and his success as a bureaucrat culminated in his elevation in 1882 to the Genrōin (Council of Elders). His chief responsibilities as a Hyōbushō official included translating information about military academies in the West, drafting a history of the department, assisting in compiling a five-language dictionary of military terms, and serving for several years as the chief of the department's planning office.[21] He also helped to write the Conscription Law of 1873 and the *Imperial Rescript to Soldiers and Sailors* in 1882. One of his most interesting assignments was serving periodically as a briefing officer, lecturing candidates for army commissions on politics and history. In addition, when he joined the Military Department in 1870, Nishi simultaneously became an examiner for the Education Office (Gakuseikyoku),[22] and he also served the Imperial Household

[20] Mori Ōgai, *Nishi Amane den, Ogai zenshū* (Tokyo, 1923-1927), VII, p. 182; Roger F. Hackett, "Nishi Amane—A Tokugawa-Meiji Bureaucrat," *Journal of Asian Studies*, XVIII, 2 (February 1959), p. 216. For Yamagata, see biographical notes.

[21] Ōgai, *Nishi Amane den*, p. 183ff.; Hackett, "Nishi Amane," p. 216; Kazue Kyōichi, "Nishi Amane no shōgai to sono shisō," *Tetsugaku kaishi*, 9 (1958), pp. 18-25. For an excellent chart detailing Nishi's bureaucratic career, compiled from several sources, see "Nishi Amane," *Kindai bungaku kenkyū sōsho*, ed. Shōwa Joshi Daigaku (Tokyo, 1956), III, pp. 115-117.

[22] Yano Kuromichi, a leading National Learning scholar, wrote that Nishi's connection with the Education Office ended in the intercalary tenth month. Most of the officials in this bureau were advocates of National Learning, in conformity with the bias of the government's educational efforts before the Monbushō was established in

Ministry at various times as an adviser and occasionally as a lecturer to the Meiji Emperor. Nishi's major accomplishments during his interesting and highly responsible official career will be evaluated in a subsequent chapter.

Since his duties in the Military Department did not at first require full-time attention (Japan as yet had no national army worthy of the name), Nishi seized the opportunity to reopen the private academy which he had operated during 1867 in Kyoto. Matsudaira Shungaku (1828-1890), a Tokugawa collateral and the lord of Fukui, supported this venture because he was pleased with the education which his retainers had received at Nishi's Kyoto school.[23] Accordingly, the academy was reopened on Christmas Day 1870, near Nishi's home at Asakusa-bashi. Among the pupils at the Ikueisha (Educational Hall), as Nishi called his school, were a number from Matsudaira's fief. There were daily lectures in English, mathematics, Japanese, Chinese, history, and a variety of other subjects, and there were also six special lectures each month on the topic "encyclopedia," a general introduction to Western knowledge.

One of the pressing questions facing the Western-oriented educator in restoration Japan was that of personal morality. Underlying the vigorous national drive to modernize the nation was a deep undercurrent of insecurity among the *keimō* intellectuals concerning Japan's precipitate rejection of her feudal tradition. Although these scholars were among the harshest critics of the "evil customs" of the past, they were anxious to insure that some standard of morality would be maintained in the vortex of their attacks on the discredited Shushi Confucianism. Hence Nishi made it clear in the regulations for the Ikueisha that he considered individual moral training essential for his pupils: "since morals are the principles practiced by individuals in daily life, you should neither neglect them nor stray from them for a moment. Although morals will not be especially taught in my school,

---

the autumn of 1871. Nishi was not comfortable in such surroundings. See Ōkubo Toshiaki, "Kaisetsu," *NAZS* 1961, pp. 757-760.

[23] Ōkubo, "Kaisetsu," *NAZS* 1945, pp. 21-27.

each of you should cultivate them by yourself."[24] Throughout Nishi's writings the theme of personal morality recurs. He was convinced of the need for moral direction from above, but he also believed that moral teachings should not prejudice objective scholarship. Therefore, although he denied Neo-Confucian ethics, he did not deny the importance of morality itself. Indeed, his *Jinsei sanpōsetsu* (Theory of the Three Human Treasures), published in 1875, demonstrated that he considered morality crucial for building a modern society in Japan.[25]

Nishi elaborated on his ideas about education, as well as the general question of national reform, in a series of questions and answers with his Ikueisha pupils called *Tōei mondō* (Dialogue of Enlightenment).[26] When a pupil inquired whether only bright persons should be educated, Nishi replied:

"People generally have the same heaven-bestowed intellect, but some are naturally able and some are dull . . . though they be dull, they must be educated. Though they be stubborn and obstinate when you teach them, they can be put to some use. However, no matter how much you teach those who are naturally dull or force them to learn, they cannot be superior to others or become men of talent. Thus what is needed is to teach them right away some other trade which they can do, paving the way for their own career, rather than wasting money and effort trying in vain to make them scholars."[27]

Nishi is saying here that there is definite value in extending the scope of education as broadly as possible among the people, because even the dull-witted have a function in society

[24] *Ikueisha nori*, quoted in Ōgai, *Nishi Amane den*, p. 183. This document also appears in *NAZS* 1961, pp. 509-515.

[25] This theme, of course, is not unique to the Meiji period or to Japan. Cf. the search by Japanese intellectuals for the moral basis of "democratization" after World War II, especially in such works as Osaragi Jirō, *Homecoming*, tr. Brewster Horowitz (Rutland, Vt., and Tokyo, 1955).

[26] *Tōei mondō*, *NAZS* 1961, pp. 247-277.

[27] *Ibid.*, pp. 266-267.

which can be learned. "What below-average people need is to serve as merchants, craftsmen, or farmers, to have the way opened to pursue whatever livelihood they want."[28] The freedom of occupational choice was already a legal fact by 1871, when Nishi spoke these words, but the requisite education was not yet generally available. As a *keimō* scholar, Nishi conceived of his task in terms of educating all men, "though they be stubborn and obstinate when you teach them," but he was not so quixotic as to believe that all persons had the same potential for learning. Nonetheless, these words clearly show that Nishi rejected any suggestion that a traditional educated elite should be maintained to the exclusion of exposing the public at large to instruction that in the early Meiji context meant a *keimō* education.

As to the general goals of *bunmei kaika,* Nishi said, "the people should be governed with clemency, and we must develop industry, encourage all sorts of learning, nourish men of talent, and enrich the nation by not needlessly wasting wealth."[29] Governing men with clemency and fostering men of talent were ideals that had been sought at various times throughout Chinese and Japanese history, but they did not conflict with the other more modern objectives that Nishi cited here. The obligation of the state in promoting *bunmei kaika,* he taught, was to ensure equality and freedom: "In general, those who participate in the national government should treat all men equally; they should look down upon none, always befriend the people, and instruct and guide them . . . let each have his freedom, let industry be encouraged, and let not wealth be snatched away."[30] How should the people be given freedom? "Each individual has a free nature, and so long as you do not rob him of this spirit, he will be free."[31]

If this is the case, Nishi asked, how are we to avoid outright anti-social behavior by the man who gives vent to his own spirit of freedom? Here is where government is needed:

[28] *Ibid.,* p. 267.   [29] *Ibid.,* p. 249.
[30] *Ibid.,* p. 250.   [31] *Ibid.,* p. 252.

89

A Leader in Enlightening Japan

"Although people generally possess their own individual liberties, when they take selfish advantage of them, it is like having no government. Since government is established by selecting a ruler from among the people, the people must respect it. In order to create respect for the ruler, the people must entrust him with a portion of the rights which each of them possesses. Because they have entrusted him with this portion, each person will have to uphold the ruler's orders and not violate them. Furthermore, people cannot conduct themselves entirely freely. Since the ruler has been entrusted with a portion of the people's individual rights, he must distinguish right from wrong and judge matters according to law. This is the essence of government."[32]

The state, through impartial administration of justice, protects against an excessive spirit of liberty that would infringe on others' rights. This notion that individual freedom would not lead to social anarchy if supervised by a disinterested state accorded well with the utilitarian principles which Nishi later advocated in *Jinsei sanpōsetsu*.

The goals of *bunmei kaika* which Nishi stated to his pupils were basically opposed to the Confucian values that had dominated Japanese society during the period of Tokugawa administration. The idea of "treating all men equally" represented a direct contradiction of the warrior-farmer-artisan-merchant (*shi-nō-kō-shō*) stratification of the Edo era. The emphasis on freedom, industrial development, and private wealth similarly conflicted with the norms of the ideal group-centered, agrarian Confucian society. The matter of "instructing and guiding" the people was an element remaining from the Confucian master-pupil tradition, but the content and objectives of this instruction were in keeping with what Nishi held to be the requirements of a modern society.

The Ikueisha was not so well known as the private schools run by Fukuzawa Yukichi and Nakamura Masanao, but in subject matter it was as progressive as any academy in Ja-

[32] *Ibid.*, p. 255.

90

A Leader in Enlightening Japan

pan.[33] The Ikueisha was significant because it served as Nishi's forum for introducing European philosophy to Japan. His lectures included many pioneering expositions of European thought and scholarship. To judge from the manuscripts and lecture notes from the Ikueisha period, these were mainly years of importation and transmission, although it must be granted that as outlines for elementary classroom lectures on Western knowledge, Nishi's notes understandably contain little truly creative scholarship. The surviving texts clearly reflect the influence of his tutors in Holland. The instruction at the Ikueisha contained rudiments of virtually every scholarly discipline then known in Europe; it was Japan's first true liberal arts curriculum.[34] Yet despite the richness of the course content, the task of spreading European philosophic thought required an audience beyond the classroom, something Nishi rarely achieved until the Meiji Six Society began its work in 1874. Of nine important Nishi manuscripts from the years 1870-1873 dealing with Western knowledge, only one was published immediately.[35] Therefore there is every

[33] Ōkubo, "Kaisetsu," *NAZS* 1945, p. 29. Nakamura's Dōninsha opened in 1873, eight years after Fukuzawa's celebrated Keiō Gijuku. In mid-1871, according to a contemporary account, there were sixteen private academies in Tokyo which concentrated on Western studies, with a total enrollment of 908 students. See "Toka shijuku ichiran," *Shinbun zasshi* (1871, sixth month), quoted in Kumashiro Shūryō, "Meirokusha zasshi kaidai," *MBZ*, XVIII, p. 3. This is probably a very frugal estimate, since the number of students listed for the Ikueisha, thirteen, is much smaller than its actual enrollment. See Kazue, "Nishi Amane no shōgai to sono shisō," pp. 18-19. Kumashiro also casts doubt on the accuracy of the figures in "Toka shijuku ichiran," in "Meirokusha zasshi kaidai," p. 3. See also Ōi Sei, *Nihon kindai shisō no ronri* (Tokyo, 1958), pp. 253-255.

[34] There was greater breadth than at Fukuzawa's Keiō Gijuku, although Nishi's school offered little specialized work. This is so, despite Fukuzawa's inflated claim that between 1868 and 1873, "ours was the only center in the country where Western learning was being taught." Fukuzawa, *The Autobiography of Fukuzawa Yukichi*, tr. Eiichi Kiyooka (Tokyo, 1960), p. 213. Nishi moved his school to Kanda in October 1871, where it remained until its demise two years later.

[35] Only *Chichi keimō* from this period was published immediately (1874). It appears in *NAZS* 1960, pp. 390-450.

A Leader in Enlightening Japan

reason to doubt that his early efforts exposed an appreciably large segment of the population to Western ideas. The real value in examining his lectures and writings from the Ikueisha period is in understanding the development of Nishi's own thinking and scholarly values. His ideas are not always apparent throughout these summary works that objectively introduced European learning, but it is possible to appreciate how his mind worked by examining his selection and arrangement of information for exposition.

The most interesting and significant of Nishi Amane's works from the Ikueisha years is *Hyakugaku renkan* (Links of All Sciences), to which Nishi added the English subtitle *Encyclopedia*.[36] This fascinating document stems from Nishi's special lectures at the Ikueisha on the content and organization of contemporary scholarly knowledge in the West. It is supplemented by notes taken by Nagami Yutaka, one of Nishi's pupils. *Hyakugaku renkan* is a detailed classification of the scholarly disciplines and represents a conscious attempt to demonstrate the integral harmony of all knowledge.

Despite the assertions of some Japanese cultural historians,[37] *Hyakugaku renkan* is not a reference work in the manner of the eighteenth-century French encyclopedists. Its spirit is much closer to nineteenth-century positivism. Its contents clearly resemble the subjects that the positivists Opzoomer and Vissering had taught Nishi in Leiden. Indeed, their lectures seem to have constituted Nishi's main source of information in compiling *Hyakugaku renkan*. What is more, even at the height of his attraction to French thought during the Ikueisha period, Nishi depended almost exclusively on English language works for documentation. He cited the English *Encyclopedia of Political Science* as a source for his

[36] The text, together with photographic reproductions of the entire original notes, was first published in *NAZS* 1945, pp. 3-562. Hereafter *Hyakugaku renkan* will be cited as *HGRK*.

[37] Kōsaka Masaaki, e.g., overemphasizes the resemblance between Nishi's *HGRK* and the encyclopedias of the eighteenth century in France. *Japanese Thought in the Meiji Era*, pp. 100-113. See also Gino K. Piovesana, *Recent Japanese Philosophical Thought, 1862-1962, A Survey* (Tokyo, 1963), p. 16.

92

A Leader in Enlightening Japan

material.[38] Although his text is not systematically annotated, the scholar Asō Yoshiteru has established that in addition to Lewes' *Biographical History of Philosophy* Nishi's sources included translations of Comte's *Cours de philosophie positive* (1830-1842), numerous writings by J. S. Mill, and scattered works by Cousin, Chateaubriand, Flaurens, and Littri.[39] However, there is little resemblance between *Hyakugaku renkan* as a whole and any of these works save Comte's *Cours*. The fragmentary nature of the Western language terms in his text, the lack of precise documentation, and the dissimilarity between Nishi's work and any of the books cited by Asō (except for Comte's *Cours*) indicate that Nishi put the Ikueisha lectures together without frequent reference to his personal library of Western works. English language terms stand out on nearly every page of the main text, while phrases from other languages are relatively scarce. This suggests that when he did use other sources to supplement the material incorporated from Opzoomer's and Vissering's lectures, the sources were written in English. Although his reliance on English language works does not rule out encyclopedist influences, it points unmistakably toward inspiration by contemporaneous British social thought.

Hyakugaku renkan consists of a twenty-five page introduction and two books devoted to "common science" and "particular science," respectively. The table of contents indicates the huge scope of Nishi's lectures:

Introduction

Book I. Common Science (*futsūgaku*)

    A. History (*rekishi*)
    B. Geography (*chirigaku*)
    C. Literature (*bunshōgaku*)
    D. Mathematics (*sūgaku*)

---

[38] London, 1840. Nishi acknowledged the influence of this book in the introduction to *HGRK*, p. 11.

[39] Asō Yoshiteru, *Kinsei Nihon tetsugakushi* (Tokyo, 1942), pp. 126-127.

A Leader in Enlightening Japan

Book II. Particular Science (*shubetsugaku*)

A. Intellectual Science (*shinrijōgaku*)
1) Theology (*shinrigaku*)
2) Philosophy (*tetsugaku*)
3) Politics, Science of Law (*seijigaku*, *hōgaku*)
4) Political Economy (*seisangaku*)
5) Statistics (*keishigaku*)

B. Physical Science (*butsurijōgaku*)
1) Physics (*kakubutsugaku*)
2) Astronomy (*tenmongaku*)
3) Chemistry (*kagaku*)
4) Natural History (*zōkashi*)

While Nishi was almost surely the first Japanese to attempt a discussion of such a broad range of subjects, much of the European learning he treats had already been introduced to Japan in previous works, including those which he and Tsuda prepared for the *bakufu* after returning from Leiden. The common sciences were those which were universal in scope and known to all civilizations. Nishi's remarks about the four common sciences reveal little that was fresh to Japan in 1870, although the section on history tells us a good deal about his own intellectual leanings at this time. Of the particular sciences, Western theology (i.e. Christianity) was already well known in Japan. Nishi himself helped to introduce political science and law in *Seihōsetsu yaku* (Outline of Natural Law Theories, 1867) and *Bankoku kōhō* (International Law, 1868), while Tsuda published *Taisei kokuhōron* (Discussion of Western Constitutional Law) in 1868. Tsuda likewise dealt with statistics (and to some degree with economics) in *Hyōki teikō* (Charts and Classifications), a translation of Vissering's lectures that he began in 1868 and published in 1874.[40] Moreover, the material on the physical sciences summarizes recent Western scholarship in disciplines that were already fairly well known in Japan, thanks in large

[40] See ch. 3 above.

measure to the early scientific studies by scholars of Western learning (Rangakusha) in the late Edo period.

The truly important and striking innovation in *Hyakugaku renkan* is Nishi's discussion of European philosophy. His lectures on this subject not only transmit new schools of thought to Japan, but also include much criticism of the Confucian intellectual tradition that Nishi was hoping to displace. The introduction to *Hyakugaku renkan,* containing some glimpses of Nishi's theory of knowledge, and the portions on philosophy constitute the most fertile grounds for understanding both the manner in which he interpreted positivism and inductive logic and the ways in which his own intellectual development occurred during the Ikueisha years.

Nishi's introduction to *Hyakugaku renkan* deals with the meaning, methods, and purposes of knowledge, amply embellished with quotations in English. Here he distinguishes between science (*gaku*) and art (*jutsu*) by explaining the difference as that between knowledge and application. He cites the English scholar, Sir William Hamilton (1788-1856), who wrote that "Science is a complement of cognition having in point of form, the character of logical perfection, and in the point of matters, the character of real truth. . . . Art is a system of rules serving to facilitate performance of certain actions. . . . Therefore science and art may be said to be investigations of truth, but science is required for the sake of knowledge, art for the sake of productions, and science is more concerned with the higher truth, art with the lower."[41] Hamilton's writings on art and science were influential in the development of J. S. Mill's inductive logic; Mill in fact devoted an entire volume to *An Examination of Sir William Hamilton's Philosophy* (1865). Although there is no evidence that Nishi ever read this book, he was especially attracted to Mill's logic and presumably derived his interest in Hamilton

[41] Quoted in *HGRK*, pp. 43-44. (Spellings have been corrected.) Hamilton, the son of Sir William Hamilton (1730-1803), the noted collector of Greek, Roman, and Etruscan vases, was a well-known scholar of metaphysics and a pioneer in empirical logic.

through that medium.[42] Nishi's distinction between the two basic components of learning, science and art, was unfamiliar to scholars trained in the Neo-Confucian orthodoxy, and the fact that his introduction to the nature of knowledge begins with such a dichotomy indicates his debt to English philosophy.

Nishi next relates the science-art distinction to two more familiar polarities in East Asian thought. One is theory (*kansatsu*) and practice (*jissai*), and the other is knowledge (*chi*) and action (*kō*). Theory, he states, is parallel to science and practice is parallel to art. Knowledge is a result of "the impressions of the five senses being gathered from without," and action "emerges from within based on that knowledge."[43] Since the Chinese philosophic tradition, including Confucius himself, recognized the theory-practice and knowledge-action dichotomies, Nishi concludes, it should not be difficult to understand that the basic elements of Western learning center on science and art. It is typical of Nishi's scholarship that he cites numerous examples from Chinese history to illustrate unfamiliar analyses. His stress on the common ground between the European and East Asian intellectual heritages helped to smooth the way for a new outlook on the nature of knowledge that emphasized the ultimate social usefulness of all scholarship.

A large part of the introduction to *Hyakugaku renkan* concerns the "means of scholarship." Here Nishi credits the West with three crucial discoveries that led to her cultural superiority: the invention of printing, Columbus' discovery of America, and Galileo's theory that the earth revolves.[44] One might question Nishi's judgment, but he clearly acknowledges that the spirit of invention and scientific discovery was essential to much of Western knowledge.

Two important sections of the introduction are devoted to

[42] On Mill's ideas on art and science, see *John Stuart Mill's Philosophy of Scientific Method*, ed. Ernest Nagel (New York, 1950), pp. 7, 352, 439.

[43] *HGRK*, p. 45.

[44] *Ibid.*, p. 47. Western scholars have long acknowledged that printing originated in China.

the philosophy of Auguste Comte and John Stuart Mill. Comte is commonly known in the West as the founder of positivism and a pioneer in the social sciences. Philosophic positivism was a mid-nineteenth-century theory of knowledge, based on the principles of natural science, which held that all that can be known of reality must be based on actual observation. It denied the possibility of understanding religious and metaphysical problems, since they could not be empirically observed.[45] During much of his life Comte believed in philosophic positivism and actively applied the methods of the natural sciences to the study of society. He developed a three-stage theory of uniform social development, whereby humanity advances from the theological level to the metaphysical level, and finally to the positive level. Comte's major work was the *Cours de philosophie positive,* based on his private lectures in Paris, in which he classified all branches of knowledge according to their value as positive sciences. His chief interest was the nature of society, which he held could be known through the methods of the biological sciences, and he was concerned only secondarily with the individual.[46] In his later years Comte abandoned philosophic positivism in favor of the Religion of Humanity, as religious positivism is known. Throughout his writings there are major inconsistencies which have led some to question whether he was ever a true positivist.[47]

Mill never accepted the dogmas of philosophic positivism, but he shared in the general positivistic spirit of scientific investigation. He was his generation's leading exponent of utilitarianism, which is normally considered to be that branch of social ethics which regards anything useful as good. Utilitarianism assumed that pleasure was good for its own sake and that the pleasures of all men were equally good. Morality, according to utilitarianism, was determined by achieving the

[45] See D. C. Charlton, *Positivist Thought in France During the Second Empire, 1852-1870* (Oxford, 1959), pp. 5-6.
[46] See Iris W. Mueller, *John Stuart Mill and French Thought* (Urbana, 1956), pp. 128, 133.
[47] See Charlton, *Positivist Thought,* pp. 34-48.

greatest happiness for the greatest number of persons.[48] It is true that Mill did not consistently adhere to these principles, but his thought was in basic accord with the mainstream of utilitarian radicalism in nineteenth-century England. He agreed with Comte that phenomena were related and that causal relations could be detected, although both avoided a strictly teleological position.[49] Mill for a time accepted Comte's idea of uniform historical development but later rejected it, claiming that individuals and nations show distinctive patterns of advancement. Mill did, however, accept the basic positivist premise that knowledge must be gained by observation. He is remembered principally for his inductive logic, his concern for individual liberty under democratic government, and his defense of the utilitarian principle of the greatest happiness for the greatest number.[50]

In his introduction to *Hyakugaku renkan,* Nishi confines his discussion of Mill to *System of Logic.* He explains that the inductive method has only recently been developed: "A new method of logic is what the Englishman John Stuart Mill discovered. The work he wrote is called *System of Logic,* a very weighty thing. From this point onward, the scholarly world was greatly reformed . . . the doctrine of this reform was induction."[51] However, Nishi writes:

"In order to understand this inductive method, we must first understand the previously existing doctrine known as deduction. . . . [Deduction] is like a cat eating a rat. When a cat eats a rat, it starts with the most important thing, the head, and gradually consumes the body, four legs, and tail. In our study of the ancient sages . . . those who have studied *Mencius* have taken *Mencius* as their sole evidence, and those studying the *Analects* have concentrated on the *Analects,* and they have extracted various truths from this. Like the cat eating the rat, this is the deductive method."[52]

[48] John Plamenatz, *The English Utilitarians* (Oxford, 1958), pp. 2-8.
[49] Charlton, *Positivist Thought,* p. 7.
[50] See Plamenatz, *The English Utilitarians,* pp. 122-144, for a useful summary of Mill.
[51] *HGRK,* p. 54.   [52] *Ibid.,* pp. 54-55.

A Leader in Enlightening Japan

Nishi then examines the limitations of the traditional deductive method: "Because scholarship has been deductive since antiquity, and because (as I stated previously) all things have been undertaken on the basis of only one type of evidence, men were never able to escape their limitations or attain excellence. Usually they lapsed into conservatism and obstinacy. This then was not practical knowledge but merely study relying on book learning. It is impossible to press one's books into actual service. Thus they became enslaved by this method."[53]

The inductive method, on the other hand, leads to the truth: "The inductive method, in contrast with the deductive method, is like a man eating a fish. When a man eats a fish, he eats its delicious parts bit by bit, and finally eats all that is supposed to be eaten. In like fashion [the inductive method] approaches the truth by working from the parts to the whole, from the outside to the inside. . . . Some time ago in the West there was a person named Newton who observed an apple falling to the ground from a tree and discovered the earth's gravity. Apples are not the only things that fall to the ground; the same is true for stones and leaves. Nothing falls from above to above; the fact that everything falls downward is the principle of gravity. This we call 'fact.' This is to say that when we try to gather many facts wherever we can, we will understand that there is a single truth common to them all. For example, when we throw a rock into the air, it falls to the ground. The same is true for leaves, feathers, lead, and iron. We know that they each fall to the earth—these then are facts. That they all fall to the earth is one truth. In ancient times in the West too all science was deductive, but recently this inductive method has become standard."[54]

Here is Nishi's most forceful endorsement yet of the new learning. Here too is a deliberately direct denunciation of the existing Neo-Confucian system, which was mere empty book learning and of little social usefulness. To suggest that scholars in China and Japan had become conservative, obstinate, and enslaved by their narrow approach to knowledge

[53] *Ibid.*, p. 55.   [54] *Ibid.*, pp. 55-56.

was far more than a call for academic reform: Nishi attacked the heart of the Confucian methodology and introduced a radically new discipline to replace it. The heretofore dominant Neo-Confucian orthodoxy assumed that all knowledge existed a priori and that there were no new truths in the universe still to be discovered. Nishi, inspired by Mill, assumed instead that there were always more principles to be uncovered, and the way to find them was to use inductive logic. Simple experimentation with rocks and feathers would lead to many more truths than would adhering to the stuffy bibliophilia of the Confucianists, all of whom followed the deductive method.

Nishi's defense of induction in this introduction to *Hyakugaku renkan* is neither detailed nor cogent, but it is indicative of the larger purposes of the entire work. *Hyakugaku renkan* is most important for the Western thought it transmits, and yet it is also significant as a critique of Confucian idealism.[55] It was crucial to Nishi's outlook on learning to break the mold of Shushi epistemology, so that philosophy and social science from Europe could take root and flourish. He did not deny the historical similarities between Western learning and Confucian thought, but for the present it was essential to replace traditional approaches to knowledge with induction, because induction would help men discover new truths useful to society. Learning for its own sake, Nishi thought, was useless: "It is impossible to press one's books into actual service." One of Nishi's principal criteria in selecting elements of Western thought for introduction to Japan was social utility. Just as he had dismissed Sung metaphysics at age seventeen because they "served no purpose for people's daily lives,"[56] so he was now requiring scholarship to be relevant to man's condition. This basic premise clearly shaped Nishi's approach to Western learning throughout his scholarly career, and it helps us to appreciate why he was more devoted to Mill's

[55] See Ōkubo, "Kaisetsu," *NAZS* 1945, pp. 46-47.
[56] *Soraigaku ni taisuru shikō o nobeta bun*, quoted in Kazue Kyōichi, "Nishi Amane no shūgyō jidai," *Nihon oyobi Nihonjin*, 1428 (April 1964), p. 46.

logic than to his writings on liberty or parliamentary government.

Hyakugaku renkan, however, is primarily a work of transmission, and it was not until 1874, in *Hyakuichi shinron* (New Theory of the Hundred and One), that Nishi prepared a logical, detailed criticism of Neo-Confucianism. In *Hyakuichi shinron,* he used the inductive method for examining the works of Confucius, and he specifically rejected the Sung interpretations of Confucius as contrary to empirical verification. In the meantime, he devoted a separate lecture series at the Ikueisha to a comprehensive study of *System of Logic.* A book based on these lectures was published in 1874, entitled *Chichi keimō* (Logic and Enlightenment). Nishi explained in this work that logic was the basis of scholarship and, in another section, that it was intended for practical use in "general academic discussions, public debate, lawyers' appeals, and judges' decisions."[57] The twenty-five topics in *Chichi keimō* cover all aspects of Mill's method, making this book Japan's first outline of formal logic.[58]

The final section of the introduction to *Hyakugaku renkan* is devoted to an exposition to Comte's three-stage theory of social development and an analysis of his system of knowledge. Nishi writes:

"According to the discoveries of the modern Frenchman Auguste Comte . . . there are three stages. Men begin with the first, gradually pass to the second, and finally reach the third. The first is the theological stage, the second is the metaphysical stage, and the third is the positive stage. . . . Although there are differences in the length of time spent in stages one and two and the speed with which the positive stage is reached, all [societies] must pass through the first two stages in order to reach the third. . . . For example, stage one was in early times when thunder was thought to be caused by the gods. This was the theological stage. Later, in

---

[57] Quoted in Kawahara Hiroshi, *Tenkanki no shisō—Nihon kinda-ika o megutte* (Tokyo, 1963), p. 329.

[58] Ōkubo, "Kaisetsu," *NAZS* 1960, p. 638. See also Asō, *Kinsei Nihon tetsugakushi,* pp. 294-302.

stage two, it was attributed to the interplay of *yin* and *yang*. This was the metaphysical stage. Now that electricity has been discovered, we reach the third, or positive, stage. Passing through the first two stages, we finally attain the third. This methodology is ineluctably valid. Once we pass through the first two stages, we will understand the positive stage. This is positive knowledge. These three stages are highly relevant to all scholarship. In general, scholarship is what discovers truth . . . however, even when truth is discerned, it is not always directly applied and utilized. . . . Because even when we discover the truth it is difficult to apply it directly, we must study and investigate, and begin to accumulate various means and apply our skills. Such applications are called art. The importance of using these skills is evident in the discovery of the telegraph from the principle of magnetism, the invention of the windmill from the principle of wind, and the workings of other such machines. All of these represent the application of art. As a rule, it is essential in all scholarship to seek the truth, and then to apply it."[59]

This extract indicates how Nishi simultaneously set forth and endorsed Comte's historical scheme. His analysis of Comte bears out his earlier distinction between science and art, which derived from Hamilton and Mill. Furthermore, this paragraph confirms the utilitarian criteria for scholarship which he developed for judging Mill's inductive logic: mere discovery of truth is useless unless it is "directly applied and utilized." Nishi's approach leaves little doubt that he supports the scientific-mechanical ecumene which grew out of these methods in Europe, as evident in the development of the windmill and the telegraph. Here is further implicit criticism of the Confucian tradition: Nishi's assumption, unlike that of most Confucianists, is that "it is essential in all scholarship to seek the truth, and then to apply it."

Nishi next presents the related doctrine that experience (*kōmon*), not abstract theory (*kanmon*), is the key to learning. Truth and its concrete application, the objects of schol-

[59] *HGRK*, pp. 62-64.

102

A Leader in Enlightening Japan

arship, must be investigated by positivistic (*jitsurijō*) means.[60]
Finally, he discusses Comte's use of scientific methods in
studying society. Nishi elaborated on Comte's positivism in a
series of articles written between 1870 and 1873, the most
important of which was *Seisei hatsuun* (The Relation of the
Physical and the Spiritual).[61]

It is thus evident that Nishi introduced only limited portions of Comte's and Mill's thought in *Hyakugaku renkan*,
partly because he seized first upon those teachings which
seemed most applicable to Japan, but also because he was
probably not yet conversant with the full range of their philosophies. Only Mill's *System of Logic* is discussed in this
document; it was not until several years later that Nishi first
referred to *Utilitarianism*, which had been published in 1863,
and he apparently never read such works as *Principles of
Political Economy* (1848) and *Liberty* (1859). It is likely that
he obtained the greater part of his understanding of both
Comte and Mill at second hand, through Opzoomer's and
Vissering's lectures in Leiden and English language secondary
works on European philosophy. The definitions and epistemological concepts in this introduction to *Hyakugaku renkan*
derive mainly from Comte and Mill; Nishi's chief contribution
was the arrangement of topics and the addition of numerous
examples from East Asian history to clarify obscure points.
Despite his limited grasp of the material and the meager size
of his audience, these lectures to the Ikueisha constituted
the earliest discussion of European positivism in Japan.

The main body of *Hyakugaku renkan,* containing the classification of all branches of knowledge, shows more originality. Its inspiration was Comte's *Cours de philosophie positive,* but the organization and sequence were Nishi's work.
Comte's system centered on five fundamental sciences, starting with that which was the least relevant to humanity (astronomy) and ending with the most "positive" or socially

[60] *Ibid.*, pp. 66-67.
[61] *Seisei hatsuun, NAZS* 1960, pp. 29-129. Part two of this work
includes a long translation of the section on the somatology of Comte
in Lewes, *Comte's Philosophy of the Sciences* (London, 1845).

applicable (sociology). Nishi, however, distinguishes between "common" and "particular" sciences. He chose to put history first among the common sciences, an indication of his respect for the subject. He cites the usual positivist idea that causal relationships exist in history: "History is a methodical record of important events, which concern a community of men, usually so arranged as to show the connection of causes and effects."[62] His justification for studying history is this:

"History is a common [read 'universal'] science because it records all the evidence since antiquity and it is suitable for learning lessons from the past. If a scholar wants to know anything at all of the present, he must consider the past.

"For example, in ancient times it was thought that the sun was a mass of fire. However, when men looked at it with the telescope, there were three black dots on it which sometimes changed position. Therefore it was thought in medieval times that the sun was originally like the earth, an opaque form always enveloped with an atmosphere. Therefore they said that since its atmosphere had light and shade, it was the reflection of its shady parts which produced the black spots. However, nowadays we have for the most part reverted to the ancient theory that it is a great mass of burning fire. In the same manner, what gives history its common [read 'universal'] character is that it applies both anciently and at present.

"In all scholarship, when you seek to understand the present you must consider the past. Because scholarship of course seeks to understand all things, past and present, it is history that makes this possible in all branches of learning."[63]

Comte also believed that a knowledge of history was essential to social science,[64] but in the philosophy section of *Hyakugaku renkan* Nishi specifically denies Comte's theory of uniform historical development. Instead he acknowledges that Japan is ill-prepared to utilize Western laws and forms

---

[62] *HGRK*, p. 74. [63] *Ibid.*, pp. 73-74.
[64] Comte's theory is contained in *Cours de philosophie positive* (Paris, 1830-1842), v.

A Leader in Enlightening Japan

of government: "when we adopt the political and legal systems used in the civilization of the West and carry them out in our country, it is like trying to apply third-level government and laws to a second-level civilization. In general, political and legal systems must be fitted to the [degree of] civilization of the country."[65] Nishi's beliefs about historical causation were quite clearly of European, not Confucian, origin, since he conceived of levels of civilization in much the same manner as Fukuzawa Yukichi, a devotee of Buckle and Guizot.[66] He treated history as an objective, scholarly discipline, classing it as merely one of many sciences; this was a direct rejection of the Confucian attitude toward the study of the past. He acknowledged that all disciplines must take note of former events, but he did not accept the Confucian world-view, with its moralizing effects on all scholarly inquiry and denial of progress in human events. But if Nishi as historian was no Confucianist, it is equally plain that he could not accept the mechanistic implications of Comte's theory of historical development. This is an indication of how an intellectual in the Meiji period did not need to be slavishly Western in order to be thoroughly modern.

Nor was Nishi any less modern for all the Chinese terminology and historical examples which he used to convey Western ideas. Nishi was a writer who created a new language by trying (in the words of Bagehot) "to express various meanings on complex things with a scanty vocabulary of fastened senses." *Hyakugaku renkan* is full of terms created from Chinese graphs, many of which are still used in modern Japanese. For example, he gave the present meaning to the words for deduction (*en'eki*) and induction (*kinō*) to convey the novelty of Mill's logic.[67] The word he used for "philosophy" in his brief history of Western philosophy, written on

[65] *HGRK*, p. 166.
[66] For Nishi's attitude toward history, see Ōkubo Toshiaki, "Nishi Amane no rekishikan," *Meijishi kenkyū sōsho*, series 2, vol. 4, *Kindai shisō no keisei*, ed. Meiji shiryō kenkyū renrakukai (Tokyo, 1956), pp. 241-282. Ōkubo overemphasizes the deterministic tendencies in Nishi's historical thought.
[67] *HGRK*, p. 54.

A Leader in Enlightening Japan

shipboard in 1862, was *kitetsugaku,* "to seek clarity."[68] In *Hyakugaku renkan* he uses both *hirosohī* (the English word "philosophy" in phonetic transcription) and *kitetsugaku* to explain that philosophy "means to love and seek wisdom."[69] Although the modern term, *tetsugaku,* was the most famous of Nishi's neologisms and appears occasionally in *Hyakugaku renkan,* he did not consistently use it until he wrote *Hyakuichi shinron* (1874).[70]

Nishi also invented or gave the modern meaning to the words for subjectivity (*shukan*), objectivity (*kyakkan*), reasoning power (*risei*), reason or understanding (*gosei*), reality (*jitsuzai*), phenomenon (*genshō*), psychology (*shinrigaku*), a priori (*senten*), and a posteriori (*kōten*).[71] Of these, *shukan, kyakkan, genshō, shinrigaku,* and *senten* were entirely new terms.[72] Before the Meiji era, *risei* had the ancient Buddhist meaning of "the true nature of all things," *gosei* had a Buddhist meaning of "the nature of enlightenment," *jitsuzai* meant simply "existing in the world," and *kōten* was used in the *Book of Changes* in the sense of "environment." Nishi thus made a considerable contribution to modern philosophical scholarship in Japan by introducing this new terminology. Inoue Tetsujirō later perfected Nishi's philosophic terms in the *Tetsugaku jii,* or Dictionary of Philosophy, published in 1881.[73]

Nishi borrowed Chinese terminology, both Confucian and Buddhist, because Chinese was the scholarly lingua franca in mid-nineteenth-century Japan. (His was the last generation consistently to use Chinese compounds to translate new con-

[68] *Seiyō tetsugakushi no kōan danpen, NAZS* 1960, pp. 16-17.
[69] *HGRK,* p. 145.
[70] Kazue Kyōichi, in private conversation, indicated that Nishi never used *tetsugaku* until *Hyakuichi shinron* was written, meaning that a later hand added it to *HGRK.*
[71] Kazue, "Meiji jidai no shisō," p. 297; Kazue, "Nishi Amane no shōgai to sono shisō," p. 1; Asō, *Kinsei Nihon tetsugakushi,* pp. 315-316.
[72] Kuwaki Gen'yoku, *Nishi Amane no Hyakuichi shinron* (Tokyo, 1940), p. 18. The *Dai kanwa jiten* lists no classical antecedents for these words.
[73] *Tetsugaku jii.* See Piovesana, *Recent Japanese Philosophical Thought,* p. 11.

cepts from abroad; by the 1890's it was customary simply to transliterate European words with indigenous phonetic symbols.) However, Chinese was merely the medium of expression, not the temper of his thought. What Nishi did was to transform the Chinese terms from literal to metaphorical meanings.[74] Removing them from their familiar context, he clipped away their usual connotations and denotations and infused them with new Western meanings, so that *jitsuzai* (reality) only figuratively still resembled its Chinese counterpart, *shih-chi* (to exist in the world). This transition from literalism to nominalism signified the demise of the classical tradition, not any inhibition or compromise of Nishi's basic commitment to the West.

Another important section of *Hyakugaku renkan* deals with philosophy. Here Nishi reiterates his earlier belief that philosophy is the most important of the Western sciences:

"As to the definition of philosophy [he uses the English word in phonetic transcription], we may say that philosophy is the science of sciences and that it is chief among all sciences.

"There is a general principle governing all things, which inevitably controls all affairs. Therefore, like king and subject, philosophy controls all sciences, and they must all be controlled by it."[75]

Nishi, under the influence of the English utilitarians, thus grants philosophy the leading position that Comte reserved for sociology. He nonetheless treats it as a *primus inter pares,* the most essential of many important disciplines. This is a modification of his understanding of "philosophia" in his letter to Matsuoka in 1862, in which he thought of it as the Western functional equivalent of Confucianism: no longer does Nishi imply that an alternative can be found in the West to replace Confucianism as a monistic thought system. Now philosophy is no airtight world-view; it is simply the primary academic discipline, one that is essential for all scholarship.

[74] I am indebted to the late Professor Joseph R. Levenson for suggestions on this point.
[75] *HGRK*, p. 146.

A Leader in Enlightening Japan

Here we have the emergence of Nishi's own mature *Weltanschauung*. Henceforth his scholarship is characterized by a quasi-evolutionist outlook that consistently accords philosophy the uppermost berth among the various branches of human knowledge.

Nishi's conception of what constitutes the boundaries of philosophy is evident from the eight sections he devotes to it in *Hyakugaku renkan*: logic, psychology, ontology, ethics, political philosophy, esthetics, the history of philosophy, and positive philosophy (*jitsurijō tetsugaku*). Of these various aspects of philosophy, Nishi evidently considers logic extremely important. He cites it first among the branches of philosophy and reiterates his conviction that Mill's logic is superior to previous deductive methods: "Since antiquity all logic has been deductive, but logic reached its pinnacle with the system of logic developed by Mill. Here we have the highest stage of this science. Scholars by all means must rely on the inductive method."[76] Nishi also emphasizes the contributions of psychology to philosophy, explaining the uses of such terms as soul, mind, emotion, and will.[77]

The concluding pages of the section on philosophy contain some meaningful comparisons of the East Asian and European intellectual traditions. In one place Nishi states: "Philosophy in the Orient is called Confucianism; the originators of Confucianism were Confucius and Mencius. Confucian scholars since the time of Confucius and Mencius have continued to preserve the teachings of these men without change. However, while scholars in the West are the heirs of an ancient intellectual continuum, with each new discovery they have been active in attacking the theories of previous writers. Therefore philosophy has gradually developed and been made over."[78] Again, he notes: "In my explanations throughout this volume, I have ranked Japan, China, and the West side by side, but when it comes to philosophy, the West stands first. In our country there is nothing that deserves to be

[76] *Ibid.*, p. 149.   [77] *Ibid.*, pp. 149-152.   [78] *Ibid.*, p. 169.

called philosophy; China too does not equal the West in this regard."[79]

But there were at least glimmerings of empirical studies in imperial China: "In Chu Tzu's time there was a man named Lu Hsiang-shan [Lu Chiu-yüan, 1139-1192]. After that there was Yang-ming [Wang Yang-ming, 1472-1529]. Their scholarship, which derived from self-knowledge, was much more practical than that of Chu Tzu. When Chinese Confucianism is reformed in the Western manner, it should be exceedingly outstanding."[80]

He concludes the thirty-eight page discussion of philosophy on an optimistic note: "What prevents the Chinese Confucianists from attaining preeminence is the phrase 'attachment to antiquity.' Once the finger is put on the sore spot, they will become enlightened and equal the West."[81]

By the time he wrote this section of *Hyakugaku renkan,* Nishi clearly believed that philosophy was essential for making Japan intellectually modern. To Nishi philosophy meant a rational, practical approach to knowledge, using inductive logic to investigate phenomena. Since he entirely excluded metaphysics and speculative thought from his description, Nishi's conception of philosophy was a limited one that was more relevant to practical epistemology than to the formal study of the basic principles of reality. The quasi-evolutionary character of his historical outlook is confirmed in his discussion of philosophy in China: although she "does not equal the West in this regard," Nishi is confident that once the Chinese lose their fondness for antiquity, "they will become enlightened and equal the West." By implication the same holds true for Japan: she will reach the "enlightened" or "positive" stage of development when she adopts rational, empirical approaches to knowledge. Just as Tokugawa Japan was overwhelmingly feudal, Japanese scholarship was grievously antiquated by the end of the Edo era. Vast changes in intellectual attitudes and scholarly assumptions were vital if Japan was to complete the transition from feudalism to

[79] *Ibid.,* p. 181. [80] *Ibid.,* p. 182. [81] *Ibid.,* pp. 182-183.

modernism—changes symbolized by the exchange of feudal Confucianism for modern empiricism.

To what degree, then, did Comte's interpreter differ from Comte himself? It is usually asserted that of all the major works of Nishi Amane, *Hyakugaku renkan* shows the greatest influence of Auguste Comte.[82] Its model was unquestionably Comte's *Cours de philosophie positive*. Both Nishi and Comte searched for unity in knowledge; both believed that the object of theory was practical action. The study of history as a secular science was central to both men's thought. Both Nishi and Comte deserted a strictly positivistic position by claiming that tutelary moral leadership of the common people was desirable; Comte would agree with Nishi's statement in 1874 that "if the men of wisdom and talent within a country do not rescue the people from their social evils, they cannot be blamed for them."[83]

Yet there are a number of striking differences between Comtian positivism and the ideas expressed in *Hyakugaku renkan*. First, Nishi agreed with Comte that the study of history was essential, but he joined Mill in rejecting the notion that there were uniform laws of social and historical development.[84] Second, Nishi made philosophy, not sociology, the culminating science in his scheme. Natural science, and particularly biology, was the underpinning for Comte's study of society, but Nishi consigned biology to a very minor position in *Hyakugaku renkan*. Although Nishi had far more interest in the natural sciences than most subsequent Japanese philosophers, his theories were man-centered, not nature-centered, and for this reason he was not an active participant in the early Meiji discussions of natural law. Third, Nishi gave great weight to logic and psychology, the latter of which Comte ignored on the ground that biology could accomplish the

[82] Ōkubo, "Nishi Amane no rekishikan," pp. 250-254; Kazue, "Nishi Amane no shōgai to sono shisō," pp. 19-20.
[83] "Yōgaku o motte kokugo o shosuru no ron," p. 577.
[84] For Mill's rejection of uniform historical laws, see *Principles of Political Economy*, ed. W. J. Ashley (London, 1909), pp. 795-796.

same ends.[85] Nishi's many pages in *Hyakugaku renkan* on the inductive method stem from Mill, as does his general emphasis on logic as the keystone of philosophy.

Nishi's writings do not satisfactorily explain why he preferred Mill to Comte, but his preference may derive in part from his greater familiarity with the English language than with French and the immense prestige of Britain in Japanese intellectual circles after 1868.[86] It is more likely, however, that the general humanizing effects of Confucianism (especially the Jinsai-Sorai heritage of concern for man as opposed to nature, reflected in Nishi's youthful shift to Soraigaku from Sung metaphysics) may have predisposed him to eschew the coldly scientific Comtian approach to the study of society. Moreover, it is probable that his interest in inductive logic, the hallmark of Mill's thought in Nishi's opinion, was foreshadowed by the school of empirical investigation that arose in the mid-Edo period under the influence of Rangaku and the utilitarian successors of Sorai. At any rate, Nishi's thought during this period was in harmony with the general positivistic spirit of the times. He did not agree, however, with the philosophical positivists, who held that science supplied the sole key to knowledge and that all that could be known was that which could be observed.[87] To the extent that Comte shared this broad positivistic spirit, his thought was congenial with Nishi's, but both men eventually abandoned strict positivism and went in separate directions, so that the only exclusively Comtian element in *Hyakugaku renkan* was its organizational structure.

Why was it that positivism was introduced to Japan, and what foundation existed for accepting its spirit? An obvious factor is that it was the current philosophy in Leiden when Nishi and Tsuda studied there; it was the current melody, as it were, when the Japanese first tuned their dials to the West.

[85] For Comte, see *Cours*, VI.
[86] See Mikiso Hane, "English Liberalism and the Japanese Enlightenment, 1868-1890," Ph.D. dissertation in history, Yale University (New Haven, 1957), pp. 8-25.
[87] See Charlton, *Positivist Thought*, pp. 5-7, for a summary of the various types of positivism.

A Leader in Enlightening Japan

Second, as an *état d'esprit,* positivism supplied an appropriate outlook for understanding the rapidly changing events of the early Meiji period. Its attitude was one not of upheaval but of progress and order, which could help to stabilize a nation undergoing revolutionary changes.[88] The intellectual revolution that was crucial for the reforms of the Meiji era had already started in the 1860's with the quest for some all-inclusive explanation for the superiority of the Western morality or spirit (*dōtoku*) as well as the preeminence of its more tangible technology (*geijutsu*). As the *keimō* scholars' understanding of the West deepened, so did their perplexity at the enormous complexities and contradictions in European thought. Positivism stood as a halfway house between the monolithic, panacean approach of the 1860's and the narrow specialization of Japanese scholarship in the later Meiji period. It offered systematic, rational guidelines for grappling with vast, inchoate corpus of new knowledge and new influences flowing into Japan in the 1870's. Third, positivism was something of a European counterpart to the school of practical studies (Jitsugaku) that had developed indigenously during the late Edo period, so that there were points of contact with the native tradition when positivism first entered Japan. Fourth, the classifying spirit of positivism was meaningful to a nation with a wide variety of intellectual choice. Positivism was by no means in harmony with orthodox Confucianism, but its emphasis on a hierarchy of knowledge was intelligible to anyone trained in Chu Hsi Confucianism. Positivism lent sanction to the idea that Buddhism, National Learning, Western studies, and the many varieties of Confucianism could exist within the same system,[89] although certain of these schools were more positivistic than others.

In Nishi's case, another factor leading him to positivism was the strong effect of Ogyū Sorai's thought, to which Nishi had become converted at seventeen. Although there are few references to Sorai in *Hyakugaku renkan,* there are a num-

[88] Funayama Shin'ichi, *Meiji tetsugakushi kenkyū* (Tokyo, 1959), pp. 6-7.
[89] See Funayama's comments on this point, *ibid.,* pp. 7-8.

112

ber of similarities between his thought and Anglo-French positivism. Like Comte, Sorai was more concerned with social development than the nature of the individual. Both men emphasized the importance of political institutions in achieving social progress. Sorai rejected metaphysics and personal morality, as did positivism, and he emphasized the study of history quite as strongly as Comte.[90] Sorai believed that anything benefiting the common people was good; such utilitarian social ethics corresponded remarkably closely with Mill's ideas in *Utilitarianism,* which Nishi later translated.[91] Although Nishi did not agree at every point with Sorai or the Europeans, Sorai's general approach to knowledge along rational and empirical lines of inquiry had prepared Nishi for understanding European positivism and created a sound basis for introducing positivistic ideas to Japan.

Hyakugaku renkan is a significant manuscript because it is evidence of the earliest introduction of many branches of knowledge previously unknown in Japan. More importantly, it demonstrates that Nishi's mind had developed within the positivistic context during and after his study abroad. Epistemologically the document was extremely iconoclastic, because it represented an attempt to abandon Confucian patterns of learning and knowledge in order to create a modern intellectual outlook. *Hyakugaku renkan* is not an accurate index of the whole range of Nishi's thought during the Ikueisha period, since it deals mainly with the nature of knowledge, but it is a most illuminating guide to the manner in which a *keimō* scholar who was personally committed to values derived from the West utilized the Japanese tradition as a tool for conveying the new knowledge, long after that tradition had lost its intellectual vitality and claim to moral exclusivity.

[90] *Sources of Japanese Tradition,* ed. Wm. T. de Bary (New York, 1958), pp. 423-424; J. R. McEwan, *The Political Writings of Ogyū Sorai* (Cambridge, Eng., 1962), pp. 7-14; Mueller, *John Stuart Mill,* p. 128.

[91] McEwan, *The Political Writings of Ogyū Sorai,* p. 4; Mill, *Utilitarianism,* in *Utilitarianism, Liberty, and Representative Government,* ed. A. D. Lindsay (New York, 1951), pp. 42-50. Nishi's translation, entitled *Rigaku,* was published in 1877.

five

Attack on Neo-Confucianism

One of the cardinal tasks facing the ideologues of Japan's new age was to dispel the lingering academic prestige of Neo-Confucianism by exposing the threadbare fabric of Shushi ethics to the bright light of reason. As a viable political ideology, Shushigaku had been interred in joint rites with the fallen *bakufu* in 1868, but as an ethical system and intellectual outlook it still carried great weight among many scholars. If Confucianism could no longer be employed to excuse the Tokugawa grasp on the Japanese polity, many persons thought, perhaps it might still survive as a moral or epistemological system. This to the *keimō* scholars was anathema. Unable or unwilling to perceive that Confucian morality could not effectively outlive the decline of Confucianism-in-political-action, Nishi and his associates trained their sights on the shortcomings of the old Confucian society and undertook a comprehensive re-evaluation of the nature and role of morality itself.

What, indeed, was wrong with Japan's feudal society? Among other things, the *keimō* intellectuals believed, was the stubborn fact that it had persisted virtually intact through the political upheavals of the 1860's—that is, it was bad because it had not yet undergone a transformation. More substantively, these scholars generally agreed that the common people were deplorably base and morally apathetic. Some, such as Nishimura Shigeki (1828-1902), refused to condemn the Shushi ethics outright, merely criticizing the lack of nationality consciousness in the feudal polity and society.[1] A few others, like Nakamura Masanao (1832-1891)

[1] David Abosch, "Katō Hiroyuki and the Introduction of German Political Thought in Japan: 1868-1883," Ph.D. dissertation in history,

114

Attack on Neo-Confucianism

decried the spiritual poverty of Tokugawa Japan in comparison with the ethics of Christianity.[2] But most of the *keimō* thinkers joined Katō Hiroyuki in reviling the obscurantism of both the National Learning school and Shushigaku and agreed with Fukuzawa that the moral obligations (*meibun*) growing out of the unequal status relationships of feudal society were reprehensible.[3] The consistent thread throughout these criticisms is the same concern with morality that Nishi had exhibited in his lectures at the private academy in Tokyo. As men who understood that certain Western values as well as Western machines were indispensable for Japanese self-strengthening, these scholars universally believed that some sort of morality was needed in the social organism that they hoped to reform. This tendency to stress the importance of morality was probably a reflection of their education in the Confucian tradition, but what mattered was not their emphasis on morality itself but the content of the teachings they advocated and the role they expected morals to play. In fact, this was a motive force behind the Meirokusha: according to Nishimura's conversations with Mori Arinori, one of the charter objectives of the society was to correct the recent decline of ethical standards among the Japanese people by establishing a new set of moral principles.[4] While the *keimō* scholars never reached a satisfactory consensus on the question of what the new standards should be, their intense interest in the problem, as revealed in their journal, *Meiroku zasshi,* indicates how vital they considered a new morality for modern Japan.

University of California (Berkeley, 1964), pp. 227-229. For a study of Nishimura, see Donald H. Shively, "Nishimura Shigeki: A Confucian View of Modernization," *Changing Japanese Attitudes Toward Modernization,* ed. Marius B. Jansen (Princeton, 1965), pp. 193-241.

[2] Carmen Blacker, *The Japanese Enlightenment: A Study of the Writings of Fukuzawa Yukichi* (Cambridge, Eng., 1964), p. 29.

[3] For Katō, see *Kokutai shinron* (1874); for Fukuzawa, see *Gakumon no susume.*

[4] Tōyama Shigeki, "Meiroku zasshi," *Shisō,* 447 (September 1961), p. 117.

Attack on Neo-Confucianism

THE SEPARATION OF POLITICS AND MORALS

Nishi Amane's primary contribution to modern Japanese thought is normally considered to be his sustained effort to introduce contemporary European philosophy, and in this respect he was a true pioneer. An attempt to reconstruct the intellectually significant Nishi, however, requires that we look beyond the comparatively straightforward process of transmission, as evident in *Hyakugaku renkan,* to the manner in which he applied the new learning to the major problems confronting his nation. Nishi was not directly involved in setting political, diplomatic, or economic policy in the 1870's, since he was not a member of the Meiji oligarchy or its small coterie of modernizers in the realm of statecraft. For Nishi, like many of the other *keimō* writers, the most urgent national problems involved a redefinition of public morality.

Nishi's contributions to the debate on morality reveal a Confucianist's concern for public ethics, but not the Confucian prescriptions. His position was that of the reformer who seeks a controlled social revolution along reasoned guidelines, without the disorientation and anarchy of violent change. Just as the law sometimes sleeps but never dies, morality too cannot be permanently evaded, Nishi seemed to believe. His case indicates how an early Meiji intellectual could think that morals were important without remaining attached to the traditional ethics: the enlightenment of the public mind did not mean emancipation from public responsibility. What is crucial for appreciating the degree of modernism in Nishi's thought is to understand his formulation of the place morals should occupy in human society and the content of the morality he advocated. He dealt with the first of these matters in *Hyakuichi shinron* (New Theory of the Hundred and One), which was published in 1874.[5] He treated the

---

[5] It is contained in *NAZS* 1960, pp. 232-289. Nishi began work on *Hyakuichi shinron* in Kyoto, and its publication was underwritten by his associate, Yamamoto Kakuma (see biographical notes). Ōkubo Toshiaki, "Kaisetsu," *NAZS* 1960, p. 635. The book was widely circulated in the Meiji period and has been reprinted in several collections of Meiji era writings and representative works in Japanese thought.

Attack on Neo-Confucianism

second question in a series of *Meiroku zasshi* articles in 1875, entitled *Jinsei sanpōsetsu* (Theory of the Three Human Treasures). *Hyakuichi shinron,* which will be discussed in this chapter, contains Nishi's criticism of the old society; *Jinsei sanpōsetsu,* the topic of the next chapter, includes his moral program for the new society. Together with *Hyakugaku renkan,* these two works represent the most outstanding achievements of his scholarly career and demonstrate that he did far more than merely introduce Western thought in a Japanese setting.[6] He utilized that thought to attack the ethical values of the pre-modern era and to create new guidelines for moral action in Japan's radically transformed society.

Hyakuichi shinron is an example of Nishi's most original scholarship. It is a systematic refutation of the Shushi orthodoxy, centering on two issues: the separation of ethics from politics and the distinction between human and scientific principles. It is quite characteristic of Nishi, the most scholarly of the *keimō* intellectuals, that he took the time to construct an elaborate denial of the ideology of the *ancien régime,* while others often merely denounced it and concentrated on plans for a modern society. *Hyakuichi shinron* represents the fulfillment of Nishi's attempts to establish a basic outline for moral teaching that was Western in inspiration but universal in application. Although the mark of his early Confucian education is visible in the terminology and documentation of this work, the arguments and conclusions seem totally in keeping with the most advanced Western studies of his generation and demonstrate beyond all doubt that his philosophical position was as progressive as any in early Meiji Japan.

Far from being a defender of tradition, Nishi was intellectually something of an iconoclast, despite his personal reserve and penchant for thorough scholarship. He had broken the feudal code of loyalty at twenty-four to study Dutch in Edo,

---

[6] In choosing to emphasize *Hyakugaku renkan, Hyakuichi shinron,* and *Jinsei sanpōsetsu,* I am grateful for the advice of Professors Ōkubo Toshiaki and Kazue Kyōichi. Professor Kazue's research seminar on Nishi Amane at Chūō University in 1964 focused on these three works.

a sign that his allegiances had shifted from the confines of his clan to the national realm. In 1870 he had written a trivial but vigorous denial of National Learning, asserting that it was opposed to the development of new knowledge and the rational study of Japan's ancient myths.[7] What is more, his occasional commentaries on poetry reflected the anti-formalist spirit of the Gesakuha (school of low-brow literature) of that period, and his lectures were often given in the colloquial, punctuated with jokes and anecdotes.[8] *Hyakuichi shinron* was written in the same vein: it resembles a Socratic dialogue between master and pupil, an unorthodox form in the Meiji period. But Nishi was not merely a gadfly; his approach was constructive, and he attempted to create positive alternatives to the Neo-Confucian attitudes toward knowledge and morality.

The term *hyakuichi* implies a unity (*ichi*) among the diverse (*hyaku*) moral teachings that exist throughout the world, but *Hyakuichi shinron* deals only tangentially with this theme. Nishi offers little more than a summary of his idea in *Hyakugaku renkan* that there is basic harmony among all scholarly disciplines: "precisely because I end up with the same meaning when I consider the mysteries and meanings of various teachings, I call it 'unity.' "[9] Under the strong influence of Comtian positivism, Nishi was the first Japanese to detect unity in all academic investigation, both Western and Eastern. The important questions in *Hyakuichi shinron,* however, concern the relationship of morals with politics and

[7] *Fukubōshisho.* See Ōkubo Toshiaki, "Nishi Amane no rekishikan," *Meijishi kenkyū sōsho,* series 2, vol. 4, *Kindai shisō no keisei,* ed. Meiji shiryō kenkyū renrakukai (Tokyo, 1956), pp. 273-276.

[8] Kuwaki Gen'yoku, "Kaisetsu," *NAZS* 1945, p. 71; Kazue Kyōichi, "Nishi Amane no shūgyō jidai," *Nihon oyobi Nihonjin,* 1,428 (April 1964), pp. 42-45. On Nishi's literary inclinations, see Kano Masanao, "Fukuzawa Yukichi to Nishi Amane," *Kokubungaku,* VI, 11 (August 1961), pp. 84-88.

[9] *Hyakuichi shinron,* p. 234. Henceforth *Hyakuichi shinron* will be cited as *HISR.* See also Kuwaki Gen'yoku, *Nishi Amane no Hyakuichi shinron* (Tokyo, 1940), p. 28. Kuwaki suggests that Nishi derived his title from the *Thousand and One Nights.*

the basic principles underlying human and natural phenomena.

One of the central doctrines of Shushigaku was the unity of government and moral teaching. In the ideal Confucian society, virtue rested in the hands of the political leaders, and their administrative role was one of moral influence rather than the exercise of actual power. From the eighteenth century onward, the Japanese spirit of rationality and nascent consciousness of nationality helped to undermine this Chinese doctrine by denying that the members of the ruling elite were the sole moral exemplars. By the time of the Meiji Restoration, many Japanese scholars were prepared to assert that moral instruction was no longer a proper concern of the government. It was Nishi Amane, in his *Hyakuichi shinron,* who brought this process to culmination by permanently severing the philosophical connection between morals and politics, thus formally scuttling a thought system which Japan's politicians had in practice already rejected.

In this work Nishi uses the word *oshie* to mean moral instruction, or simply morals, in a slightly different sense from the conventional Confucian term for morals, *dōtoku.* Although *oshie* normally signified educational or religious instruction in nineteenth-century Japan, Nishi gives it a new meaning: "*Oshie* may appear in the meaning of a certain teaching, a certain school, or a certain cult, but the *oshie* I am using here means solely teaching the way of man [*hito no hitotaru michi*]."[10] The term thus does not stand for morality in the accepted Confucian manner but instead indicates a more general ethic of humanity. Nishi claims to have derived his vague definition of *oshie* from the West; he cites the word for "morals" in several European languages and concludes, "although these words originate from Latin usage, in their present sense they all designate teaching the way of man."[11] Nishi hence assumes that morality in the broadest sense is something that exists throughout the world, not merely within the context of Confucianism.

Moral teaching, he continues, must not be confused with

[10] *HISR,* p. 236.   [11] *Ibid.,* p. 236.

politics. He differentiates between the still current idea that politics and morals are in conformity and the consequent inference that they are the same: "People today often say 'the conformity of politics and morals [*seikyō itchi*].' While this phrase is easily coined, there are many people who mistake the meaning a bit and understand this as 'the one path of politics and morals [*seikyō itto*].' "[12] His point is that politics and morals are two distinct phenomena, using entirely different methods, but that they share a common objective: "Now the phrase 'conformity of politics and morals' is very suitable for separating the confused ideas mentioned above. Politics and morals are necessarily two distinct paths. If they were not, the term 'conformity' would be unnecessary. Thus politics and morals differ in origin and emerge as different paths, but their results—their ultimate objectives—may be said to be identical. The methods employed in governing and teaching morality are completely different, but there is final conformity in their objectives: to better people's lives, to promote their welfare, to prevent death, to make life comfortable, and to insure that even after death no resentment remains."[13] Nishi thus argues that there is a conformity (*itchi*) of purpose in both politics and morals, but that they do not follow the same path (*itto*) to achieve it.

There is a superficial resemblance between this position and the teachings of Ogyū Sorai, but the real basis for these ideas was English utilitarianism. Sorai unquestionably anticipated the distinction between politics and morals in his criticism of *Mencius*,[14] and he agreed that social welfare should be a major concern of the state. However, Sorai had far too much respect for strong government to accept the limits on state authority over moral questions implied in Nishi's argument. Sorai merely sought to channel energies in this realm toward benefiting society.[15] He also revered classical Chinese

[12] *Ibid.*, p. 236. [13] *Ibid.*, p. 237.
[14] See *Sources of Japanese Tradition*, ed. Wm. T. de Bary (New York, 1958), p. 423.
[15] See Albert M. Craig, "Science and Confucianism in Tokugawa Japan," *Changing Japanese Attitudes Toward Modernization*, ed. Marius B. Jansen (Princeton, 1965), pp. 156-159. Murakami Toshi-

Attack on Neo-Confucianism

civilization too greatly to accept Nishi's insistent criticism of the East Asian heritage. Furthermore, Nishi explicitly acknowledges that he derived this argument from his study of James Mackintosh (1765-1832), an English legal historian: "This man first discovered the fact that morals and law are of separate derivation."[16] In fact, Mackintosh's *Dissertation on the Progress of Ethical Philosophy* (London, 1830) was a principal source for Nishi's manuscript. It is not coincidental that John Stuart Mill made a similar distinction, acknowledging that the two were not clearly differentiated in less advanced societies;[17] Nishi was almost surely aware of Mill's writings on the subject. Moreover, the purposes that Nishi ascribes to morals and government—"to better people's lives," "to make life comfortable"—are in harmony with English utilitarianism, which held that happiness was good for its own sake and that it should be secured for society as a whole. If Soraigaku helped to orient Nishi toward his criticism of Chu Hsi Confucianism, the major inspiration for the policy-morality distinction was nonetheless Western.

To buttress his argument, Nishi offers a detailed interpretation of Chinese history to refute the Sung idea that politics and morality are united. The later Confucianists, he writes, "confuse the ideas of politics and morality. First, to cite the root of this evil, the later Confucianists are mistaken in contending that cultivating the self and ruling others are the same thing, based on the doctrine in the *Ta hsüeh* [The Great Learning] of cultivating one's self, ordering one's family, governing the country, and pacifying the world. They think that if we just cultivate ourselves, others will be governed, and that if we possess sincerity and integrity, the world will be pacified. They believe that if sincerity and justice are somehow possible in all material and intellectual matters, the

haru fails to note these differences between Nishi and Sorai in "Nishi Amane no shisō ni taisuru Soraigaku no eikyō," *Kyōto Gakugei Daigaku kiyō*, series A, 25 (October 1964), p. 112.

[16] *HISR*, p. 262. See also Kuwaki, "Kaisetsu," *NAZS* 1945, p. 70.
[17] *Utilitarianism*, in *Utilitarianism, Liberty, and Representative Government*, ed. A. D. Lindsay (New York and London, 1951), pp. 51-80.

121

work of ruling the country and pacifying the world will naturally be possible, without special study or understanding advantage and disadvantage."[18]

Self-cultivation, according to Nishi, is not a proper way to set about ruling the world: "To think that politics is like a Zen priest's meditation is a painful misconception."[19] This error, he believes, results from a false interpretation of the *Ta hsüeh*: "This point in the *Ta hsüeh*—saying that one should first cultivate one's own virtue—is not to state a method of ruling the state and pacifying the world, because rulers are personally immoral and unyielding in their authority over the people. The *Ta hsüeh's* clause about ruling the people and pacifying the world says a few words about regulating people's property, but no method is cited."[20]

Nishi thus denies the usefulness of the *Ta hsüeh* as a guide to good government, dismissing it as "a kind of instruction book."[21] Nishi's approach to this question is best described as realistic. He scoffs at the fiction that rulers can rule benevolently and assumes that, being "immoral and unyielding," they will use their powers to promote their favorite ethical teachings. The implication is that such was the case throughout the Edo period.

Nishi similarly denies the Sung interpretation of the ancient rites and music as effective tools of political control: "Now as to etiquette and music, the latter was everything from playing harps, bells, and drums to songs and dance. . . . It seems to have been extremely popular in the Chou period. In the West it was the same, since music achieved a very high level among the Greeks. We may conclude that it reached heights of skill and ingenuity in the Chou civilization. However, the Confucianists in later centuries overemphasized it, saying that music together with etiquette constituted the principal tool for transforming the world. Thus they

[18] *HISR*, pp. 237-238.   [19] *Ibid.*, p. 238.
[20] *Ibid.*, p. 238.
[21] *Ibid.*, p. 238. See Benjamin Schwartz, "Some Polarities in Confucian Thought," *Confucianism in Action*, ed. David S. Nivison and Arthur F. Wright (Stanford, 1959), pp. 52-54, for a cogent discussion of self-cultivation and government.

held that ancient music must be revived. It is unfortunate that they spewed forth such roundabout arguments."[22] Instead, he argues, music should be encouraged for its intrinsic esthetic virtues, not because it is a fit technique for ruling. Wang Yang-ming, he notes parenthetically, was even more unrealistic in interpreting the Confucian classics. Nishi praised Wang's philosophy as more nearly empirical than Chu Hsi's in *Hyakugaku renkan*,[23] but here he condemns Wang's tendency to confuse morality and politics as worse than the teachings of the Sung scholars themselves.[24] There was thus precious little in any branch of the Confucian tradition that suited Nishi on this matter.

Orthodox Neo-Confucianism taught that the essence of morality was personal cultivation, but Nishi thought that it was designed both for the individual and for society. In support of this position, Nishi presents an unusual interpretation of Confucius as a man whose "main shop" was teaching about politics and whose "sideline" was morality. In Confucius' time, he believes, morals did not merely constitute self-cultivation; they had practical applications in society as well. In order to understand Confucius, Nishi says, we must study both his moral teachings and the history of his period:

"Therefore the person who truly wishes to study Confucius must understand that his moral teachings about benevolence and righteousness explain the laws and civilizations of all historical periods, and he will understand their merits and demerits. He must investigate things which were ignored at the time. The later Confucianists thought that such [historical] matters were of the lowest priority in their work and ridiculed the study of utility. They made explaining human nature and morality their main business. . . . Those who truly wish to study Confucius must conduct field work; they must decide which [Confucian ideas] are most advantageous, which are most profitable, which are most unprofitable, and which will serve the present purpose."[25]

22 *HISR*, p. 240.
23 *Hyakugaku renkan*, *NAZS* 1945, p. 182. See ch. 4 above.
24 *HISR*, p. 275.   25 *Ibid.*, p. 242.

Attack on Neo-Confucianism

Here Nishi is applying utilitarian standards to analyze Confucius' teachings, stating that we must understand Confucian doctrines in context. This relativism was quite alien to the Chu Hsi tradition and represents very striking evidence of Nishi's commitment to a set of values drawn from the West.

An important related question was the genesis of law, as distinguished from morality, in the centuries after the death of Confucius. Nishi notes that in the Chou period, the term etiquette (*rei*) included ceremony, manners, and law (*tenshō*), the latter of which he identifies as "the legal system for administering the state and the world."[26] Thus, until his old age, Confucius was not primarily a moralist, as the Sung scholars had claimed, but an adviser on etiquette, which included law. By the Han dynasty, however, ceremony and manners had become separate from etiquette, and "etiquette in the sense of a tool to rule the world changed its name" to law. The Han concept of law "was limited to criminal law [*keihō*], but this included all the regulations and codes for managing the world."[27] He writes:

"By the Han period, law and etiquette were already distinct and gradually became two separate paths. Etiquette was a matter for the *I chu* [a volume of prescribed ceremonies], which regulated family relationships, and ruling the world was called law. In precisely the same fashion, the ancients called water an element, but later generations, as new discoveries grew more frequent, divided it into hydrogen and oxygen. I believe that it was only later generations [the Han] who discovered that, rather than calling everything etiquette as had the Chou, etiquette meant ceremony and law meant the rules and institutions for governing the world."[28]

Thus the idea of ruling by law was now quite distinct from morality, according to Nishi, and it was only the later Sung Confucianists who "both confused the paths of self-

26 *Ibid.*, p. 246.   27 *Ibid.*, pp. 247-248.   28 *Ibid.*, pp. 248-249.

cultivation and ruling others and also did not understand the difference between politics and morals."[29]

It is important to note that Nishi has not rejected the Confucian tradition *in toto* here. Rather, he has reinterpreted it according to the precepts of Western political theory. His argument that law and morality were distinct by the time of the Han dynasty is unconvincing, as is his relentless castigation of the Sung viewpoint. His intent was not merely destructive, however. By finding such ancient precedents for the divergence of government from ethics, he was trying to demonstrate that a process of secularization that (in Nishi's opinion) did not occur until the late eighteenth century in Europe[30] had taken place in East Asia nearly two millennia previously. In fact it was not Han Wu Ti but Nishi who severed the nexus of politics and morality, a link that had remained quite secure in Japan until the mid-nineteenth century.

Having established the separation of law from morality, Nishi discusses at considerable length the merits of rule by criminal punishment, which "is the proper path for governing the world and the state."[31] Under the Chou, he notes, people were simple and easygoing, so that rule by etiquette sufficed. As civilization advanced, men grew more cunning and learned to evade the general regulations that existed. Therefore, more detailed laws became necessary, and by Han times "government by punishment was the standard method of ruling, so as people became enlightened (*kaika itaseba*) this standard path became evident."[32] This Nishi regards as the "natural" (*tōzen*) course of events, and he illustrates it with numerous examples from the Han and Warring States eras.[33] (By *tōzen* he meant something closer to "inevitable" than a strictly physical nature, since he did not use the term *shizen* [nature].) He considers Confucius in his old age a bit "orthodox" (i.e., reactionary) because he did not perceive this natural development and instead sought a return to the

[29] *Ibid.*, p. 251.   [30] *Ibid.*, p. 262.   [31] *Ibid.*, p. 252.
[32] *Ibid.*, p. 256.   [33] *Ibid.*, pp. 256-257.

ideal Confucian societies of Yao, Shun, and Chou.[34] Nishi praises Shen Tzu (?-337 B.C.), Shang Tzu (?-338 B.C.), Han Fei Tzu (?-233 B.C.), and Li Szu (third century B.C.) as the founders of Chinese law, commenting: "We must not mistake this as meaning something bad. Without law the world is of course difficult to rule. It is fair to say that at least Shen's and Shang's opinions that etiquette was too old-fashioned were better than those of Confucius and Mencius. But this is by no means to say that the laws established by Shen and Shang and those thought up by Li Szu were good."[35] In other words, Nishi thinks that the growth of law was a good and necessary development in Chinese history, even if the laws themselves were cruel and unreasonable. In his opinion, Confucius was shortsighted in not recognizing the necessity of law in ruling the state. One's impression is that Nishi has seriously misjudged Confucianism by demanding that it fit a pattern that occurred only in the West. In fact Nishi doubtless understood Confucianism quite well; what he was trying to do was to destroy its Sung interpretation, replacing it with a highly Western theory of legal development which was nonetheless applicable to the East Asian context, thereby demonstrating that Japan was at least on the right path toward enlightenment.

It is also significant that Nishi's interpretation of Chinese history is progressive, not cyclical. He denies that the classical Chou civilization was more admirable than the world of imperial China, when "men became enlightened." The belief that civilization advances reflects the teachings of Comte and other positivists; this was a widely shared interpretation of history among the *keimō* scholars. Nonetheless, the problem was that East Asian civilization had not developed so fast as that of the West. Nishi notes that once law had been discovered in China, it never developed beyond the Draconian legalism of its early pioneers:

"Later generations used the laws of Shen and Shang and

[34] Nishi uses the English word "orthodox" to mean reactionary. *Ibid.*, p. 258.
[35] *Ibid.*, p. 260.

understood their legal implications; but the fact that no one at all noticed that it would be good to reform the structure of the laws in order to attain the highest good means, I think, that theirs is a country which has taken pleasure since antiquity in people's enslavement and a national character which has never thought a thing of squandering people's human rights [*hito to shite hitotaru ken*]."[36]

The remedy, Nishi argues, is to divorce politics ("ruling men by law") from ethical instruction ("leading them by morals"),[37] which will permit legal reform. This thinly veiled criticism by indirection was inspired in part by Rai San'yō, who had likewise condemned his own country obliquely in writings on Chinese history.[38]

An important difference between politics and morals relates to the values with which each is concerned: "I shall explain the essence of my argument that law and morals are separate. It will be fairly clear if we distinguish between them by saying that law is a tool for ruling others and morality is a tool for ruling one's self. But both are intellectual [i.e., nonmaterial] phenomena based on human nature. Since they have their origins in human nature, they are likely to be confused and misunderstood. First, to describe the concept of law, it is rooted in the term 'right' [*sei, tadashii*]. The concept of morality is rooted in the term 'goodness' [*zen, yoi*]."[39]

Nishi cites Han Fei Tzu as a legalist who graphically distinguished right from wrong "with an inked marking string." He then comments that "law is like a carpenter's square: it must neither bend nor warp, buckle nor relax." Honesty (*shōjiki*) and justice (*kōhei*) are its principal attributes. By contrast, "the concepts of goodness, beauty, ability, and taste [*zenbi nōkō*] become the basis of morals."[40] Morality is omnipresent and affects all human activity, but law is strictly lim-

---

[36] *Ibid.*, p. 261.   [37] *Ibid.*, p. 261.
[38] Nishi greatly respected San'yō. See Ōkubo, "Nishi Amane no rekishikan," p. 254.
[39] *HISR*, p. 263.
[40] *Ibid.*, p. 265. The reference to Han Fei Tzu derives from Ssu-ma Ch'ien.

ited to defined aspects of men's interpersonal relations. Although the scope of morality is broader than that of law, morality alone is not enough to achieve the common aim of improving men's lives. In "ruling the world, you simply first govern them with punishments and then improve them through morals."[41]

There is good evidence in the history of East Asia to substantiate Nishi's assertion that the distinctive values associated with law and morals were understood by some Chinese and Japanese in earlier centuries. The Sung Confucianists nonetheless often subsumed the ideas of "good" and "right" in a single category, because to them virtue and proper government were synonymous. Nishi's criticism of this attitude strongly resembles the doctrine in nineteenth-century psychology that law, with propriety as its object, was based on knowledge and experience, whereas morality, with goodness as its object, was grounded on human volition. His circumscription of the range in which law was effective is in harmony with the legal thought which he had learned from Vissering in Holland. The novel position here, however, is that morality can and should teach men certain doctrines in areas beyond the effectiveness of state rule. Morality must rely on the government for keeping order, but it penetrates much more deeply into the private life of each person, to teach morally desirable values. This theme is a direct reflection of English utilitarianism, and it indicates that Nishi was by this time thinking of the separation of public and private interests. "Law," he wrote, "establishes its control over externally revealed forms, but morality makes clear the precepts of the inner heart."[42] He soon developed the theme of private versus public more fully in *Jinsei sanpōsetsu* (see next chapter).

Nishi also introduces in *Hyakuichi shinron* the related issue of rights and obligations, which he feels is the essence of law. In his parliamentary draft of 1867, he had outlined the "rights" of the imperial court, *bakufu,* and daimyo. Now he uses the same term for "rights" (*ken*), contrasting it with the word for "obligation" (*gi*). In China's feudal period,

41 *Ibid.*, pp. 266-267.　　　42 *Ibid.*, p. 271.

Nishi asserts, the lord-retainer relationship gave rise both to obligations and to rights, but they were each called *gi*.[43] He explains that in the West each was known by a separate term and that servants had rights as well as obligations vis-à-vis their lords: "Therefore this idea of rights and obligations is in harmony with the spirit of self-interest and self-reliance with which we are naturally furnished. People respect their own rights and do not lose them, and yet they are tolerant of others' self-interest and self-reliance and honor their obligations to others. . . . In this way we should give rise to enlightened government."[44]

In order to seek the common aim shared by politics and morality, political leaders should use good laws to protect both individual rights and the rights of society as a whole. If Japan was to adopt a modern, constitutional form of government, it would be essential for the people to understand their rights and duties. Despite his attempt to find precedents in the East Asian past to convey this idea to his countrymen, Nishi is advocating something quite alien to the Japanese social tradition. The concept of individual rights was familiar fare for the *keimō* intellectuals in the 1870's, something they derived from the political philosophy of revolutionary Europe. Nishi, however, recognizes that an enlightened government acting alone cannot guarantee that people's personal rights and obligations toward society will be upheld. The people themselves must accept the responsibility of observing their own prerogatives and duties: "But when self-interest and self-reliance become too strong and people fight over their rights, they neglect others' rights of self-interest and self-reliance, and finally they violate the harmony of rights and obligations. We have morals to assuage this evil. It suppresses the spirit that stresses rights, assists the spirit that emphasizes obligations, and acts so that the harmony of rights and obligations is not destroyed."[45] Politics, as it were, is the machinery and morality is the lubricant that keeps it in running order. When "civilization becomes enlightened, people's knowledge increases, and the sphere of government grows

[43] *Ibid.*, p. 272.   [44] *Ibid.*, p. 273.   [45] *Ibid.*, pp. 273-274.

129

wider, government is not conducted just by morals but rather by a blend of morals and law."[46]

Here is the nub of Nishi's criticism of the Confucian orthodoxy: Shushigaku did not recognize that politics provided a framework without which morality was merely a quixotic approach to overseeing society. At the same time, at the risk of appearing stuffy,[47] Nishi sincerely believed that morals could not be ignored, because they were indispensable for balancing and adjusting the mechanism of state. Yet morals must not be the handmaiden of political control, lest the former lose its effectiveness at the individual level.

This section of Nishi's *Hyakuichi shinron* is a skillful application of new knowledge to old problems. It demonstrates that Nishi subscribed to utilitarian and positivistic ideas from Europe, but also that he did not completely reject the indigenous tradition. Japan, he thought, needed such European concepts as limited state power, individual rights, and a separation of politics from moral doctrine, but it equally needed morality (which was neither Eastern nor Western) to stabilize and ennoble men's lives. Much as Nishi railed against Shushi dogmas, he did not attempt to blot out the whole Confucian tradition; instead, he deliberately divided the Sung symbiosis of government and morals but retained both elements in the culture. That he did so consciously indicates that his intent was modernizing, not traditionalistic. As in *Hyakugaku renkan,* he used Chinese history to explain Western ideas to Japan and to demonstrate his positivistic notion that certain desirable developments in European culture had their parallels, however rudimentary, in East Asian civilization. Of the most lasting importance, nonetheless, was the new role Nishi advocated for morality. The contents of that morality will be examined in the next chapter, after consideration of the second major issue in *Hyakuichi shinron,* natural and human principles.

[46] *Ibid.,* p. 274.
[47] The *keimō* scholars, despite their intellectual modernism, often seemed aloof and conservative to less well-educated Japanese who participated in the craze for Western things.

Attack on Neo-Confucianism

NATURAL AND HUMAN PRINCIPLES

The second prong of Nishi's attack on Shushi Confucianism deals with the philosophical question of universal principles, or *ri*. As a preliminary to considering his remarks on the subject, it may be helpful to take up briefly the genesis of this conception of *ri*. The Sung Confucianists had long ago established a dichotomy between *ri* (principles or ideal forms) [48] and *ki* (matter), which were nonetheless two aspects of the same thing. *Ri* were uniform, unchanging principles which prevailed equally in all natural and human phenomena, from which all facets of the material and non-material world derived their form. *Ki,* the matter of which all phenomena were composed, was considered inferior to (although inseparable from) *ri*. As Chu Hsi put it, "Principle has never been separated from material-force. However, principle is above the realm of corporeality whereas material-force is within the realm of corporeality. . . . Principle has no corporeal form, but material-force is coarse and contains impurities." [49] Human civilization was thought to be a reflection of the cosmic order, with which it shared *ri*. All investigation of nature and society had as its object the comprehension of *ri*. Since man's mind was in harmony with the principles of the universe, he was capable of perceiving these a priori *ri,* which represented preexisting human and natural truths that were continually being rediscovered. Accordingly, in the Neo-Confucian tradition all scientific scholarship aspired toward an understanding of these ideal principles and assumed that there were no new truths to be uncovered.

The Sung unity of metaphysical and scientific inquiry came under severe attack in Japan at the end of the seventeenth century. Itō Jinsai denounced the search for ideal metaphysical forms and believed instead that *ri* constituted the order that existed in human society. Soon thereafter Ogyū Sorai joined Jinsai in rejecting the Shushi split between *ri* and *ki,*

---

[48] J. R. McEwan uses the translation "ideal forms" in *The Political Writings of Ogyū Sorai* (Cambridge, Eng., 1962), p. 5.

[49] Chu Hsi, *Chu Tzu ch'üan-shu,* 49:Ia-b, quoted in *Sources of Chinese Tradition,* ed. Wm. T. de Bary (New York, 1960), p. 536.

131

Attack on Neo-Confucianism

distinguishing instead between ethical and natural principles.[50] Neither Jinsai nor Sorai was interested in scientific investigation itself; rather they were concerned with applying *ri* to human questions.[51] For Jinsai this meant individual ethics, whereas Sorai focused on social and political matters. By 1800, however, many Confucian writers and scholars of Western learning had begun to inquire into the principles of the scientific world not for their moral value in elucidating ideal forms but as indices of the *modus operandi* of nature itself. They borrowed the Neo-Confucian term *kyūri* (study of ideal forms) and used it to mean the scientific method.[52] This led to a great debate, unresolved before the Meiji era, over whether Western science was capable of discovering *ri,* since the West knew nothing of the metaphysical principles that were central to Shushigaku. Men such as Sakuma Shōzan, who admitted the utility of Western science, were incapable of acknowledging that the West could discover moral *ri,* even though the Confucianism to which Shōzan subscribed taught that physical and moral *ri* were the same.[53]

Like most *keimō* intellectuals, Nishi Amane was deeply concerned with the question of *ri,* but his use of this traditional category did not mean that he was attached to Neo-Confucian analyses. Instead, Nishi borrowed from the ideas he had learned in Holland to destroy the Shushi interpretation of *ri* and to provide an entirely new outlook on the nature of morality by permanently separating physical and human principles. In this way he was able to establish that morality had no connection with the cosmic order and that social development was unrelated to the laws underlying natural phenomena.

Nishi had acknowledged as early as 1862 that the West

[50] See McEwan, *The Political Writings of Ogyū Sorai,* pp. 6-9. Maruyama Masao, *Nihon seiji shisōshi kenkyū* (Tokyo, 1952), deals with this question in some detail.
[51] Craig, "Science and Confucianism," p. 154.
[52] Sagara Tōru, "Kindai shisō juyō no gakumonteki zentei," *Kōza kindai shisō,* ed. Kaneko Musashi and Ōtsuka Hisao (Tokyo, 1959), IX, pp. 78-84.
[53] See Craig, "Science and Confucianism," p. 154.

knew a great deal about moral as well as scientific *ri*: "The explanations of life's principles [*ri*] in the science 'philosophia' are superior even to Sung Confucianism. . . ."[54] He had offered an outline of the Chinese, Japanese, and European conceptions of *ri* in his *Shōhaku sakki*, written during the Ikueisha years.[55] In *Hyakugaku renkan*, moreover, he had classified "particular sciences" under the two headings of intellectual sciences (*shinrijōgaku*) and physical sciences (*butsurijōgaku*), foreshadowing the theory that he was now advancing in *Hyakuichi shinron*. Nishi uses the term *ri* mainly to mean "principle" or "rule," rather than in its Shushi sense of "ideal forms": "Now when someone says *ri*, he might mean the propriety of reason, the principles of nature, or such principles as loyalty to lords and filiality to parents, or the fall of rain and shining of the sun."[56] There were, in fine, many kinds of principles, and Nishi devoted the latter portion of *Hyakuichi shinron* to clarifying them under two main headings, natural and human.

Nishi notes that there has normally been no distinction, in China or Japan, between human (mental or intellectual) principles (*shinri*) and physical principles (*butsuri*).[57] As a rationalist, he takes delight in ridiculing the traditional confusion of mechanical and human laws: "For example, in China it was thought that when there was an eclipse, heaven was displaying the configuration as an admonition because the ruler's government was improper. In Japan, many people believed that, because of the *kamikaze* of Ise or the influence of Nichiren's prayers, a typhoon arose to capsize the Mongol

[54] Nishi to Matsuoka Rinjirō, June 12, 1862, quoted in Mori Ōgai, *Nishi Amane den, Ōgai zenshū* (Tokyo, 1923-1927), VII, p. 152.

[55] This work was published in March 1882. It was based on lectures at the Ikueisha and includes short translations from several Western books on sociology. The title cannot be meaningfully translated. It appears in *NAZS* 1960, pp. 165-172.

[56] *HISR*, p. 275.

[57] The term *shinrigaku* means "psychology" in modern Japanese, but Nishi used it to translate the nineteenth-century discipline known as "mental science." *Shinri* to Nishi meant the principles underlying man's intellectual and spiritual activities, as opposed to the laws of the external world. *Shinri* were thus moral principles and *butsuri* were non-moral ones.

133

warships, or that Kiyokura Kisho, through the mysteries of Shingon, raised the leaning Yasaka tower by prayer, or that rain fell on the drought by virtue of the *Ise* [*monogatari's*] poems."[58] Until people become enlightened and rid themselves of these superstitions, "it is impossible to talk about true morals," because moral and natural truths are quite different.[59]

All *ri,* according to Nishi, are divisible into *shinri* or *butsuri*: "Although we call all principles by the same name, in fact there are two kinds. We must realize that they are not related in the slightest. To identify this distinction, one is called human principle and the other physical principle. Physical principles are the principles of nature. At their largest, they are the vastness of the universe and the remoteness of the stars; at their smallest, a drop of water or a pinch of earth. Whether living beings from man to the birds and animals or vegetation like grass and trees, none can exist without these properties with which each is endowed. It is utterly impossible to defy these principles in the slightest."[60]

Physical laws, Nishi contends, are a priori prerequisites for the existence of society, and human laws are necessarily derived from them. However, human principles are not invariable; man's choice dictates how these principles will operate in each set of circumstances: "However, human principles are not so broad. They prevail only among humans, and humans alone can understand them. Only humans can obey them. Although they are based on nature, you can defy or alter them if you wish. . . . Therefore physical principles are called a priori and human principles are called a posteriori."[61]

Nishi illustrates *butsuri* with numerous examples from physics and chemistry, but *shinri* cannot be empirically documented so easily. Instead, he observes that "human principles can be flouted considerably, and thus it is possible to be immoral and improper. Furthermore, even when you are immoral and improper, it is often possible to flee heaven's

---

[58] *HISR*, p. 277.   [59] *Ibid.*, p. 277.
[60] *Ibid.*, p. 277.   [61] *Ibid.*, pp. 277-278.

vengeance."⁶² Far from being rigid extensions of the *ri* in nature, human laws offer infinite possibilities which defy codification.

Despite their greater flexibility when compared with *butsuri,* Nishi claims that human principles are not entirely man-made, and they cannot be created or discarded at will: "it is simply impossible to destroy the *shinri* which humans obey." The reason for this is that "humans possess the same nature; to obey this is called morality, and it cannot be changed. What is this identical nature? We can discern it when we examine man's feelings. All men have the same feelings, and no one can remake them. When someone suddenly strikes us or tries to kill us, or even slanders us or scorns us, are we happy about it or do we dislike it? Naturally we think it is bad, and such feelings are true of birds and animals too. Surely there is no one on earth who says thank you when he is struck or kicked."⁶³

Nishi's argument is that all men share such emotions as fear, indignation, hate, and sympathy, and that "humans cannot lead solitary lives like tigers or wolves, but rather possess a social nature like geese or sheep. This necessarily gives rise to mutual sustenance."⁶⁴ He contends that, owing to these constant factors in the human experience, human principles (however flexible) cannot be fundamentally altered or permanently defied by willful men. Evil rulers, he asserts, always become victims of their own wickedness.⁶⁵ Hence, the application of *shinri* depends on men's will, but the principles themselves are constant.

The reason for making this sharp distinction between *shinri* and *butsuri* was to establish that "both law and morals belong to the realm of *shinri* and are based on human nature, with no relation at all to physical principles."⁶⁶ Although they must remain separate themselves, both law and morality are considered to be phenomena capable of change and development, without reference to the cosmological *ri* of Shushigaku. In this way Nishi belittled the old Tokugawa claim

⁶² *Ibid.,* p. 281. ⁶³ *Ibid.,* p. 283. ⁶⁴ *Ibid.,* p. 284.
⁶⁵ *Ibid.,* p. 285. ⁶⁶ *Ibid.,* p. 288.

that the position of the *bakufu* as the temporal power and moral leader was perpetually justified by the unchanging natural order.

The implications of this dualism were crucial for the early Meiji intellectual community. *Hyakuichi shinron* contributed greatly to destroying the Shushi theory of knowledge, which had delayed truly empirical scholarship in Japan, by conclusively emancipating society and moral philosophy from their repressive links with the Sung cosmology. Both natural and social science could now pursue their respective *ri*, no longer forced to yield a common product. *Ri* itself was now liberated from its Confucian overtones to become something ethically neutral, like its English counterpart, "principle." Furthermore, if human society was no longer a reflection of the invariable structure of the universe, men would be capable of perfecting themselves and need not accept as inevitable the hierarchy of society. Nishi was the first to express these new attitudes toward scholarship in the Meiji era, and his work cleared the track for genuinely modern studies of both scientific and human truths in Japan.

We must not forget, however, that Nishi's theory and its ramifications had various antecedents in Japanese thought, especially in the teachings of Sorai. It was Sorai who first enunciated a clear distinction between the laws of man (*jindō*) and those of nature (*tendō*),[67] and Nishi duly acknowledged his debt to Sorai in *Hyakuichi shinron*. Nishi commented, however, that "it is difficult to say that his view was fully developed."[68] The *jinsei* (benevolent rule) thought of later Neo-Confucianism, which held that men could perfect their own society without relying on heavenly intervention, was likewise a significant forerunner of Nishi's belief that the application of human principles depended on men's will, not on *butsuri*.[69] Nonetheless, the scholar Funayama Shin'ichi is

---

[67] See Furuta Hikaru, "Nishi Amane, keimōki no tetsugakusha," *Asahi jyānaru*, IV, 16 (Apr. 22, 1962), p. 95; Murakami, "Nishi Amane no shisō," p. 112.

[68] *HISR*, p. 275.

[69] See Sagara, "Kindai shisō," pp. 70-71.

probably correct in concluding that Nishi derived his analysis mainly from the Western thought that he had studied at Leiden.[70] He made it clear in *Hyakuichi shinron* that there was no confusion in the West between human and physical *ri*.[71] English utilitarianism, to which Nishi was very devoted, similarly emphasized the asymmetry of physical and moral laws, teaching that man was capable of improvement and perfection. It was Anglo-French positivism which encouraged Nishi's interest in science, although he patently rejected the positivist faith in purely scientific explanations of social behavior on the ground that they excluded men's will.[72]

Albert Craig has likewise argued in a fascinating essay that Nishi derived his concept of *shinri* and *butsuri* not primarily from Sorai but from Western philosophy. He bases this conclusion on the fact that when Sorai separated natural laws from human laws, he did so in order to direct attention toward political realities and away from the investigation of scientific phenomena.[73] Craig believes that Nishi, however, divided the two kinds of *ri* so that each could stand as an independent subject of scholarly inquiry. Craig is undoubtedly correct in noting that Nishi "wrote in a tradition that took the universe as an object of knowledge as well as respect,"[74] but in fact Nishi's primary concern was most assuredly human society and morality, not natural science. Regardless of the origin of his analysis, which was indeed principally European, Nishi's chief objective in *Hyakuichi shinron* was to destroy two Shushi doctrines: the unity of politics and morality and the uniformity of *ri*. Because he concentrated on the independence of morality from government in the former case and upon the separation of human and moral

---

[70] Funayama Shin'ichi, in *Nihon no kannenronsha* (Tokyo, 1956), pp. 42-43, sustains this position, as does Craig on p. 159 of "Science and Confucianism."

[71] *HISR*, p. 288.   [72] *Ibid.*, pp. 278-281.

[73] Craig, "Science and Confucianism," p. 159. See also Blacker, *The Japanese Enlightenment*, pp. 102-103. For a later perspective on Nishi and *ri*, see Albert Craig, "Fukuzawa Yukichi: The Philosophical Foundations of Meiji Nationalism," *Political Development in Modern Japan*, ed. R. E. Ward (Princeton, 1968), pp. 113-114n.

[74] Craig, "Science and Confucianism," p. 159.

principles from scientific truth in the latter, Nishi's thought resembled Soraigaku more closely than Craig would seem to allow. Likewise it was more in harmony with English utilitarian ethics than with the strictly scientific orientation of philosophic positivism.

As a corollary to his theory of two kinds of *ri,* Nishi puts forth the idea that there are two branches to moral instruction, one theoretical and one practical. "Since the practical school [*kōmon*]," he asserts, "is based on human nature and is that which established law, it does not concern physical principles, but the theoretical school [*kanmon*] must refer to physical principles. . . . In saying that we must refer to physical principles, [we mean that] man is one of the phenomena in the natural world, so he must take physical principles into account."[75] Nishi is stating that morality in a practical sense, such as the etiquette (*rei*) of the Chou that was used to govern China before law became separated from morals, is unrelated to scientific *ri.* Moral man must nonetheless acknowledge his place in the natural order. Nishi thus believes that, in an abstract, historical sense, people must recognize that humanity and its laws have developed from the laws of the external world, but in everyday human society scientific principles are irrelevant. This curious *obiter dictum* on the theoretical and practical branches may represent an attempt, inserted as an afterthought, to reconcile to some degree the two kinds of *ri* that he had so carefully separated. The *obiter dictum* itself makes sense, but it vitiates the force of his main argument. Perhaps it was added to mollify some unknown or anticipated critic.

Equally peculiar is his abrupt conclusion that it is philosophy which unites all these ideas. Philosophy, he states, is that which "refers to human principles and makes clear the ways of man and nature, and at the same time establishes the methods of moral instruction. To translate this, we call it *tetsugaku.* It has existed in the West since antiquity."[76] (It is here that Nishi first uses *tetsugaku* as the Japanese equiva-

[75] *HISR,* p. 288.   [76] *Ibid.,* p. 289.

138

lent of the English term "philosophy.") He offers this statement without further explanation or justification, and apparently it was likewise an afterthought, tacked to the end of his book in defense of the title. While it is unclear what relation Nishi thought philosophy had to the main issues in *Hyakuichi shinron,* he gave it a very positivistic purpose: "To discuss all teachings generally and to make clear their identical purpose. . . . Thus philosophy must deal with both physical and mental principles."[77] These words confirm Nishi's tendency in *Hyakugaku renkan* to use "philosophy" to mean general positivistic philosophy. In *Hyakuichi shinron,* as in his earliest writings, Nishi seems once again to be using philosophy as something of a functional substitute for Shushi metaphysics: just as Neo-Confucianism held that there was a single *ri,* philosophy was the doctrine which could explain both human and natural truths. He never developed this argument, however, and it is doubtful, in the light of the more limited role which he assigned to philosophy in *Hyakugaku renkan,* whether he could have done so to his own satisfaction. His sophistication in European learning after studying in Holland was probably too great to permit him a sound defense of philosophy as the Western equivalent of Confucianism.

Hyakuichi shinron was Nishi's chief contribution to *keimō* thought in Meiji Japan and demonstrates the remarkable degree to which he thought in Western terms about Japanese problems. Its progressive attitude toward historical development and positivistic approach to problems of knowledge were totally in keeping with the enlightened spirit of the 1870's. (Katō Hiroyuki, for instance, made a similar distinction between natural and moral law.)[78] Most of the other Meiji Six Society members agreed generally with Nishi's ideas in *Hyakuichi shinron,* and the facts of the first twenty years of Meiji history conformed to his thesis: Confucian analyses were largely dropped in favor of the dual concep-

[77] *Ibid.,* p. 289.
[78] Kuwaki, *Nishi Amane no Hyakuichi shinron,* p. 36. Abosch, in "Katō Hiroyuki," p. 438, refers to the related problem of Katō's distinction between popular and national rights.

139

tion of human and natural *ri,* and the new government pursued a hands-off policy with respect to moral instruction. Ultimately, however, Nishi's theories fared less well. Even during the *bunmei kaika* period such persons as Nishimura Shigeki and Nakamura Masanao maintained that ethical teaching should be a responsibility of the state.[79] Their position prevailed after 1885, the start of a trend that finally led in the 1930's to the government-enforced moral training known as *shūshin.*[80] Nevertheless, the split between the *shinri* and *butsuri* persisted and gradually became more refined, enabling the Japanese intellectual community to escape traditional regimens in favor of a more practical and rational approach to scholarship.

[79] Warren W. Smith, Jr., *Confucianism in Modern Japan: A Study of Conservatism in Japanese Intellectual History* (Tokyo, 1959), p. 53; *Japanese Thought in the Meiji Era,* ed. Kōsaka Masaaki, tr. David Abosch (Tokyo, 1958), pp. 124-127.

[80] See R. K. Hall, *Shūshin: The Ethics of a Defeated Nation* (New York, 1949).

six

Ethics for the New Society

Life in Meiji Japan was exciting, although as for most brilliant eras the glamour now associated with the period is partly apocryphal. The first ten years of Meiji were filled with reforms and innovations that seemed all the more bold against the dull backdrop of Tokugawa Japan. Although the changes were initiated primarily by the political elite, they were supported by almost all the significant elements in the post-restoration balance of forces, for Japan had reached, with surprisingly little dissent, a consensus on the need for economic and military modernization. With her course thus clearly charted, Japan in the early Meiji years experienced a feeling of great public exuberance, a sense that she had embarked on a perilous but rewarding expedition into the unfamiliar realm of enlightened, civilized nations. This grand venture demanded—and obtained—the full energies of the Japanese people, who proved remarkably eager to assist with building a modern nation. This creative public mood was characterized by one of its greatest admirers, Fukuzawa Yukichi, as the "spirit of civilization."[1]

However well-developed Japan's plans for economic and military *aggiornamento* may have been, her future norms of social behavior were much less clearly defined. As a succession of edicts by the Meiji oligarchs steadily unraveled the country's ties with its past, even the most serious students of Western culture began to perceive that the public preoccupation with the tangible efforts toward modernization lacked any real justification in value. They believed the modern economy and polity to which Japan aspired must be firmly grounded in an appropriate social morality. Some higher value than mere wealth or power must be discovered if Japan

---

[1] See Carmen Blacker, *The Japanese Enlightenment: A Study of the Writings of Fukuzawa Yukichi* (Cambridge, Eng., 1964), p. 31.

Ethics for the New Society

was to become a truly modern nation. Thus, although the *keimō* scholars were the leading critics of the feudal ideology and supported most of the Meiji reforms vigorously, they became anxious when they could not detect in the abrupt and arbitrary decrees of the oligarchy any suitable substitute theoretical justification for the new state and society. Nishi expressed this uneasiness in these terms:

"The grand work of the restoration . . . amounts to achieving impartial rule: abolishing fiefs, samurai positions, differences in rights among the four classes, and the various boundaries between *han*. In a single morning the whole world underwent sudden change. . . . This is to uproot the trunk and let the branches die. The elements of 2,500 years of moral education have been secretly destroyed . . . this is decreed by the course of events and cannot be stopped by anyone."[2]

In this climate of moral uncertainty, John Stuart Mill immediately gained a wide circle of admirers in Japan. In 1871 Nakamura Masanao brought out a complete translation of *Liberty,* under the title *Jiyū no ri*. Other scholars published translations of *Representative Government* and *Principles of Political Economy,* both of which appeared in 1875.[3] These works had reappeared in many editions by the end of the century, and their popularity is in a sense a testament to Japanese interest in the more tangible Western institutions such as government and economy. Asō Yoshiteru has argued that Mill's renown resulted from the appeal of his ideas to the merchants: they were "adopted as an ideological prop

---

[2] *Kōfuku wa seireijō to keikaijō to sōgōsurujō ni naru no ron,* NAZS 1960, pp. 556-557.

[3] *Liberty* was first published in England in 1859, and Nakamura's translation was a complete one. Nagamine Hideki published a partial translation of *Representative Government* (1861), as *Daigi seitai* in 1875. Hayashi Shigeru and Suzuki Jūkō brought out a complete translation of *Political Economy* as *Keizai ron* in 1875. See Asō Yoshiteru, *Kinsei Nihon tetsugakushi* (Tokyo, 1942), p. 177; Kazue Kyōichi and Sagara Tōru, *Nihon no rinri* (Tokyo, 1959), pp. 175-176; and Funayama Shin'ichi, *Nihon no kannenronsha* (Tokyo, 1956), pp. 48-49.

by the townsman class, recently come to power as a force opposed to the feudal system. . . ."[4] The historians Ienaga Saburō and Ino Kenji have observed that utilitarianism was by no means the most radical European doctrine available for import into Meiji Japan and that it therefore represented an attempt to inculcate such bourgeois values as freedom and independence. According to Ienaga and Ino, utilitarianism was dominant because it was the most effective ideology for combatting feudalism.[5]

These theories do not take full account of the fact that it was principally the intellectuals of aristocratic birth, not the merchants, who preached the merits of Mill's thought and that utilitarian ideas were central to the government policy of *bunmei kaika* in the mid-1870's. Something by Mill was read in virtually every government school during this period. Rather than being taken up as an "ideological prop by the townsman," utilitarianism was promoted from above in order to supply a rationale for the industrial and commercial economy which Japan's leaders were creating. Utilitarianism was a splendid alternative to Confucian ethics, the *keimō* scholars reasoned, not merely because of its economic implications but mainly because it was the leading philosophy of Europe's most advanced nation, England. Most importantly, mid-nineteenth-century utilitarianism was essentially a social, not an individual, philosophy, and it was therefore more easily grasped by Confucian-trained minds than the thought of Calvin or Rousseau. Beginning with Adam Smith, English empiricists had enunciated the doctrine that the sum of selfish interests equaled the general interest of society. It was this collective, functional principle that was seized by the Japanese amid the chaotic changes of the 1870's. For all these reasons Mill was unquestionably the most widely read European philosopher in the early Meiji era.

[4] Asō, *Kinsei Nihon tetsugakushi*, p. 83.
[5] Ienaga Saburō and Ino Kenji, "Kindai shisō no tanjō to zasetsu," *Kindai Nihon shisōshi kōza*, ed. Ienaga Saburō, I (Tokyo, 1959), pp. 51-52.

Ethics for the New Society

If Japan was to become a modern civilization, most of the *keimō* group thought, it would be imperative to make citizens aware of their individual rights and responsibilities. This conviction gave rise to the natural rights (*tenpu jinken*) theory, of which Fukuzawa's *Gakumon no susume* (The Encouragement of Learning) was the most persuasive expression.[6] Nishi, however, did not fully support the *tenpu jinken* goals of equality, freedom, and individual self-consciousness, because of his preoccupation with English utilitarianism. Whereas Fukuzawa and others drew freely on many European schools of thought, Nishi limited himself mainly to the social philosophy of Mill, adopting only those ethical values which had direct relevance to Japanese society. Although he was less concerned with many theoretical aspects of Western thought than the advocates of the *tenpu jinken* theory, Nishi was better read in utilitarianism than French *droit naturel* and more precise than the natural rights advocates in applying specific doctrines to Japanese needs. His most creative use of Mill's thought is contained in *Jinsei sanpōsetsu* (Theory of the Three Human Treasures), parts of which were published serially in *Meiroku zasshi* during 1875.[7] This book was a landmark in Japanese philosophical scholarship because it represented the first attempt to apply utilitarian dogmas to Japanese social thought.

On the first page of *Jinsei sanpōsetsu,* Nishi praises Mill's philosophy: "Among the theories of the various great thinkers, many of which are at last being based on practical principles, I think that John Stuart Mill's expansion of Bentham's

---

[6] Published in 1872, *Gakumon no susume* by 1884 had gone through seventeen editions, totaling 220,000 copies. See Kazue Kyōichi, "Meiji jidai no shisō," *Nihon no rinri shisōshi,* ed. Kazue Kyōichi (Tokyo, 1963), pp. 289-290.

[7] Parts one through four appeared in *MRZS,* 38, 39, 40, and 42. They are contained in *MBZ,* xviii, pp. 236-239, 241-243, 246-249, and 258-259. Parts five through eight appeared in a collection of Nishi's writings prepared in 1880 by his students, entitled *Nishi sensei ronshū.* All eight parts are included in *NAZS* 1960, pp. 514-554, to which version subsequent notes refer. Henceforth *Jinsei sanpōsetsu* will be cited as *JSSPS.*

Ethics for the New Society

utilitarian moral theory (which resembles the Greek Epicurean school) is a great revolution in modern moral thought."[8] We must be cautious in treating the utilitarianism which Nishi used and admired, for there is rather less substance in Mill's social philosophy than in his logic or political writings. *Utilitarianism* was not so much an "expansion" of Bentham's theory as an involuted defense of it, one that is almost apologetic in tone.[9] Mill's main concern was to defend "inductive" morals against the attacks of "intuitionists" (or transcendentalists) who held that ethical principles, while not empirically verifiable, were self-evident. Much of *Utilitarianism* is given over to a discursive examination of happiness, which is the object of morality, although Mill in the end turns to a consideration of justice and sympathy as legitimate concomitants of pleasure. Indeed, in many respects it would be more apt to call Mill's utilitarianism a variety of naturalistic ethics.[10]

If Mill's social ethics were highly elliptical, it is understandable that Nishi followed his guide only in a general way. Nishi used Mill as a springboard for creating a new theory of social behavior for Japan that is harmonious in spirit with *Utilitarianism* but does not conform to it point by point. After explaining in *Jinsei sanpōsetsu* that the aim of utilitarianism is the greatest happiness for the greatest number, he states, "the main point I wish to discuss here is the method of attaining this general happiness which we have established as mankind's number one objective."[11] Nishi uses this familiar utilitarian doctrine as a starting point for developing his own theory of morality, which can be divided into three categories: the ethical theory of the three treasures, the relation between society and the individual, and the moral responsibilities of the state. His approach to each of these problems reveals the extent to which he had become estranged from the ethics of orthodox Neo-Confucianism.

"There are three precious things in human life," Nishi says, that "are the means, the agency for attaining the ulti-

---

[8] *JSSPS*, p. 514.
[9] John Plamenatz, *The English Utilitarians* (Oxford, 1958), p. 134.
[10] *Ibid.*, p. 144.　　　　[11] *JSSPS*, p. 515.

Ethics for the New Society

mate objective, general happiness." These three "treasures" are health (*mame*), knowledge (*chie*), and wealth (*tomi*).[12] They are the *sine qua non* of a harmonious modern society. Nishi is quick to point out that the treasures are not themselves the ultimate aims of society, for this "would be the philosophies of thieves and coolies." Health, knowledge, and wealth should replace the lamentably archaic values of feudal society, namely the "virtues of docility, naïveté, humility, deference, unselfishness, and freedom from avarice that constitute the primary duties of what we call morality today."[13]

What were the origins of these grievous defects in the Japanese national character that Nishi hoped to mend? They stem, Nishi argues in another essay, from two things: the "servility" imposed by seven hundred years of military government and the "asinine" hierarchical nature of Shushi Confucianism.[14] The Japanese people have traditionally been faithful and compliant, resulting in the persistence of their subordination. Furthermore, they have been content to "have despotic rulers above them and regard themselves as slaves."[15] Now that the Meiji political upheaval has taken place, Nishi concludes, this subservient character must be corrected and the people taught to claim their rights.[16] Curiously, he assumed that this popular tractability could easily be cured by instruction from above, now that feudalism, politically and philosophically, was at an end, although it was precisely this pliant subservience to higher authority that he was trying to purge.

Nishi states in *Jinsei sanpōsetsu* that the treasures are natural gifts to man and that it is each person's obligation to nature to seek health, knowledge, and wealth:[17]

[12] *Ibid.*, p. 515. Nishi used the modern characters for health (*kenkō*) but appended the rare reading *mame* in *furigana*. For knowledge he used the modern *chishiki* but added the reading *chie*, which today implies wisdom rather than knowledge. He clearly meant knowledge in a quantitative, accumulative sense. For wealth he used the compound *fuyū* but added *tomi*.

[13] *Ibid.*, pp. 515-516.

[14] "Kokumin kifūron," *MRZS* 32 (March 1875), *MBZ*, xviii, pp. 207-208.

[15] *Ibid.*, p. 208.   [16] *Ibid.*, pp. 208-209.

[17] *JSSPS*, pp. 516-517.

Ethics for the New Society

" 'How is health a treasure?' I would reply, 'there is no living being which does not value its life. This fact is visible before our very eyes. This is inborn moral nature. It is clear that man's first obligation to heaven is to preserve his life by protecting his health.' If one asked, 'how is knowledge a treasure?' I would reply, 'there is no living being that does not like to surpass others. This fact too is evident before our own eyes. Accordingly this is inborn moral nature. . . . if we seek to excel in individual mental power, how can we fail to attain knowledge? Therefore man's second obligation to heaven is to broaden his knowledge.' If one said, 'how is wealth a treasure?' I would say, 'there are no living beings which do not obtain goods for their own use. This fact too is visible before our eyes. Accordingly it is inborn moral nature. Although birds and animals need think only of food, men cannot lack the necessities of food, clothing, and shelter for a single day. . . . Man's third obligation to heaven is to seek all sorts of wealth.' "[18]

Hence "if each individual truly values these three treasures, and does not nullify his natural gifts, the foundation of morality will be established, and we shall be able to achieve the maximum general happiness."[19]

At first glance, this concept of the three treasures may appear to be a bland and artless statement of the obvious, cloaked in the guise of English thought. Indeed, Nishi forthrightly accepted responsibility for its shortcomings, stating at the outset that "this theory of the three treasures is of course a personal view, taken from my own mind; I do not dare hope to transmit the theories of the Western philosophers."[20] If Nishi did not take the idea of the treasures directly from European thought, neither was it entirely novel in Japan. Fukuzawa had stressed men's right to protect their lives, honor, and property in *Gakumon no susume* (1872), in which he also placed great emphasis on learning.[21] On this point both Fukuzawa and Nishi of course owed a

[18] *Ibid.*, p. 517.　　[19] *Ibid.*, p. 519.　　[20] *Ibid.*, p. 515.
[21] See Blacker, *The Japanese Enlightenment*, p. 105.

great debt to the ideology of the French and American revolutions. The importance of Nishi's argument in *Jinsei sanpō-setsu* is that in place of the feudal social ideals of loyalty, subservience, frugality, and the like, he attempted systematically to justify the pursuit of health, knowledge, and wealth as legitimate goals for the Japanese people. Each was a birthright enjoyed by all men, and the moral person would attain general happiness by cultivating each of them.

To espouse utilitarian goals, however, did not require a total apostasy from the Japanese tradition. It is significant that Nishi tried to find Confucian precedents for his theory. In one place he states that "although the way of Confucius and Mencius has never asserted the three human treasures, it does not follow a path completely apart from them."[22] In another, he defends the moral worth of moneymaking, noting that "the Confucian teaching that you should be content with poverty is merely saying that you should not indulge in illicit wealth. It does not forbid obtaining money by expending labor."[23] Here is further evidence that Nishi is using his unburned bridge back to the East Asian heritage to help reconcile foreign concepts with the native past. There is little doubt of his basic antipathy to the main Confucian tradition, but by finding some evidence that these utilitarian values of health, knowledge, and wealth had been respected, however rudimentarily, in Chinese and Japanese history, Nishi could avoid condemning his own tradition for completely ignoring the civilizing virtues of the West. He thus shifted the blame to the Sung Confucianists for retarding the development in East Asia of values that had fully emerged in early modern Europe. In this manner he could maintain that China and Japan had been on the path toward an enlightened civilization and that it now was simply a question of catching up with Europe. This progressive attitude toward history, evident through all of Nishi's works, was itself a denial of Confucian historiography.

[22] *JSSPS*, p. 515.   [23] *Ibid.*, p. 519.

Ethics for the New Society

In preparing a new set of ethical standards for Japan, it was particularly important for Nishi to account for the interests of society as a whole, because most previous Japanese moral teachings had been characterized by a high degree of group consciousness. Private profit was ordinarily beneath the dignity of the Confucian gentleman because it was acquired at the expense of others. The mid-Edo period doctrine known as *shingaku* helped to weaken the Confucian interdiction of profit, but as an ideology for the feudal merchant class *shingaku* was quite as group oriented as Confucianism.[24] The *shishi* thought of the later Edo period, which emphasized sincerity and individual action, similarly denied a great portion of Shushi ethics, but its appeal was limited to aristocrats and it had almost no relevance to the commercial economy. Thus Nishi was especially obliged to reconcile the idea that each individual should pursue his own treasures with the prevailing Japanese notion that one should subordinate personal ambitions to the interests of society as a whole. It was essential that Nishi place the individual in proper social perspective, lest his theory be mistaken as license for selfishness or greed.

The individual, Nishi says in *Jinsei sanpōsetsu,* has two responsibilities in his associations with other men. One is the negative, legal duty of not tampering with others' health, knowledge, or wealth; the other is the positive, moral obligation of assisting other men in their pursuit of the three treasures:

"Therefore the rules [of morality] first say, 'you must not harm others' health, knowledge, or wealth.' These are called the three negative provisions, because they all say 'don't!' When you express a desire to regulate, restrain, and protect yourself, this does not concern other peoples' three treas-

---

[24] For an interesting discussion of *shingaku*, see Robert N. Bellah's investigation of the thought of Ishida Baigan (1685-1744) and others, entitled *Tokugawa Religion: The Values of Pre-Industrial Japan* (Glencoe, Ill., 1957).

Ethics for the New Society

ures. Thus these are things to be achieved by completing the latter half of the rules. They are called the three positive provisions, for they all say 'do!' They authorize us to aid, assist, and support the three treasures of other persons. Therefore the three negative provisions have their origin in law, as distinct from morals, while the three positive provisions constitute moral application."[25]

This problem involves the concept of rights and obligations which Nishi had discussed in *Hyakuichi shinron*, elaborating on ideas put forth by Katō Hiroyuki. Like Katō, Nishi asserts that every man has the right to defend his treasures from violation by others, but he also has the obligation of "respecting the three treasures of other persons and not violating them in the slightest."[26] Hence, at the individual level, man has a moral obligation to nature to pursue health, knowledge, and wealth, together with the legal right of protecting them from depredation. Similarly, at the social level, each person must observe both his legal obligation not to interfere with the treasures of others and also his moral duty to help others secure their treasures.

Nishi offers a detailed description of the development of society to support his belief that "the basis of human morality lies in respecting the three treasures. . . . No other rules are necessary for personal conduct or for associating with others."[27] All societies, whether advanced like Europe's or primitive like those of Taiwan and the Ainu, are composed of human beings, and the forces uniting them are greater than those dividing them. Societies differ only in size and level of attainment, not in substance, Nishi believes. The more men attain the treasures, the more society will become enlightened. This civilizing process he regards as the "natural course of events [*risei no tsune nari*]."[28] Nishi undoubt-

[25] *JSSPS*, p. 521.
[26] *Ibid.*, p. 522; Katō, *Shinsei tai-i* (1870). See David Abosch, "Katō Hiroyuki and the Introduction of German Political Thought in Japan: 1868-1883," Ph.D. dissertation in history, University of California (Berkeley, 1964), p. 360.
[27] *JSSPS*, p. 524.   [28] *Ibid.*, p. 526.

edly means that these values of health, knowledge, and wealth prevail in all societies and that with the proper amount of effort Japan can reach a civilized stage of development.

In order to fulfill their obligations to nature and to each other, Nishi maintains, all individuals must equally cultivate the three treasures. He argues in favor of the equality of economic opportunity, holding that each person is "like the loop of a chain or rosary": there may be differences in relative size or strength, but each is equally indispensable to society.[29] This idea is an outgrowth of his Ikueisha lectures in 1871, in which he had stressed the value to society of even the most dull-witted worker.[30] Therefore, he concludes, there are two great principles for society: (1) The three human treasures have uniform value, without distinction between rich and poor or superior and inferior. (2) If the three treasures are not harmed in the slightest, all human actions will be free and independent.[31]

General happiness, the goal of society, is thus characterized by freedom and equality. The effect of utilitarian teachings may be observed in Nishi's understanding of these terms: he means freedom of occupational choice and equality of economic opportunity rather than the broader, more theoretical definitions of these words. He rarely discussed such abstract ideals of European civilization as these without reference to tangible situations, a fact which at least had the virtue of making his ideas exceedingly intelligible to the early Meiji reader. The result, despite the florid distraction of the treasure metaphor, was a meaningful but limited explanation of what "freedom" and "equality" really meant. It was one of the shortcomings of Nishi's understanding of Western thought that he never squarely confronted the meanings of these terms as absolutes, because of the relativistic nature of the utilitarianism to which he adhered. Utilitarianism ignored human values apart from their social usefulness.

If everyone is morally bound to seek private profit, what

[29] *Ibid.*, p. 527.
[30] *Tōei mondō, NAZS* 1961, pp. 266-267.
[31] *JSSPS*, p. 528.

safeguard is there to prevent conflicts of interest among men? Nishi gives no satisfactory answer to this dilemma. He merely reiterates the stock utilitarian explanation that private and public interests are in harmony:[32]

"The public interest is the aggregate of private interests. . . . Therefore, the object of society is the public interest, which is the sum of private interests. Private interests result from individuals' [pursuit of] health, development of knowledge, and fulfillment of wealth. Both private profit, as an individual matter, and public profit, as a social matter, boil down to advancing the three treasures. Therefore, if men seek to cultivate morality, they should begin by respecting their own three treasures."[33]

By "public" Nishi clearly means society as a whole, not the state. Even the miserly old farmer must yield his wealth to society when he dies, and therefore, Nishi concludes, there is no conflict so long as men observe their legal and moral obligations toward the treasures of others.

Another tie between public and private interests is Nishi's dictum that "man lives for others."[34] He attempts to show that by laboring on society's behalf, men can advance their own health, knowledge, and wealth: "Even if we devote ourselves to others' affairs and plan for their benefit, still we do all these things for our own sakes. Where there is no personal profit, what man would toil for the sake of another?"[35] Thus "living for others" is synonymous with seeking one's personal profit. This curious argument was patently designed to encourage a spirit of initiative and boldness among individuals

[32] On this point see Mikiso Hane, "English Liberalism and the Japanese Enlightenment, 1868-1890," Ph.D. dissertation in history, Yale University (New Haven, 1957), pp. 43-45.

[33] *JSSPS*, pp. 532-533. See Benjamin Schwartz, *In Search of Wealth and Power: Yen Fu and the West* (Cambridge, Mass., 1964), pp. 116-129, for Yen Fu's defense of individual profit.

[34] A precept, Nishi notes, of Christianity. *JSSPS*, p. 530. Nishi was not particularly attracted to Christianity except as a historical phenomenon. See also Murakami Toshiharu, "Nihon kindaika no katei ni okeru ten no kannen," *Kenkyū ronbunshū*, ed. Bunkakei Gakkai Rengō, xvii (1966), pp. 9-23.

[35] *JSSPS*, p. 531.

Ethics for the New Society

that was, in Nishi's opinion, all too rare in Japan. He did not mean, however, that the individual's interests should take precedence over those of society as a whole, either from an ethical point of view or from practical considerations. In "Aitekiron," for example, he advocated altruism on moral grounds and said that men "in dealing with others must have a loving nature. . . . The phenomena of indignation and resentment are largely to be found among women and petty persons."[36] In the routine events of daily life, he asserted in *Jinsei sanpōsetsu,* the ultimate aim of personal gain was to benefit the public interest.[37]

Having established that every man has an equal right to promote his health, knowledge, and wealth, Nishi must account for the inequalities within human society. There are, he declares, no natural differences among men nor distinctions as to individual worth:[38] "Every individual is equal with his companions, and the basic nature of the three treasures has no differences between high and low or rich and poor."[39] The Sung Confucianists were misguided in ascribing human inequalities to the presence or absence of *ki.*[40] The real reason for hierarchy in society is that, although all men have equal rights to the treasures, some have exercised these rights more fully than others, thus gaining a greater measure of health, knowledge, or wealth. Just as the laws of gravity prevail everywhere or as the cat's strength exceeds the rat's, those who possess the treasures dominate those who lack them: "The strong control the weak, the wise control the foolish, and the rich control the poor."[41] Mencius stated a similar principle, according to Nishi, but Mencius did not ascribe to it the regularity of physical laws that Nishi does.[42] The important point is that any man can rise to prominence simply by accumulating the treasures.

The reason why European countries dominate Asian lands, Nishi says, is that they possess the three treasures in greater

[36] "Aitekiron," *MRZS,* 16 (September 1874), *MBZ,* xviii, p. 136.
[37] *JSSPS,* p. 532.
[38] *Ibid.,* pp. 544-545. See Kazue, "Meiji jidai no shisō," pp. 305-306.
[39] *JSSPS,* p. 545.   [40] *Ibid.,* p. 554.
[41] *Ibid.,* p. 544.   [42] *Ibid.,* p. 545.

abundance. Speaking of the principle that those who have the treasures control those who lack them, he comments with respect to Japan that: "When the institutions and customs of a country and the freedom of its people are fettered, we can see that this rule will necessarily come close to perishing. However, in later generations the institutions and customs of such countries will of necessity be reformed, and this rule will gradually resume its influence. This has been so throughout all history."[43] Hence Nishi thinks that during Japan's long centuries of military rule, when men's freedom was "fettered," this principle fell into eclipse, but that when the government is reformed, men will rise to the top of society through personal accomplishment, a fact that "is in accordance with the laws of nature and protects equal rights for the whole of society."[44] He assumes that ideally those who rise to high station will do so without infringing on the rights of others.

The *Jinsei sanpōsetsu* sections on the individual's relation to society were based on an elliptical and somewhat unsatisfactory adaptation of utilitarian precepts, but the dialectical shortcomings did not diminish the force of Nishi's argument on behalf of individual initiative, occupational freedom, and economic opportunity. In lieu of the feudal virtues, Japan needed men who would increase their knowledge and wealth, because this would benefit society as a whole. Similarly, at the international level, Japan would elevate her position among the nations once she escaped the shackles of feudalism and pursued her three treasures. It was consistent with Nishi's progressive outlook on history that he regarded the feudal period as a temporary setback in the drive for wealth and power; he thought that the institutions and customs of feudalism would "of necessity be reformed" and that the principle of the three treasures would once again become operative. Furthermore, it is interesting to note that, in *Jinsei sanpōsetsu,* Nishi confused the distinction between human and physical principles which he had made in *Hyakuichi shinron* by classifying as "natural law" the rule that those

[43] *Ibid.,* p. 547.   [44] *Ibid.,* p. 548.

Ethics for the New Society

with treasures control those without them. Such a rule, no matter how invariable, would belong to *shinri*, according to *Hyakuichi shinron*, because it is a law of human society. Nishi's statement that it is a natural right of all men to search for the three treasures is as close as his thought ever came to the *tenpu jinken* theories of early Meiji, since ordinarily he eschewed any statement arguing that human rules had the unchanging, a priori character of natural principles. Finally, it is essential to bear in mind that Nishi's endorsement of such liberal, humane values as freedom, equality, and personal initiative was limited to the context of social and economic opportunity. The interests of society, he believed, were ultimately of greater value than those of the individual. This assumption was in harmony with both the general group orientation of traditional Japanese ethics and the teachings of utilitarianism, which held that the smaller values of the individual could be turned into the greater values of society.[45] Nevertheless, there is a basic historical difference between utilitarianism and Nishi's thought. The social philosophy of the English empiricists emerged after centuries of concern for freedom, equality, and individual rights, whereas Nishi's Japanese heritage was one of group-centered systems. The drift of European utilitarian thought was thus from individual to society, whereas Nishi's was moving from group to individual. That he ultimately upheld the primacy of society's interests was therefore less significant for modern Japanese thought than his considerable efforts to rationalize the individual's pursuit of private gain.

THE MORAL BASIS OF GOVERNMENT

Nishi had devoted nearly two-thirds of *Hyakuichi shinron* to destroying the Sung connection between politics and morality. However, to deny that moral instruction was a

---

[45] See Kawahara Hiroshi, *Tenkanki no shisō—Nihon kindaika o megutte* (Tokyo, 1963), p. 354; Minamoto Ryōen, "Meiji ishin to jitsugaku shisō," *Meiji ishinshi no mondaiten*, ed. Sakata Yoshio (Tokyo, 1962), pp. 116-117; Funayama Shin'ichi, *Meiji tetsugakushi kenkyū* (Tokyo, 1959), pp. 67-69.

Ethics for the New Society

proper concern of the state did not, of course, mean that politics and politicians should lack moral principles. In fact, as Nishi argued in *Jinsei sanpōsetsu,* morality was a much broader and more profound phenomenon than government, and politics was merely one of many elements included within its scope. Nevertheless the state was an important and powerful component of society, and Nishi believed that it was essential to identify the effects of morals on politics and to establish a moral foundation for government.

First Nishi dismisses the Chinese idea that the family is the cornerstone of the state, relying on both Asian and Western history to demonstrate that government did not exist until society was well established. Once the state emerged, it became merely one kind of society (*kaisha*) within human society at large (*ningen shakō*).[46] It differs from other societies only in size, since all have fixed objectives, prescribed rules, managers, administrators, and divisions of responsibility. Furthermore, Nishi claims, all societies except religious groups pursue at least one of the three treasures, and therefore "the object of government as a society [within society at large] is to provide protection for all three treasures simultaneously."[47] Just as individuals are morally bound to conserve and increase their health, knowledge, and wealth, the most important moral duty of the state is to safeguard the treasures of all members of society. Both the idea that the state is merely one unit within society at large and the theory that government's role should be that of a guardian of society's interests were quite opposed to the orthodox Shushi concept of the state based on the family and show the impact on Nishi's political thought of European theories of limited government.

More significant for understanding the mechanics of Nishi's mind is his assertion that "so long as the three treasures are protected, it does not matter whether government is monarchic, republican, or by clan rule. In general, different forms

[46] *JSSPS*, p. 533. *Kaisha* means corporation in modern Japanese, but Nishi used it to mean any association, company, society, or subculture within *shakō*, which is human society at large.
[47] *Ibid.*, p. 534.

156

of government such as these should stress the great advantages and benefits of patronizing the three treasures in all matters, in accordance with the degree of national social progress, historical development, and the condition of state affairs. (In our country, for example, serving the unbroken imperial line is very convenient and advantageous for the people's three treasures.) Therefore, the theory of the three treasures is unrelated to the political structure. But if the government ignores the three treasures or is lax in protecting them or harms them, then it immediately loses its justification for governing."[48]

This extraordinary statement that any form of government is desirable, so long as it promotes the three treasures, is an apt summary of Nishi's lifelong political position. It is consistent with his insouciant neutralist stance during the restoration, when he had been willing to settle for any government that would "diminish samurai pensions, abolish lineages, and reform the army."[49] There is some merit in this unorthodox position that what matters is the policy and not the form of government, but Nishi was at the very least quixotic, if not indiscriminating, in failing to recognize that in actual practice a country's form of government and the philosophy underlying it are usually crucial to the protection of men's health, knowledge, and wealth. However sanguine a position he took on this question, Nishi correctly perceived that enlightenment and national strengthening did not require a European form of rule; civilized society, of which Western Europe was the archetype, could be accomplished just as well through native political institutions, a fact that was not yet generally apparent in 1874. This belief that any form of government will do has exposed Nishi to charges that he worshipped the powerful, a question that will be considered in the next chapter.

Nishi's attitude demonstrated a utilitarian disregard for precise forms of government, so long as the proper aims

[48] *Ibid.*, p. 534.
[49] From the diary of Koyama Masataka, quoted in Mori Ōgai, *Nishi Amane den, Ōgai zenshū* (Tokyo, 1923-1927), vɪɪ, p. 165.

were realized,[50] but he failed to acknowledge that English utilitarianism developed within the matrix of post-revolutionary European political philosophy. Only a limited range of political systems existed in nineteenth-century Europe, and the utilitarians were generally dealing with some form of constitutional state. Mill, in fact, wrote under the assumption that democracy would inevitably become England's form of government and believed that, despite its dangers, it was the best political system.[51] No such narrow consensus on political philosophy existed in Japan in the 1870's, and therefore Nishi would have argued his case for the three treasures more convincingly had he taken account of the differences between the English and Japanese situations. The form of Japan's government would one day matter much more than he realized when he set about prescribing new ethical values for the Japanese people.

It is interesting that Nishi considered Japan's imperial system "convenient and advantageous for the people's three treasures." Always a critic of National Learning and never swayed by loyalist thought during the Bakumatsu era, he nonetheless conceded that monarchy was an expedient institution upon which to build a state that would guarantee the treasures, which had been ill-guarded during the period when the Tokugawa family ruled in the name of the throne. Like most *keimō* intellectuals, he accepted the emperor as a symbol of national reunion. The link which he had established in *Jinsei sanpōsetsu* between the imperial institution and utilitarianism was probably prompted by the example of England, whose "civilization and institutions" he had admired ever since 1862.

Nishi continues his analysis of the three treasures by describing the European fondness for national constitutions and

---

[50] Utilitarianism taught that men's duties toward the state were unrelated to how the government took power or preserved its position, so long as it responsibilities were fulfilled. See Plamenatz, *The English Utilitarians*, p. 2.

[51] As expressed in *Representative Government*, in *Utilitarianism, Liberty, and Representative Government*, ed. A. D. Lindsay (New York and London, 1951), pp. 271-292.

cites Montesquieu's theory of the threefold separation of powers. After detailing the manner in which constitutional states guarantee the integrity of the three treasures, he denies that this form of government is requisite for safeguarding the treasures or achieving general happiness. He concludes: "The threeway division of powers is merely a technique for suppressing arbitrariness and is not related to morality. Further, the legislative authority must establish laws which respect the three treasures, and the executive [branch] must administer laws which uphold the three treasures."[52]

Policy, rather than structural form, is thus the key to good government, and policy must center on enhancing the general happiness. This outlook is the keystone of Nishi's attitude toward constitutional movements in Japan. Since he did not consider constitutionalism at all necessary for achieving the country's major goals, he had little interest in the early Meiji efforts to draft a constitution or establish parliamentary government. Thus one suspects that apart from introducing the concept of "rights," Nishi drafted *Gidai sōan* in 1867 perfunctorily as an intellectual handyman for the shogun and not as a champion of parliamentary democracy. This indifference toward constitutionalism was evident also in his testy denunciation of the *minsen giin* (popularly elected assembly) proposal of 1874, which will be considered in the next chapter.

To achieve a moral basis for politics, Nishi contends, there are four major responsibilities which all governments, regardless of form, must discharge. Each of these duties relates to the three treasures and constitutes an obligation of government as one society (*kaisha*) to society at large. First is the domestic responsibility of enforcing the laws. Included in this category are sanitation, cadastral and police work, and civil and criminal adjudication. Each of these protects at least one of the treasures, although Nishi carefully differentiates between civil and criminal law by observing that "civil adjudication comes after the fact, but it can make full restitution. Criminal adjudication has no way to restore previous

[52] *JSSPS*, p. 535.

damage, but it protects against future damage to other things."[53]

Second is government's external obligation to conduct diplomacy and maintain an army for society's defense. Although war and diplomacy use different techniques, they share a common aim, "namely to protect the life and strength of the people, to protect their wisdom and prevent falsehood, and to protect their property and not permit its loss."[54]

The third responsibility concerns safeguarding the state's own three treasures. Government must protect its vitality by conserving the strength of its officials; it must choose wisely when appointing men to high positions, in order to protect its knowledge; and it must guard against graft and peculation. Since financial stability is the most obvious of these governmental obligations to its own three treasures, Nishi believes that the state is likely to emphasize it to the exclusion of the others. He warns that all three must be equally observed if government is to remain secure.[55] In a later section of *Jinsei sanpōsetsu* he elaborates on this point, maintaining that "the first and most important measure to be taken to achieve the objectives of society as a whole is this third category, namely government's protecting its own three treasures."[56] The state, he thinks, must put its own house in order before meeting its other obligations, a difficult but vital task for a modern government. Nishi's particular emphasis on this point should not be understood as a criticism of the new Meiji state of which he was a part; rather it probably stems from the great Bakumatsu period anxiety on the part of both Western studies scholars and many *shishi* concerning the decadent administrative system of the *bakufu*. Internal political reform was a constant demand of all but the most reactionary intellectuals during the 1860's; this may account for Nishi's especial concern for clean government in 1875.

To attain the goal of general happiness, it is not enough for a government merely to discharge these responsibilities in domestic administration and foreign affairs and to safe-

53 *Ibid.*, p. 535.   54 *Ibid.*, p. 536.
55 *Ibid.*, pp. 536-537. 56 *Ibid.*, p. 540.

160

Ethics for the New Society

guard the state's own treasures. There is a fourth group of moral obligations which government must also fulfill: the various bureaucratic departments must encourage agriculture, industry, education, trade, and finance. Such work should be done by the state not to increase its own power but to benefit society at large:

"To discuss this matter with respect to each of the three treasures, governmental encouragement of industry and agriculture is surely the means to create the basis of the people's livelihood. The first treasure relates to health. Although there is no single method to promote the public welfare, as a rule agriculture and industry are the basic way. It is easy to understand the principle that when this basis is achieved, people will be prosperous and healthy. Next, the government's activity in education is surely the origin of popular enlightenment. This relates to the second treasure, knowledge. Although there is of course no single path to public enlightenment and progress, its basis is in education. Hence it is easy to understand the principle that when we achieve this basis, the people will be enlightened and possess knowledge. Next, the government's activity in trade and finance is surely the foundation of public abundance. This relates to the third treasure, wealth. Although there is no single method for the people to accumulate and circulate wealth, as a rule trade and finance are the basic way. Accordingly, it is easy to understand the principle that when we establish methods convenient for this basis, public abundance and wealth will increase.

"Therefore, if the government seeks to achieve morality, it must make the people's three treasures materialize."[57]

Nishi hence gave his unqualified support in *Jinsei sanpōsetsu* to the Meiji oligarchy's efforts to promote industry during the 1870's. Indeed, he argues that when a government looks after its domestic and international duties and its own treasures, yet still topples, the reason usually is that it has neglected this fourth category.[58]

[57] *Ibid.*, pp. 541-542.   [58] *Ibid.*, p. 542.

161

Ethics for the New Society

Essential as economic development is, however, even more crucial is the responsibility of educating the public, because it "is the basis of public enlightenment and progress."[59] Nishi thus shared with Fukuzawa the conviction that education was the most essential key to national development.[60] While he recognizes in *Jinsei sanpōsetsu* that the growth of trade, industry, finance, agriculture, education, and the like are interrelated and that the government must coordinate its efforts to encourage each of them, he concludes that of the three treasures "education is senior to the other two. It is the most important moral duty which the government can undertake."[61] This belief in the supreme importance of education was typical of the man who was the most scholarly of the *keimō* intellectuals.

There is considerable similarity in mood between this prescription of the government's duties and the "rights" which Nishi had enumerated eight years earlier in *Gidai sōan*. The definite implication in both works is that all duties and privileges not clearly specified are forbidden to the state. In other respects Nishi's list of governmental responsibilities was noteworthy in 1875 because of the tie which he established between the duties of the state and the utilitarian idea of the three treasures.

Nishi once characterized his theory of the three treasures as "the study of prosperity" (*jinsei sanpōsetsu wa fukushi no gaku nari*).[62] Although the term *fukushi* means welfare as well as prosperity, Nishi certainly did not advocate anything approaching the modern welfare state. He was conversant with European socialism and may have lectured the Meiji Emperor on the subject,[63] but his concern for human welfare

59 *Ibid.*, p. 541.
60 See Carmen Blacker's discussion of *Gakumon no susume*, in *The Japanese Enlightenment*, pp. 57-58.
61 *JSSPS*, p. 542.   62 *Ibid.*, p. 543.
63 Asō Yoshiteru claimed that Nishi delivered *Shakaitōron no setsu* in 1872 or 1873 as a lecture to the young emperor, but Ōkubo Toshiaki demurs on the ground that Nishi did not use the term *shakai* for "society" until after 1875, a fact that is substantiated by his use of *shakō* and *kaisha* in *JSSPS*, which was written in 1874-1875. See Asō, *Kinsei Nihon tetsugakushi*, pp. 263-266, and Ōkubo, "Kaisetsu,"

was more in the tradition of Sorai than Saint-Simon. The major ideological basis for *Jinsei sanpōsetsu* was nonetheless English utilitarianism. Although the concept of the three treasures itself is oversimplified and Nishi's argument is often redundant, the importance of this work lies in the philosophical justification which he sought to provide for the new values of a modern, enlightened society.

Nishi was not wholly unsuccessful in this venture. Carmen Blacker has observed that despite the *keimō* scholars the West—having destroyed the traditional Japanese morality— failed to supply a new ethical basis for society.[64] While it is true that such Western doctrines as Christianity, philosophic positivism, utilitarianism, and evolutionary thought proved unable to offer an appropriate substitute morality, Nishi's writings gave great impetus to the successful internalization of such familiar European concepts and attitudes as the individual profit motive, the spirit of practicality, and rational approaches to the study of both science and society. None of these was an exclusive province of the West; all had authentic precedents in Edo period Japan. Together they did not add up to a morality to replace Neo-Confucianism, but each has played an important part in creating the modern Japanese nation.

NAZS 1961, pp. 740-744. *Shakaitōron no setsu* appears in *NAZS* 1961, pp. 420-432.

[64] Blacker, *The Japanese Enlightenment*, pp. 57-59, 139.

seven

Nishi on Politics and
Current Events

There is a certain timelessness about the thought of Nishi
Amane at the height of his scholarly productivity, a quality
of semi-detachment from both the events of early Meiji history and his official duties in the Military Department and
its successor, the Ministry of War (Rikugunshō). To some
extent this apparent withdrawal from day-to-day affairs was
characteristic of the *keimō* scholars as a group; in Nishi's case
it was heightened by his utilitarian indifference toward concrete political policy. However, it is more accurate to ascribe
Nishi's intellectual posture to the particular focus he chose
for his most important scholarly works: the problem of social
enlightenment. His writings are all the more significant for
their broad, non-specific approach to the questions that he
regarded as crucial for Japan's modernization. It can hardly
be said that Nishi was unconcerned with the rapidly changing
world about him. He spoke out vigorously on a group of
leading issues in the 1870's, including the role of the intellectual vis-à-vis the state, the nature of Japan's foreign policy,
the relationship of politics and religion, and the creation of
a parliamentary assembly. Because his most provocative essays on contemporary affairs were prepared within the context of the Meiji Six Society, we shall first examine the nature
and function of the society.

NISHI AND THE MEIJI SIX SOCIETY

The Meiji Six Society (Meirokusha) claimed Nishi's energies and capabilities as a charter member precisely when his
eminence as a spokesman for *bunmei kaika* came into fullest
flower.[1] The society's two most active years, 1874 and 1875,

[1] The best study in English of the Meiji Six Society is to be found

Nishi on Politics and Current Events

coincided with the appearance of Nishi's most influential works, *Hyakuichi shinron* and *Jinsei sanpōsetsu*. The Meirokusha emerged to provide institutional framework for his scholarly activities less than a year after his private academy, the Ikueisha, had foundered financially. The society and its successor, the Tokyo Academy, served as a focus of Nishi's intellectual attainments for the remainder of his career. During its active phase, the Meirokusha supplied Nishi with an unprecedented national forum, and at the same time it forced him to bring the fruit of his Western learning to bear upon current issues.

The Meiji Six Society was principally the brain-child of Mori Arinori (1847-1889), a young diplomat and educator who had received his first training in Western studies at the Kaiseijo school in Edo in the 1860's. Mori had been sent in 1865 to study in England and the United States by his clan chieftain, Lord Shimazu of Satsuma, and in 1869 he became the Japanese vice-consul in Washington, D.C.[2] He apparently had occasion while living in the United States to observe the activities of American scholarly societies.[3] When he returned

---

in David Abosch, "Katō Hiroyuki and the Introduction of German Political Thought in Japan: 1868-1883," Ph.D. dissertation in history, University of California (Berkeley, 1964), pp. 163-287. Carmen Blacker, *The Japanese Enlightenment: A Study of the Writings of Fukuzawa Yukichi* (Cambridge, Eng., 1964), pp. 32-33, touches on Fukuzawa's role in the society. *Japanese Thought in the Meiji Era*, ed. Kōsaka Masaaki, tr. David Abosch (Tokyo, 1958), pp. 50-84, contains a great deal of information on the group. Donald H. Shively, "Nishimura Shigeki: A Confucian View of Modernization," *Changing Japanese Attitudes Toward Modernization*, ed. Marius B. Jansen (Princeton, 1965), pp. 193-241, is a study of an influential member. The best of numerous Japanese language studies is Tōyama Shigeki, "Meiroku zasshi," *Shisō*, 447 (September 1961), pp. 117-128.

[2] *Nihon kindaishi jiten*, ed. Kyōto Daigaku Bungakubu Kokushi Kenkyūshitsu (Tokyo, 1958), p. 596. For an interesting series on Mori's activities abroad, see Hayashi Takeji, "Bakumatsu no kaigai ryūgakusei," *Nichibei fuōramu*, x, 1, 2, 4, 6 (January, February, April, and June 1964). Also see Hayashi, "Mori Arinori to nashonarizumu," *Nihon* (April 1965), pp. 80-86. Ivan Hall is preparing a dissertation at Harvard University on Mori, and an edition of Mori's collected works is in process in Japan.

[3] Tōyama, "Meiroku zasshi," p. 117.

Nishi on Politics and Current Events

to Japan in 1873, Mori sounded out Nishimura Shigeki and other *keimō* intellectuals about the possibility of instituting a similar society in Tokyo, with the dual purpose of promoting enlightened scholarship and establishing new moral standards.[4] Nishimura supported the project and helped to enroll eight other eminent Western studies scholars as charter members: Nishi Amane, Fukuzawa Yukichi, Katō Hiroyuki, Tsuda Mamichi, Nakamura Masanao, Mitsukuri Shūhei (1825-1886), Mitsukuri Rinshō (1846-1897), and Sugi Kōji (1828-1917).[5] In addition to the original ten, more than two dozen leading *keimō* writers regularly attended the group's sessions, and others joined as corresponding or special members.

The Meirokusha took its name from the year of its inception, the sixth year of Meiji (1873), and held its first gathering in January 1874. It was Japan's first learned society, with fortnightly discussion meetings and monthly sessions at which papers were presented for debate and subsequent publication in the group's journal, *Meiroku zasshi*. The *Yūbin hōchi shinbun* helped to publicize the group's meetings and served as distributor of its organ, Japan's first scholarly review. *Meiroku zasshi* appeared forty-three times between January 1874 and November 1875, when publication ceased, owing in part to new government restrictions on the press.[6]

[4] *Japanese Thought in the Meiji Era*, pp. 60-61.

[5] Asō Yoshiteru, *Kinsei Nihon tetsugakushi* (Tokyo, 1942), pp. 273-274, where Asō also gives a complete membership list.

[6] For viewpoints on the effect of the May 1875 libel laws (*zanbiritsu*) on the dissolution of the Meirokusha, see Ōkubo Toshiaki, "Meirokusha no kaisan," *Nihon rekishi*, 91 (January 1956), pp. 46-48; Abosch, "Katō Hiroyuki," pp. 282-284; Miyagawa Tōru, *Kindai Nihon shisō no kōzō* (Tokyo, 1956), pp. 59-60; Hirota Masaki, "Nihon keimōshugi no chōraku—Fukuzawa Yukichi no henbō," *Shirin*, xLVII, 6 (November 1964), pp. 1-37. The society continued to meet occasionally until the early 1900's, and Nishi regularly attended its sessions until crippled by a stroke. Nishi's *Nikki* (Diary) for 1883-1884 contains frequent entries to this effect. *Nikki*, *NAZS* 1966, pp. 437-488. See Kumashiro Shūryō, "Meirokusha zasshi kaidai," *MBZ*, xVIII, p. 4, for the later history of the society. Its functions were largely taken over after 1878 by the Tokyo Academy (Tōkyō Gakushi Kaiin), which later became the Imperial Academy and is now known

Nishi on Politics and Current Events

Reportedly its average circulation was 3,205 copies, an astoundingly high figure considering that the largest Japanese newspaper in 1875, the *Tokyo nichi-nichi,* averaged 8,000 copies.[7] The enlightened ideas set forth by the society therefore reached a large audience with a swiftness unparalleled in the previous history of Japanese thought.

The style and objectives of the Meirokusha were unquestionably academic, not political. Nishi, who had the distinction of presenting the first paper at the initial regular session of the organization, expressed the consensus of the group in calling for a great campaign to educate the people. "As I see it, in the end the common evil of all peoples of the world is that the wise are few and the foolish are many. The disparity is so great that it is no contest."[8] It was not merely the government's fault that the people were unenlightened; they themselves were to blame, he believed, for not seeking wisdom. It was the primary purpose of the Meiji Six Society to destroy this great army of ignorance and folly.[9]

This general belief in the need for civilization and enlightenment was common to all who took an active part in the Meirokusha. Most members considered themselves scholars of practical learning (Jitsugaku) and scorned the "empty learning" (*kyogaku*) of Buddhism and Confucianism. Jitsugaku, Tsuda wrote in the third number of *Meiroku zasshi,* "advocates principles of reality which are verified by real forms and judged by actual things."[10] Jitsugaku, in other words, was totally in harmony with European positivism, and the Meiji Six Society scholars shared in the positivistic spirit which Nishi had formally encountered in Leiden. De-

as the Japan Academy. Nishi served as its president for six years. For the history of the Tokyo Academy, see Walter Dening, "The Gakushi Kaiin," *Transactions of the Asiatic Society of Japan,* series 1, xv (1887), pp. 58-71, and *Nihon Gakushiin hachijūnenshi,* ed. Nihon Gakushiin, I (Tokyo, 1962).

[7] Tōyama, "Meiroku zasshi," pp. 118-119.

[8] "Yōgaku o motte kokugo o shosuru no ron," *NAZS* 1961, pp. 569-570.

[9] *Ibid.,* p. 570.

[10] "Kaika o susumeru hōhō o ronzu," *MRZS,* 3 (February 1874); *MBZ,* xviii, p. 65.

spite Tsuda's words, their positivism was not directed toward the scientific study of reality itself but rather aimed at awakening the public to the utility of European knowledge. The Meirokusha was therefore not so much a society for discussing scholarly research as a didactic organ for instructing the reading public about Western ideas.

In addition to their agreement on *bunmei kaika*, the Meiji Six Society members shared a number of other characteristics. Virtually all were ex-samurai who had a common heritage of early training in Shushi Confucianism. Of the charter members, only Nishimura, Mori, and Fukuzawa had not studied or taught in the Bakumatsu period at the Foreign Books Research Institute or the Institute of Development. All but Fukuzawa and Nakamura held posts in the new Meiji bureaucracy, and even these two had close liaisons with the governing elite. Although most of the Meirokusha members believed in serving the state, both before and after the restoration, none was near the center of political power and all carried their intellectual interests far beyond the scope of their bureaucratic responsibilities. Of the original ten members, all of whom exerted considerable influence in determining the society's policies, five represented different *tozama* clans, one came from a *han* that had been a Tokugawa ally, and four were born to families which directly served the shogunate.[11] The group thus represented diverse sections of the country, something that would have been virtually impossible for a school of thought in the segmented feudal society of the Edo period. This all-Japan orientation of the post-1868 scholarly world was typical of the truly national character of the entire restoration era.

The most significant aspect of the Meiji Six Society was the enormous breadth of mind and vision of its members.

[11] The breakdown, compiled from biographies in *Nihon kindaishi jiten*: Fukuzawa, Nakatsu *han* (*fudai*); Katō, Izushi (*tozama*); Mitsukuri Rinshō, Tsuyama (Tokugawa house); Mitsukuri Shūhei, Okayama (*tozama*); Mori, Satsuma (*tozama*); Nakamura, Edo (Tokugawa house); Nishi, Tsuwano (*tozama*); Nishimura, Sakura (*tozama*); Sugi, Nagasaki (Tokugawa house); Tsuda, Tsuyama (Tokugawa house). See also Iwai Chūyū, *Nihon kindai shisō no seiritsu* (Tokyo, 1959), p. 59.

Nishi on Politics and Current Events

Fukuzawa was perhaps the most versatile, but all had a general interest in the whole spectrum of Western scholarly knowledge. The society debated widely on philosophy, education, science, politics, language reform, law, and economics, and *Meiroku zasshi* was the first Japanese journal to include articles on all of these topics.[12] All members opposed the feudal social hierarchy and the custom of personal service, encouraging instead the commercial activity which Nishi had most cogently advocated in *Jinsei sanpōsetsu*.[13] The Meirokusha was a society of generalists who were both the seed and flower of *keimō* thought: they were its most effective propagators precisely because of their splendid achievements in Western studies. It was their broad intellectual compass and *savoir-faire* in an age when foreign things and ideas were fashionable which earned them such high esteem. One writer has noted that "to highbrows, the appeal of the intellectual activity of the Meiji Six Society consisted in the make-up of its membership rather than in the value of the magazine articles themselves."[14] Nonetheless the semi-monthly meetings and the journal were valuable media for their criticisms of feudal thought and the introduction of European ideas.

The Meiji Six Society members uniformly acknowledged their duty to enlighten the public, but there was less agreement about their obligation toward the state. It was crucial to their rationale as *keimō* intellectuals that they consider whether they could continue to educate the public while serving the partisan interests of the political elite. The truly enlightened person, Fukuzawa had argued in 1872 in *Gakumon no susume,* could not legitimately function as such within the governmental bureaucracy.[15] Instead, he would best

---

[12] Toyama, "Meiroku zasshi," p. 120.

[13] Ienaga Saburō and Ino Kenji, "Kindai shisō no tanjō to zasetsu," *Kindai Nihon shisōshi kōza*, ed. Ienaga Saburō, I (Tokyo, 1959), pp. 49-50.

[14] Kazue Kyōichi, "Meiji jidai no shisō," *Nihon no rinri shisōshi*, ed. Kazue Kyōichi (Tokyo, 1963), p. 288.

[15] Fukuzawa's position is expressed in part four of *Gakumon no susume* and is entitled "Gakusha no shokubun o ronzu." See Abosch, "Katō Hiroyuki," p. 272, and *Japanese Thought in the Meiji Era*, p. 87.

serve the nation by remaining outside the polity and offering independent criticism as a private individual. The scholar's chief obligation to the state was therefore to create an enlightened populace capable of understanding its political responsibilities. Fukuzawa clearly rejected the traditional Confucian concept that the educated man should aspire to bureaucratic service and eschew fractious criticism of state policies.

Almost as soon as the Meiji Six Society was organized, Tsuda Mamichi challenged Fukuzawa's theory. Tsuda minimized the differences between the polity and society, describing their relationship as that between "body and spirit."[16] He thus held that intellectuals had no particular political responsibilities in or out of government, apart from the general duty to enlighten the people. Katō Hiroyuki more forcefully refuted Fukuzawa's outlook in a brief riposte in *Meiroku zasshi*.[17] He presented the more traditional argument that intellectuals could best lead the people by holding bureacractic posts and actively influencing state policy.

Nishi similarly refused to support Fukuzawa's position, a fact that has led to charges that he was a government-patronized intellectual technician who worshipped authority.[18] Others have variously characterized Nishi's comments on *Gakumon no susume* as both the most intelligent and the weakest criticism of Fukuzawa's theory.[19] Nishi's attitude on the question of the scholar-bureaucrat was that it did not

[16] "Gakusha shokubunron no hyō," *MRZS*, 2 (February 1874); *MBZ*, xviii, pp. 59-60.
[17] "Fukuzawa sensei no ron ni kotau," *MRZS*, 2 (February 1874); *MBZ*, xviii, p. 58. See also Abosch, "Katō Hiroyuki," p. 272, and *Japanese Thought in the Meiji Era*, p. 94.
[18] For this view, see Suzuki Yasuzō, "Nishi Amane no seiji-shakai shisō kaisetsu," *Meiji bunka no shin kenkyū*, ed. Osatake Takeshi (Tokyo, 1944), p. 277; Funayama Shin'ichi, *Meiji tetsugakushi kenkyū* (Tokyo, 1959), p. 67; Furuta Hikaru, "Nishi Amane, keimōki no tetsugakusha," *Asahi jyānaru*, iv, 16 (Apr. 22, 1962), p. 96.
[19] "Higakusha shokubunron," *MRZS*, 2 (February 1874); *MBZ*, xviii, pp. 60-61. Kōsaka maintains in *Japanese Thought in the Meiji Era*, p. 94, that Nishi was the most rational critic of Fukuzawa. For a contrary view, see Kawahara Hiroshi, *Tenkanki no shisō—Nihon kindaika o megutte* (Tokyo, 1963), p. 348.

matter whether *keimō* intellectuals served the state or remained independent. "Though we are equally scholars of the West, some are in government and assist with public affairs, and others do their work privately. It is all the same."[20] There must be enlightened individuals, he maintained, in both government service and private life: "Previously I mentioned the vitalization of the government. There must be some spice to make this vitality throb. This [spice] must be the scholars who serve the government. I also mentioned stimulating the people. There must be a temperature [thermostat] to regulate the stimulation. For this we must have private scholars."[21]

Nishi thought that Fukuzawa was far too quixotic in hoping that independent critics could stimulate the state to enact reforms. If all scholars were mere private analysts, their commentaries would be hopelessly theoretical, without any relation to political realities.[22] Nishi's belief that it was unimportant whether one labored on behalf of the state or remained a private scholar was remarkably similar to his nonchalance in *Jinsei sanpōsetsu* about forms of government. Just as the protection of the three treasures, and not the type of political system, was the *sine qua non* of a moral state, so it was the scholar's role in enlightening the country, not his week-day occupation, that was of crucial importance.

Rather than being greatly concerned about the intellectual's ties with government, Nishi was far more exercised about the quality of Japan's Western scholarship: "We cannot yet say that society's great teachers have mastered the inner mysteries of Western learning," he asserted, and Japan would have to increase her understanding of the West greatly if she were to match Europe in learning, commerce, law, and the like.[23] Here is the nub of Nishi's vision of the *keimō* intellectual's role: his most essential scholarly duty was to investigate carefully the origins of Western knowledge, so that Japan could comprehend European ideas and institutions more thoroughly than the T'ang model had been understood in the

---

[20] "Higakusha shokubunron," p. 61.
[21] *Ibid.*, p. 61.   [22] *Ibid.*, p. 60.   [23] *Ibid.*, p. 60.

171

seventh century.[24] Once again Nishi's firm insistence on formal scholarship is evident, always with the clear purpose of accomplishing practical ends. Far from encouraging study for its own sake, Nishi held that it was essential only if it could make the new Western ideas and systems more secure in the reformed Japanese state and society.

Because Nishi answered Fukuzawa's theory with the contention that *keimō* intellectuals, in or out of government, should concentrate on sound research, it is unreasonable to conclude that he worshipped authority or was intellectually committed to his bureaucratic employers. Such criticism would be valid only if he had argued that all scholars should serve the state and subordinate their curiosity about the West to the requirements of public office. In fact, Nishi saw no reason why an intellectual would compromise his scholarly effectiveness by working in the national bureaucracy; indeed, such persons were needed to "add spice to the vitality of government." Certainly it was unrealistic of him to believe that there could be no conflict between a bureaucrat's scholarly and political obligations, but it is clear that this attitude was consistent with Nishi's personal philosophy of government and that his outlook was largely one of indifference rather than timorous obedience toward political authority.

The controversy among the Meirokusha members over their self-image as *keimō* scholars did no violence to the basic agreement about their role as leaders of Japan's new academic elite. Far more important than their unresolved dispute concerning scholar-bureaucrats was a fundamental unanimity about their mission to enlighten the people in a tutelary fashion and to build a strong state and society. The group therefore spent the next two years seeking to fulfill this mission. The details of Meirokusha history have been amply set forth in other works and lie beyond the compass of this study. It is important, however, to inquire into Nishi's attitudes to-

[24] *Ibid.*, p. 60. Nishi elaborated on this theme in a speech in October 1877 to a group of scholars who soon formed the nucleus of the Tokyo University faculty. The speech was entitled *Gakumon wa engen o fukakusuru ni aru no ron* and appears in *NAZS* 1960, pp. 568-573.

Nishi on Politics and Current Events

ward certain major issues in current affairs which occupied the attention of the entire society during its brief active phase, in order to understand the manner in which he applied his philosophic ideas to analyzing concrete problems.

RELATIONS WITH WESTERN POWERS

The Meiji Six Society scholars, like all intellectuals in Meiji Japan, repeatedly debated the question of relations with the various foreign powers, whose continual demands for diplomatic and commercial concessions required prompt attention. Nishi shared with his *keimō* colleagues the conviction that Western civilization was a worthy model for reforming the Japanese state and society, but he wrote nothing concrete about foreign relations until he joined the Meirokusha.[25] This lacuna did not derive from any previous isolation from diplomatic affairs: Nishi had served as a translator during the treaty negotiations with the U.S. consul, Townsend Harris, in the late 1850's, and his Foreign Books Research Institute responsibilities between 1857 and 1862 had included considerable *bakufu* duties in external affairs. His extensive study of international law and economics in Leiden and subsequent service with Keiki in Kyoto had permitted him further splendid opportunities to ponder the requirements for successful dealings with the West.

Nonetheless Nishi wrote virtually nothing about foreign affairs until encouraged to do so by his compatriots in the Meiji Six Society. The only reasonable explanation for his

[25] Nishi prepared two memoranda in the course of his work in the Ministry of War concerning Japan's punitive expeditions in the mid-1870's to Korea and Taiwan. It is unknown precisely when he wrote these reports, but they probably predate or coincide with the Meirokusha period. They are entitled *Jōrinpō heibi ryakuhyō*, NAZS 1966, pp. 128-143, and *Kihei goei no kaijo no kou jōsōbun'an (daisaku)*, NAZS 1966, pp. 151-152. Nishi also prepared a draft of an imperial rescript on the subject of punishing the Koreans, entitled *Chōsen seitō sōtoku e no chokugo sōan*, NAZS 1966, pp. 119-122. On the final version of *Jōrinpō heibi ryakuhyō*, which was put out in 1880 as *Rinpō heibi ryaku*, see Marius B. Jansen, "Japanese Views of China During the Meiji Period," *Approaches to Modern Chinese History*, ed. Albert Feuerwerker *et al.* (Berkeley and Los Angeles, 1967), pp. 167-168.

silence is that ever since 1857, when he wrote that "we must rely not upon the advantages of large weapons and the size of our ships, but upon reforms in our government,"[26] he consistently concentrated on internal reform rather than the external threat. He firmly believed in strengthening the army, and he shared Fukuzawa's profound anxiety about preserving Japan's independence.[27] But Nishi had adopted the old Kaikoku premise that foreign intercourse must be tolerated at least until Japan had effected sufficient domestic changes to insure her sovereignty.[28] Furthermore, as a positivist and utilitarian, his major interest was the dynamics of society, not the relations among political units.

During the Meirokusha years, nonetheless, Nishi became involved in a minor academic dispute over proposals to allow foreigners to travel and reside freely throughout Japan. A ten-mile land limit around the treaty ports had been established during the Bakumatsu period to guard foreign traders and other non-diplomatic personnel from the boisterous *shishi*,[29] but now that Japan had embarked upon a policy of civilization and enlightenment, many *keimō* thinkers believed that it would help to erase popular ignorance and suspicion of foreigners if the treaty arrangements were revised to permit unrestricted travel.

Nishi Amane took the initiative among the Meiji Six Society members in supporting this proposal. His views appeared in *Meiroku zasshi* under the title "Naichi ryokō" (Domestic Travel).[30] This article is significant not only because of the ideas it contains but also because it is written in a novel lecture note style, utilizing the inductive method that Nishi had introduced in *Hyakugaku renkan* and *Chichi*

[26] *Tōshi jūgatsu sōkō*, quoted in Furuta, "Nishi Amane," p. 94.

[27] For verification in 1857, see *ibid.*, p. 94; in 1867, see Mori Ōgai, *Nishi Amane den*, *Ōgai zenshū* (Tokyo, 1923-1927), VII, p. 165; in 1874, "Higakusha shokubunron," p. 60.

[28] See Blacker, *The Japanese Enlightenment*, p. 39. His remarks to Koyama Masataka, quoted in Ōgai, *Nishi Amane den*, p. 165, confirm his belief in this premise.

[29] Blacker, *The Japanese Enlightenment*, p. 34.

[30] "Naichi ryokō," *MRZS* 23 (December 1874), *MBZ*, XVIII, pp. 166-169.

Nishi on Politics and Current Events

keimō.[31] It represents an attempt to employ simplified inductive logic to demonstrate that contact with foreigners is highly desirable for enlightening the general public.

The deductive method is worthless for analyzing this question, Nishi declares, because it must grapple first with the entire foreign problem. Instead, one must initially consider specific issues such as internal travel by foreigners in order to establish a meaningful general principle for dealing with the larger question of foreign relations.[32] By way of example, Nishi first uses the deductive method, stating that since Japan is currently maintaining a policy of open ports, "it is clear that we must permit internal travel too."[33] This conclusion is unsatisfactory, he thinks, because one could argue that the pre-restoration arrangement of permitting treaty concessions is no longer valid under the new state. Furthermore, it is widely believed that the Japanese people are insufficiently enlightened for daily contact with aliens.[34]

Nishi then reargues the question inductively. He cites seven common objections to permitting free travel by foreigners:

1. If foreigners come in, they will trade.
2. They will enter places they should not.
3. It will be troublesome to protect them.
4. It will be difficult to converse with them.
5. They will bring their dogs.
6. It will be troublesome when they get into difficulties.
7. Since there are still rowdies throughout Japan, there will be incidents.[35]

He quickly dismisses each of these complaints, holding that (1) it will be disastrous to outlaw trade; (2) and (3) these problems exist in all lands and should cause Japan no particular difficulty; (4) it is the foreigners' responsibility to learn to converse with the Japanese; (5) they will not mind

[31] Tōyama, "Meiroku zasshi," p. 119; Asō, *Kinsei Nihon tetsugakushi*, pp. 306-308.
[32] "Naichi ryokō," pp. 166-167.   [33] *Ibid.*, p. 166.
[34] *Ibid.*, p. 167.   [35] *Ibid.*, p. 168.

175

restrictions on their dogs; (6) negotiation with consular officials will settle any problems; and (7) it is the duty of the Japanese government and police to curb rowdyism.[36] Thus there is no serious obstacle to allowing free travel, and there is the great advantage that the Japanese people will become increasingly enlightened from contacts with foreign travelers. Not until we try it, Nishi maintains, will we know definitely whether unrestricted travel and residence is a good thing.[37]

Nishi gained the support of Tsuda Mamichi on this issue,[38] but Fukuzawa took the position that the presence of aliens would itself hardly bring about popular enlightenment and that the Japanese spirit of independence was as yet insufficiently developed to protect the public from exploitation by foreign traders.[39] There was no hint of exclusionism in Fukuzawa's remarks; the controversy centered on the degree and timing of foreign contacts. Nishi admitted that when foreigners were permitted unlimited travel, the "complaints will be most serious, because no matter what is said, the Japanese people are ignorant and foolish, and they will find fault."[40] He, Fukuzawa, and Tsuda all agreed that the real requisite for successful foreign intercourse was to educate the people.

Nishi likewise relied on the inductive method to discuss the question of renegotiating the discriminatory tariff agreements which had been forced on Japan by the Western powers. The point at issue concerned whether a foreign nation could rightfully determine Japan's external tax structure. Nishi did not take a strong stand on the matter; he discussed it with more academic detachment than emotional conviction. In a speech to the Meiji Six Society called "Kaikanzei

[36] *Ibid.*, pp. 168-169.
[37] *Ibid.*, pp. 166-167. See also Blacker, *The Japanese Enlightenment*, p. 34.
[38] Tsuda, "Naichi ryokōron," *MRZS*, 24 (January 1875); *MBZ*, xviii, pp. 171-172.
[39] Fukuzawa, "Naichi ryokō no setsu o hakusu," *MRZS*, 26 (January 1875); *MBZ*, xviii, pp. 179-182. For a study of Fukuzawa's ideas about national defense, see Masada Ken'ichirō, "Meiji shoki ni okeru kindaika no shorinen," *Shakai kagaku tōkyū*, x, 1 (September 1964), pp. 51-70.
[40] "Naichi ryokō," pp. 168-169.

Nishi on Politics and Current Events

no setsu" (Comment on Foreign Tariffs), he maintains that empiric analysis is the best way to understand this thorny problem. After identifying various kinds of levies such as indirect taxes, protective tariffs, and revenue duties, he cites J. S. Mill to support his argument concerning unequal tariffs and concludes that "this, as I said before, is a very rare occurrence; it is within the absolute rights of a sovereign state to decide its tariff laws, and it should not concern other states in the slightest."[41] It is important for enlightened scholars to consider this question, he adds, because of the implied differences in international legal status between Japan and the West.[42]

The issues in "Naichi ryokō" and "Kaikanzei no setsu" were major ones in 1874-1875, but Nishi offered no tangible proposals for Japan's foreign policy. His comments are important mainly because they show how he tried to adapt a Western system of logical analysis to the study of specific Japanese problems. Undoubtedly Nishi used these issues as an opportunity to experiment with logical induction. Fukuzawa correctly criticized his use of inductive logic as too facile and shallow,[43] but the very fact that Nishi employed the inductive method underscores his penchant for empirical investigation of concrete facts and his suspicion of broad generalizations, particularly in areas outside his major interests. Although the course of Meiji history ultimately sustained Nishi's viewpoint on both domestic travel and tariff revision, his contribution to the development of modern Japanese thought was far less significant on these points than in his major works, in which he argued positions that had few practical results.

RELIGION AND POLITICS

Another principal topic of Meirokusha debate was the early Meiji policy of *saisei itchi* (the unity of religion and

---

[41] "Kaikanzei no setsu," *NAZS* 1961, pp. 415-416. This speech was never published in the society's journal. The words "absolute rights" and "sovereign state" are given in phonetic renderings of the English terms. Presumably Nishi borrowed these phrases from Mill.
[42] *Ibid.*, p. 416.   [43] Tōyama, "Meiroku zasshi," p. 120.

177

politics). One of the first acts of the restoration government was to revive the classical Jingikan (Department of Religious Ceremonies), in which Kamei Korekane of Tsuwano was soon appointed to high office. This unit was responsible for encouraging public adherence to the indigenous religion, Shinto, and to that end missionaries were dispatched to the local regions to promote a strengthened shrine system at the expense of Buddhism.[44] Although the *saisei itchi* policy was designed to fortify the fledgling government's base of power, by 1872 the Jingikan and its successor agency had been dissolved by the Meiji oligarchy. The demise of these institutions was due in part to pressures from foreign powers anxious to insure religious freedom for Japan's small domestic band of Christians and Western missionaries. However, as soon as the Jingikan's successor had been abolished, the government established a new unit, the Kyōbushō (Department of Religious Instruction).[45] At the same time the slogan *saisei itchi* was changed to *seikyō itchi,* with little difference in meaning.[46] The Kyōbushō accordingly assumed titular jurisdiction over all religious groups in the country, in an effort to channel their activities toward strengthening popular loyalties to the new state. It nonetheless continued the Jingikan policy of promoting belief in Shinto.

Therefore, from 1872 to 1877, the year when the Kyōbushō was abolished and the Monbushō abandoned its overt policy of enlightenment through the schools, the state simultaneously pursued the seemingly contradictory policies of

[44] *Nihon kindaishi jiten,* p. 285.

[45] Warren W. Smith, Jr., *Confucianism in Modern Japan: A Study of Conservatism in Japanese Intellectual History* (Tokyo, 1959), p. 46; *Nihon kindaishi jiten,* pp. 124-125.

[46] Technically *saisei* means "politics and [Shinto] religious ceremony," whereas *seikyō* means "politics and religion" or "politics and education." *Saisei itchi* has numerous indigenous historical antecedents that convey a domestic feeling absent from *seikyō itchi.* The latter was a slogan of Shushi Confucianism in the Edo period, meaning the "unity of politics and morality," but the Kyōbushō used it in the sense of the "unity of politics and religion" after 1872. See Murakami Toshiharu, "Nishi Amane no shisō ni taisuru Soraigaku no eikyō," *Kyōto Gakugei Daigaku kiyō,* series A, 25 (October 1964), p. 112.

Nishi on Politics and Current Events

seikyō itchi and *bunmei kaika*. This paradox may be explained by observing that although the two programs differed in outward purpose, their underlying motives were practically identical. *Seikyō itchi* was nominally intended to help supervise religious activity, but its fundamental objective was to continue the former Jingikan efforts to use the indigenous religion as a means of promoting national unity under the new government. Similarly, *bunmei kaika* was ostensibly designed to enlighten the public, but its essential purpose was to create a broad class of educated citizens whose talents could be utilized in building a strong nation along the guidelines established by the Meiji government. Schooled in Western learning, the new graduates would soon staff the national and local bureaucracies and become the managers of the new industrial economy, under the direct aegis of the political elite. By carefully prescribing a uniform pattern of instruction for all schools from Hokkaido to Kyushu, the Monbushō was able to enhance national unity at the educational level[47] and to prevent the teaching in any government school of doctrines that would jeopardize the national interest as interpreted by the Meiji oligarchy. In this sense it is possible to consider both *seikyō itchi* and *bunmei kaika* as policies designed to support a unified political authority.

However, it is important to note that the yearly budget of the Kyōbushō in the years 1872-1877 was less than one-fifteenth that of the Monbushō[48] and that the government therefore asserted the *seikyō itchi* program with minimal vigor as compared with the massive efforts to encourage Western learning through the schools. That the state continued to support this policy at all after 1872 probably represents a concession to conservative remnants within the Meiji power structure, inasmuch as the earlier *saisei itchi* campaign had already accomplished its objectives of discrediting Buddhism and encouraging national loyalty through Shinto when

---

[47] Ōkubo Toshiaki, "Bunmei kaika," *Iwanami kōza Nihon rekishi* (Tokyo, 1961-1963), xv, pp. 255, 284.

[48] In 1873, the Kyōbushō budget was 72,752 yen; the Monbushō, 1,303,535 yen. In 1874, the figures were Kyōbushō, 71,355 yen; Monbushō, 1,330,348 yen. *Ibid.*, p. 278.

the Jingikan and its successor were abolished in 1872. The real problem thereafter was to build a strong, unified nation by progressive innovations in industry, commerce, finance, government, military affairs, and education, rather than by continuing to reassert the traditional tie between politics and Shinto. Therefore, *seikyō itchi* as an active policy lost favor in the mid-1870's, so that when the Meirokusha members began to attack the union of government and religion in 1874, they were already stalking a paper tiger. Their assault resulted in part from an inability to recognize the declining importance of the policy and also from their great eagerness to destroy any remaining vestiges of political influence on the part of the National Learning school, which was intimately related to the native religion.

It is illuminating to observe the gravity of Nishi's preoccupation with this question. Between February and June 1874, he published a serialized essay in *Meiroku zasshi* entitled *Kyōmonron* (On Religion), in which he set forth his belief in the separation of politics and religious faith.[49] This work is properly regarded as a continuation of his remarks in *Hyakuichi shinron*,[50] but Nishi apparently failed to understand that whereas the unity of politics and morality was a continuing problem of major proportions, the *seikyō itchi* question had been put in cold storage (via government inaction) and would remain a minor issue for the rest of the century.

Nishi brands religion in *Kyōmonron* as "something based on faith. Faith is founded on those things to which knowledge does not extend."[51] He begins by establishing the same dichotomy between politics and religion that he had created for politics and morals in *Hyakuichi shinron*: "Government should leave religion to those things in which the people believe; it cannot cause them at all costs to believe this and not to believe that."[52] However, it is entirely proper for the

---

[49] *Kyōmonron*, *NAZS* 1960, pp. 493-513. It originally appeared in *MRZS*, 4, 5, 6, 8, 9, and 12 (February-June 1874).

[50] See Kuwaki Gen'yoku, *Nishi Amane no Hyakuichi shinron* (Tokyo, 1940), p. 38.

[51] *Kyōmonron*, p. 493.   [52] *Ibid.*, p. 493.

state to control the external aspects of religion, even though it is not "supposed to question the propriety of inner beliefs."[53] The government has the right to license shrines and temples and to determine when and where outdoor religious meetings, festivals, and funeral processions may be held.[54]

Nishi maintains that this separation of politics and religious belief will not endanger the *kokutai,* or national essence. He cites examples from world history to show that men's religious faith interferes with their political obligations only when the state is already weak.[55] "Respecting and obeying the king or emperor is the people's duty . . . if there is the slightest infringement, they will be punished and exiled outside the country."[56] Therefore, Japan's status as a unique national entity will never be jeopardized so long as the government uses its power to defend the *kokutai* from any group, religious or otherwise, which seeks to debase it.

This statement was Nishi's only significant comment in his entire career about *kokutai.* It is likely that his remarks were prompted by Katō Hiroyuki's *Kokutai shinron* (New Discussion of the National Essence), also published in 1874, in which Katō similarly argued for the separation of politics and religious belief in the course of reevaluating the concept of *kokutai.*[57] Tsuda Mamichi likewise concurred that the two must remain distinct.[58] Nishi used the term *kokutai* in its accepted sense and never denied the native religious element which it contained, but it is quite clear from his other writings that he regarded Japan as merely one member of the community of nations, not a unique national body spiritually superior to all other states, as the idea of *kokutai* implied. He never attacked the imperial institution, but he held a basically utilitarian attitude toward the throne: namely, that it was the most "convenient and advantageous [structure] for attaining the people's three treasures."[59] Nishi probably

[53] *Ibid.,* p. 496.   [54] *Ibid.,* p. 498.
[55] *Ibid.,* pp. 496-497.   [56] *Ibid.,* p. 497.
[57] See Abosch, "Katō Hiroyuki," pp. 362-389, for a discussion of *Kokutai shinron.*
[58] Tsuda, "Seiron," *MRZS,* 9 (April 1874); *MBZ,* xviii, pp. 102-103.
[59] *Jinsei sanpōsetsu, NAZS* 1960, p. 534.

included the discussion of *kokutai* in *Kyōmonron* as a sop to potential nationalist critics, lest he be accused of any lack of patriotism. He no doubt sincerely believed that religion should never conflict with Japan's vital national interests, a position generally shared by the Meirokusha members.[60]

It has been suggested that Nishi's idea of the relation between secular and ecclesiastical authority derived from the Christian precept of respecting temporal rulers as well as divine commands,[61] but in most respects Nishi's attitude toward religion was humanistic, not sectarian. For example, although he upheld the individual's absolute right to his own beliefs, he also asserted that the government should reduce the people's faith in the unknown by increasing their awareness of the known: "As education advances, the things that are believed become refined. . . . In general, by broadening human wisdom, such things as folly, coarseness, and obscene beliefs are eliminated."[62] Hence, only indirectly, through education, is government permitted to impinge upon religious belief. Nishi did not carry this reasoning to its extreme, however; he stopped short of claiming that knowledge could supplant religious faith by entirely abolishing the unknown. Instead he argued the elitist position that education would ennoble men's belief in that relatively narrow area that was beyond human knowledge. "Therefore, although the faith of a person of broad and great knowledge may not be perfect, it is a far cry from that of the man of narrow and shallow learning."[63]

Kyōmonron demonstrates that Nishi hardly stood for complete religious freedom. He not only sanctioned relatively strict external controls on religious activity but also ridiculed the faith of "petty persons in animals and insects."[64] While conceding that all men believe in something, Nishi

[60] Nishida Taketoshi, "Meiroku zasshi-Hōdan zasshi," *Bungaku*, XXIII, 1 (January 1955), p. 25.
[61] Kuwaki Gen'yoku, *Meiji no tetsugakkai* (Tokyo, 1943), pp. 18-19. The allusion is to Luke 20:25, "And he said unto them, render therefore unto Caesar the things which be Caesar's, and unto God the things which be God's." (King James version)
[62] *Kyōmonron*, p. 500.   [63] *Ibid.*, p. 501.
[64] *Ibid.*, p. 501.

clearly stated that the best faith was that of the educated man. Moreover, he was willing to acknowledge the primacy of the *kokutai* and permitted no challenge to it by any religious faith. *Kyōmonron* was therefore not an unrestrained attack on the full range of Kyōbushō activities, but merely upon its attempts to inculcate Shinto as an official dogma. Nishi approved fully of the Kyōbushō's administrative function of supervising the external functions of religious organizations. Like Katō, he had little use for Shinto or the crude beliefs of ignorant persons in natural phenomena. His attitude toward religion was consistent with the *keimō* philosophy of early Meiji: foolish faiths and superstitions should be dissolved with enlightened education, and religion should occupy a relatively minor place in the life of an intelligent person.[65] Although the title *Kyōmonron* means "on religion," Nishi never discussed such matters as sin, penance, or salvation; his personal religious beliefs were limited to those of a rational humanist.

ESTABLISHING A PARLIAMENTARY ASSEMBLY

The most consequential matter in public affairs to receive Meirokusha attention was Itagaki Taisuke's petition to the Meiji government in January 1874, seeking the creation of a popularly elected legislative body. This was not the first time that parliamentarianism had been advocated in the Meiji period; well before 1874 the animus for instituting an assembly existed within the oligarchy itself. The debate in 1874 concerned not the merits of introducing representative government but the optimum timing of such a move.[66]

[65] Both Kuwaki and Funayama identify the influence of Comtian positivism in Nishi's discussion of religion, but in fact Comte's three-stage theory of history placed religion at the lowest level, followed by the metaphysical and positive stages. Nishi's insistence that religion be preserved in an enlightened world is similar only to the later, anti-positivistic Comte. See Kuwaki, *Meiji no tetsugakkai*, p. 19; Funayama, *Nihon no kannenronsha* (Tokyo, 1956), pp. 55-57.

[66] George Akita, *Foundations of Constitutional Government in Modern Japan, 1868-1900* (Cambridge, Mass., 1967), pp. 6-14; Joseph Pittau, *Political Thought in Early Meiji Japan, 1868-1889*

Nishi on Politics and Current Events

It is generally agreed that the petition was designed not simply to establish parliamentary rule but also to express the grievances of Itagaki's opposition party, the Aikoku Kōtō, against the dominant Meiji oligarchy.[67] The proposal was immediately rejected by the government leaders, but it had already created a furor in political circles, because of its overt challenge to the legal authorities, and among intellectuals, because of the European political philosophy upon which the demands were based.

The Meiji Six Society members did not approach this problem as mere "absolutist bureaucratic scholars," as some deterministic historians have asserted,[68] although Katō, Mori, Tsuda, and Nishi recognized that Itagaki's petition was a power play to seize political control.[69] Their primary interest in the proposal was theoretical. They evaluated the parliamentary plan in terms of their general blueprint for modern society, and their constant reference point in criticizing the petition was the level of enlightenment of the proposed electorate. For Nishi, in particular, the question of his position in the military bureaucracy hardly entered into his assessment of Itagaki's petition. The most cogent Meirokusha appraisals were grounded not upon personal or occupational

---

(Cambridge, Mass., 1967), pp. 55-60. The text of the petition appears in Arthur Tiedemann, *Modern Japan, a Brief History* (Princeton, 1955), pp. 100-105.

[67] The best study of the intellectual reaction to the Itagaki proposal is Abosch, "Katō Hiroyuki," pp. 244-270. The first chapter of Robert A. Scalapino, *Democracy and the Party Movement in Prewar Japan: The Failure of the First Attempt* (Berkeley and Los Angeles, 1953), is a useful account of the political aspects of the proposal. Two books by Osatake Takeshi are especially valuable: *Ishin zengo ni okeru rippō shisō* (rev. ed., Tokyo, 1948) and *Nihon kenseishi no kenkyū* (Tokyo, 1943). The standard Japanese work on the question is Inada Masatsugu, *Meiji kenpō seiritsushi*, 2 vols. (Tokyo, 1960-1961).

[68] This is the view of such scholars as Suzuki Yasuzō, Furuta Hikaru, Hattori Shisō, Tōyama Shigeki, Miyagawa Tōru, and Morita Yasuo (see subsequent notes). Itagaki himself denounced "bureaucratic despotism" in the memorial. See Abosch, "Katō Hiroyuki," p. 244.

[69] Suzuki, "Nishi Amane no seiji-shakai shisō kaisetsu," p. 289.

Nishi on Politics and Current Events

animosities toward Itagaki's supporters[70] but upon *keimō* social and political philosophy. Katō Hiroyuki best expressed the spirit of this philosophy in a formal rebuttal of the Itagaki petition.[71] He argued that the Japanese people were as yet insufficiently enlightened to determine national policy by means of a parliamentary assembly. Even in the most civilized Western countries, he asserted, public opinion was often too unreliable to make an intelligent contribution to the governing process. While he did not oppose creating an elected house in the future, Katō's gradualist position led him to seek a temporary united front of intellectuals, wealthy merchants and industrialists, and aristocrats for ruling the country until the people were ready for parliamentary democracy.[72]

Nishi generally agreed with Katō's outlook. He wrote three articles on the question, published at six-month intervals, which show that his resistance to Itagaki's proposal came not as an apologia for the Meiji state but from intellectual conviction. The first of these articles is called "Hakkyū sōkōgi ichidai" (One Topic in Refutation of the General Public Opinion) and appeared in *Meiroku zasshi* barely three weeks after the petition was presented.[73] Here Nishi attacks the logical flaws in the Itagaki proposal, without denying the propriety of establishing an elected house at some point in the future. To institute parliamentarianism before the people are truly enlightened, he believes, would be like merely adopting trains and telegraphs—the Western technique without the underlying spirit. He restates the concept that he had

[70] Mori Arinori's opposition to the petition was expressed in an attack upon the personalities of its proponents. It is entitled "Minsen giin seiritsu kengensho no hyō," *MRZS*, 3 (February 1874); *MBZ*, XVIII, pp. 62-63.

[71] The crux of Katō's criticism is contained in "Burunchurishi kokuhō hanron tekiyaku—minsen giin fukaritsu no ron," *MRZS*, 4 (February 1874); *MBZ*, XVIII, pp. 69-70.

[72] Pittau, *Political Thought in Early Meiji Japan*, pp. 55-60; Hugh Borton, *Japan's Modern Century* (New York, 1955), p. 96; Abosch, "Katō Hiroyuki," pp. 253-256.

[73] "Hakkyū sōkōgi ichidai," *MRZS*, 3 (February 1874); *MBZ*, XVIII, pp. 66-68. The title defies adequate translation. Subsequent notes refer to the version in *NAZS* 1961, pp. 238-241.

introduced in *Hyakuichi shinron* about physical and moral principles: the laws of nature are valid throughout the world, but each civilization has its own rules for conducting human affairs.[74] The parliamentary systems of France, England, and the United States are "as different as heaven and earth."[75] Therefore, how can Itagaki claim that it is the natural right of the Japanese people to pass judgment on political matters? All taxpayers, Nishi believes, may properly expect governmental protection, but participation in the affairs of state must await a higher level of popular enlightenment. Further, he denies the Itagaki contention that all societies are based on a social contract by pointing out numerous cases in world history in which this is not so. Likewise, he contends, it is foolish to hope that a popularly elected assembly would help to enlighten the people; enlightenment via education must precede parliamentarianism, so that the people can participate responsibly in government.[76]

Nishi's position was consistent with the Meirokusha consensus that "a popularly elected assembly should be carried out in the near future, but at present the level of popular wisdom is low, so that to carry it out immediately is premature."[77] It also accorded with his belief that the primary task of the early Meiji Western studies scholars was to educate the public in the virtues of civilized society. His reaction to the Itagaki petition was firmly based on his previous analysis of the nature of *ri* in *Hyakuichi shinron*. It is interesting, however, that on this point both Nishi and Fukuzawa had shifted tactics from those used when they discussed domestic travel by foreigners. Fukuzawa favored Itagaki's proposal as a proper method for enlightening the people[78] but ridiculed the

---

[74] *Ibid.*, pp. 238-239.   [75] *Ibid.*, p. 238.
[76] *Ibid.*, pp. 239-241. Nishi probably overstated the degree to which Itagaki and his supporters believed in a social contract. See Robert A. Scalapino, *Democracy and the Party Movement in Prewar Japan: The Failure of the First Attempt* (Berkeley and Los Angeles, 1953), p. 49, and Pittau, *Political Thought in Early Meiji Japan*, p. 52, for a discussion of the Itagaki proposal on this point.
[77] Quoted in Asō, *Kinsei Nihon tetsugakushi*, p. 277.
[78] Tōyama, "Meiroku zasshi," pp. 123-124; Pittau, *Political Thought in Early Meiji Japan*, pp. 60-65.

Nishi on Politics and Current Events

thought that intercourse with foreigners could accomplish the same purpose, whereas Nishi argued precisely the opposite. In Nishi's case this contradiction may be explained by the fact that he saw no concrete objection to free travel and thought that a possible benefit could be derived from contact with foreigners, whereas he envisaged the grave danger that "the throne would gradually lose its glory, government ordinances would be of diverse origins," and "politics would become like a theatrical production" if an assembly were established before the people were better educated.[79]

Certain scholars have argued that Nishi criticized the parliamentary proposal because he was merely a "bureaucratic thinker,"[80] and also that he wrote within the framework of absolutist politics as a representative of the scholarly organization "which was inevitably the official learned society of the oligarchic Meiji government."[81] They reason that Nishi and his *keimō* colleagues, as government employees, were incapable of criticizing the Meiji political elite or joining Itagaki's attack on the new state.[82] This interpretation ignores Nishi's blunt condemnation of the Meiji oligarchy in "Himitsu setsu" (Theory of Secrets), the second of his articles on the Itagaki proposal. In this work, Nishi asserts that some things—such as military tactics and diplomatic techniques—must always remain veiled from public knowledge. There is no excuse, however, for the secretive methods of the current government: "Those of high station, now that the *bakufu* has withered away, all eat meats, wear white silk skirts [the white *hakama* reserved for peers, or *kizoku*, in

79 "Hakkyū sōkōgi ichidai," p. 240.
80 Suzuki, "Nishi Amane no seiji-shakai shisō kaisetsu," p. 291.
81 Miyagawa Tōru, "Meiroku zasshi to minsen giin mondai," *Kindai Nihon shisōshi*, ed. Tōyama Shigeki *et al.* (Tokyo, 1956-1957), I, p. 61. Tōyama, in *Meiji ishin* (Tokyo, 1951), pp. 302-304, brands the Meirokusha members as "enlightened despots," as does Hattori Shisō in *Meiji no shisō, Hattori zenshū*, VI (Tokyo, 1955). A similar view may be found in Morita Yasuo, "Meirokusha ron," *Rekishigaku kenkyū*, 254 (June 1961), pp. 39-43. See Ishida Ichirō's comments in *Nihon shisōshi gairon*, ed. Ishida Ichirō (Tokyo, 1963), p. 235, for a summary of the conflicting interpretations.
82 Tōyama, *Meiji ishin*, p. 303; Miyagawa, *Kindai Nihon shisō no kōzō*, pp. 47-60.

187

the early Meiji period], and rely on despotic government—this is why they are in power. That is to say, if they do not conceal things, they will not be esteemed; if they do not act secretly, they will not be respected; if they lose respect, they will forfeit control of the realm."[83]

Nishi's ire was provoked in part by the oligarchs' sudden decision in May 1874 to attack Taiwan,[84] but his words demonstrate that he shared in the widespread frustration with clique rule which earned considerable public support for the Itagaki proposal and the subsequent "Freedom and Popular Rights" (*jiyū minken*) movement. Far from being a diffident bureaucrat who was beholden to the policies of his employers, Nishi repudiated the close-vested statecraft of the oligarchy and agreed in principle that a parliamentary body should be established. His principal objection involved the timing and method of creating an assembly. That he rarely criticized the new government (apart from "Himitsu setsu") is explained not by his membership in a bureaucratic class that was unable to escape the manipulation of the state[85] but by his utilitarian philosophy of government as outlined in *Jinsei sanpōsetsu*: "So long as the three treasures are protected, it does not matter whether government is monarchic, republican, or by clan rule."[86]

It was therefore hard for Nishi to be enthusiastic about creating a parliament immediately. He thought that such phenomena as constitutionalism, conservatism, radicalism, and the *jiyū minken* movement should always be subordinated to the primary objectives of *fukoku kyōhei* and enlightenment. Nonetheless, he was willing to sanction the creation

---

[83] "Himitsu setsu," *MRZS*, 19 (October 1874); *MBZ*, XVIII, p. 148.

[84] *Ibid.*, p. 148. See Borton, *Japan's Modern Century*, p. 97, for the details of this expedition.

[85] Abosch, "Katō Hiroyuki," p. 191.

[86] *Jinsei sanpōsetsu*, p. 534. Ōkubo Toshiaki has argued that the Meiji Six Society members opposed the Itagaki plan not because they supported the state (they were quite critical of the Satsuma-Chōshū clique) but because the proposal was unacceptable to them philosophically. See Ōkubo, "Kindai kokka no keisei," *Nihon shi (Sekai kakkokushi*, XIV), (Tokyo, 1958), pp. 450-451.

of a national consultative body, the provisions for which he outlined in the third of his articles on Itagaki's petition, "Mōra giin no setsu" (Discussion of a Collective Assembly). In lieu of a popularly elected assembly (*minsen giin*), Nishi proposed immediately establishing a body whose members would be appointed by the government (*kansen giin*). There should be representatives of the people of each prefecture, delegates from the various government agencies, and a number of persons of "great learning and moral influence."[87] The existing *sain* would become the upper house of such an assembly, and similar consultative bodies would be established in the prefectures. For the moment, the assembly would assume none of the powers of the Meiji government, and the oligarchy could dissolve it at will.[88]

What advantage would there be in creating such an impotent parliament? Nishi manages to identify five positive benefits that would grow out of such a venture. First, it would improve communication between the state and the people: "If the government seeks to ascertain broad public opinion about matters, it should adopt this [assembly] immediately."[89] Second, such a body would stimulate a general interest in public affairs. Third, it would create more respect for government. Fourth, an assembly would focus the creative energies of Japan's intellectuals on the affairs of state. Finally, the successful operation of a governmentally appointed parliament would lay the basis for a true popularly elected assembly.[90]

Nishi's suggestions for the concrete implementation of gradualism resulted in no change of state policy, and it is fair to say that he contributed little of practical value to the *minsen giin* debate. However, the fact that he proposed a *kansen giin* as a stepping stone to a bona fide elective house

---

[87] "Mōra giin no setsu," *MRZS*, 29 (February 1875); *MBZ*, xviii, pp. 193-194. Notes refer to the version in *NAZS* 1961, pp. 242-245.
[88] *Ibid.*, pp. 243-244.   [89] *Ibid.*, p. 244.   [90] *Ibid.*, p. 245.

is further evidence that he did not simply parrot the Meiji oligarchy's perfunctory rejection of the Itagaki petition. Nishi thus reacted to this critical issue in current affairs not as a bureaucrat but as a *keimō* intellectual whose uppermost concern remained the enlightenment of the Japanese people.

eight

Civil and Military Society

Among the many reform schemes and policy innovations of the early Meiji period, none was more far-reaching in its effects on Japanese national life than the Conscription Act (Chōheirei) of 1873. Next to the formation of the Meiji oligarchy itself, the creation of a conscript army was probably the single most important event in the first decade after the restoration, inasmuch as it proved to be the vital hinge upon which the drive for national wealth and power turned. Not only did the rapid growth of a well-trained, mechanized force of more than 30,000 troops represent a major step toward the goal of *kyōhei* ("strengthen the army"), but it had a great impact on Japanese politics, society, and economy as well.[1] Command of a tactical force of these proportions strengthened the oligarchy's hand vis-à-vis the remnants of armed opposition, especially in the Satsuma Rebellion of 1877. Likewise, the conscription law produced a leveling tendency by opening careers in the military service to men from all social classes for the first time in more than two hundred and fifty years, further debasing the prestige of the declassed samurai. Even more importantly, the military reforms that flowed from this act had widespread economic repercussions, not only by causing fiscal centralization and a demand for new industrial production to equip the forces but also by creating profound changes in the patterns of population growth, urbanization, employment, technical education, and consumption.[2] Finally, and most significantly in

---

[1] For data concerning the size of the new army, see Gotaro Ogawa, *Conscription System in Japan* (New York, 1921), pp. 15-17.

[2] See Roger F. Hackett, "The Military—Japan," *Political Modernization in Japan and Turkey*, ed. Robert E. Ward and Dankwart A. Rustow (Princeton, 1964), pp. 335-337; Ogawa, *Conscription System in Japan*, pp. 73-222.

Civil and Military Society

the long run, the rise of a unified military force helped to promote a new national ideology of loyalty and service, concentrated on the imperial throne. It was in this latter respect that the writings of Nishi Amane, in his capacity as intellectual in residence in the Ministry of War, made an important contribution toward defining the role of the soldier in Japan's fledgling modern state.

NISHI'S JUSTIFICATION FOR A STRONG ARMY

It is not uncommon to find scholars such as Nishi serving their governments in the modern world, but it is unusual for them to manage to write their most important works while simultaneously holding public office. Rarer still is the intellectual who is able to maintain his scholarly integrity by putting his theoretical ideals into political practice. Most modern commentators have assumed that there was a wide chasm between Nishi the scholar and Nishi the bureaucrat, and accordingly they have disregarded his lengthy career in the Military Department (Hyōbushō) and its successor, the Ministry of War (Rikugunshō).[3] However, instead of accepting the resulting implication that he was a mere chameleon, writing *keimō* tracts while serving an oligarchic state, we shall briefly consider Nishi's most important writings as a government official in order to see the extent to which they are consistent with his philosophic thought.

Between 1870 and 1886, Nishi held several positions of responsibility and influence in the military bureaucracy, despite his disclaimer that he was merely "an office boy in the government by virtue of some small skill in translation."[4] He was the principal author of Japan's first modern code of

[3] Kazue Kyōichi, for example, disregards Nishi's military thought in his otherwise excellent "Nishi Amane no shōgai to sono shisō," *Tetsugaku kaishi* 9 (1958), pp. 1-25. The works of Asō Yoshiteru, Funayama Shin'ichi, Kuwaki Gen'yoku, and Miyagawa Tōru contain virtually nothing on this important facet of Nishi's career. Of the scholars who have studied his philosophic writings, only Ōkubo Toshiaki has taken into account his military works. See Ōkubo, "Nishi Amane no gunburon," *Nihon rekishi*, 45 (February 1952), pp. 2-10.
[4] "Higakusha shokubunron," *MRZS*, 2 (February 1874); *MBZ*, XVIII, p. 61.

Civil and Military Society

military justice, the Military Criminal Code of 1872.[5] In the same year he played a major part in designing the conscription law, which took effect in January 1873. According to General Yamagata Aritomo's biographer, Nishi was consulted not only about the legal provisions of this act but also about how to organize and administer the selection of draftees.[6] He was also one of the chief compilers of a two-volume dictionary of military terms in five languages, a project which began in 1874 and required seven years.[7] In addition, he made himself useful to Yamagata as a skilled adviser on international diplomatic practice and Western military capabilities. Other positions which Nishi held at various times included service as an Imperial Household Ministry lecturer on Western thought to the Meiji Emperor, an overseer of the Tokyo Normal School, and a member of the House of Peers (Kizokuin) in 1889.[8]

The climax of Nishi's official career occurred in the years

[5] The code was known as *Rikukaigun keiritsu.* See Osatake Takeshi, "Nishi Amane no jiseki ni oite," *Kokushi Kaikokai kiyō,* 47 (Feb. 15, 1944), p. 3. Although Nishi's draft is not extant, a related commentary of his on this code appears in *NAZS* 1966, pp. 144-147, entitled *Gunritsu sōkō hihyō.* In this work Nishi expressed his opposition to capital punishment. Tsuda Mamichi, as a leading expert on Western law, played an important part in writing the *Rikukaigun keiritsu.*

[6] Tokutomi Iichirō, *Kōshaku Yamagata Aritomo den* II (Tokyo, 1933), p. 268. With respect to the Chōheirei, Tokutomi says that "not a thing escaped [Nishi's] hand." No tangible evidence of Nishi's precise role in drafting the act exists. See Ōkubo, "Nishi Amane no gunburon," p. 5; Matsushita Yoshio, *Meiji gunsei ronshū,* I (rev. ed., Tokyo, 1956), pp. 253-254.

[7] The work was entitled *Gokoku taishō heigo jisho* and was published under Rikugunshō auspices on Feb. 8, 1881. See Osatake Takeshi, "Nishi Amane sensei," *Shin Nihon,* II, 5 (May 1939), pp. 101-102, and Mori Ōgai, *Nishi Amane den, Ōgai zenshū* (Tokyo, 1923-1927), VII, p. 187.

[8] Ōgai, *Nishi Amane den,* pp. 187-191; "Nishi Amane," *Kindai bungaku kenkyū sōsho,* ed. Shōwa Joshi Daigaku (Tokyo, 1956), III, pp. 118-119; Kazue, "Nishi Amane no shōgai to sono shisō," p. 25. For Nishi's service as an imperial lecturer, see Asō Yoshiteru, *Kinsei Nihon tetsugakushi* (Tokyo, 1942), pp. 241-266. Nishi was elected to membership in the Kizokuin on Sept. 29, 1889, but resigned the position on Feb. 17, 1890, owing to poor health. For Nishi's official ranks and salaries during this period, see Ōgai, *Nishi Amane den,* p. 187.

Civil and Military Society

1878-1881, when he was chief of the planning office of the Rikugunshō. During this period his relationship to Yamagata, the real creator of Japan's modern army, resembled the arrangement in 1867 with the last shogun, Keiki, in that Nishi served the ministry chiefly as an intellectual technician. Much of his time was occupied with translating Western books and documents relating to military organization,[9] but he also contributed to devising nearly all the army and navy regulations promulgated during the first fifteen years of Meiji. Unlike Keiki, Yamagata willingly acknowledged Nishi's outstanding service: "Once Western studies had begun, there were many who could read the books and translate them, but few as yet could appreciate their flavor and put them to use. I was desperate to get someone for a responsible position in the Military Department. . . . Fortunately, someone recommended Nishi. I discussed military affairs with him and questioned him exhaustively . . . he was made an official in the ministry, to inquire into military affairs. He was well informed on military regulations and bureaucratic structure and, needless to say, applied himself diligently."[10]

Among Nishi's significant activities during 1878-1881 was lecturing to a branch of the influential Army Club (Kaikōsha) known as the Enkikai.[11] Nishi regularly spoke to the young military officers in this organization on such subjects as European history, international relations, and the proper role of the army in Meiji Japan. Twenty-two of his lectures were published under the title *Heifūron* (Discussion of Military Service) between 1878 and 1881 in *Naigai heiji shin-*

[9] Ōgai, *Nishi Amane den*, pp. 190-191.

[10] Yamagata, preface to a biography of Nishi, quoted in Tokutomi, *Kōshaku Yamagata Aritomo den*, ɪɪ, p. 269. According to Tokutomi, Yamagata's praise for Nishi was never insincere flattery. The two were apparently quite close, and Yamagata often called on Nishi during his illnesses after 1885. See *ibid.*, ɪɪ, pp. 268-269.

[11] The Kaikōsha was founded in February 1877, and it existed until the end of World War II. Its membership was limited to army officers and Rikugunshō officials. Its main function was as a research and lecture society in the early years, and it published a monthly bulletin and other works of military interest.

Civil and Military Society

bun.[12] Theoretically, Nishi addressed the Enkikai as a civilian scholar who was well versed in military affairs, not as an official representative of the Rikugunshō.[13] Thus these talks are at least better indices of his personal opinions than those military manuscripts which he wrote for his bureaucratic superiors. Like his lectures on "encyclopedia" to his Ikueisha pupils in 1870-1872, the *Heifūron* series was designed to provide the young officers with a sound background in military history. Much of the material is therefore expository rather than analytical, but *Heifūron* is especially useful for understanding how Nishi justified the existence of a strong army in a nation that was only beginning to build a modern industrial economy.

The tone of *Heifūron* is scholarly and didactic, in keeping with Nishi's earlier writings. It begins with the premise that the world is inevitably moving toward Kant's utopian society of eternal peace: "According to Europe's late men of wisdom, this world should ultimately attain eternal peace, order, and leisure without arms."[14] Such a trend, he asserts, has in fact been taking place throughout human history, characterized by a movement both in Japan and the West toward political consolidation and unity. However, since this goal will not be realized until "10,000 years in the future at the earliest," "it is our fate to pursue this serious work of amalgamation and unity in the short span of our lives . . . in order to grant the blessings of eternal peace to our descendants ten millennia from now."[15]

Japan must realize, Nishi warns, that violence and confusion are to be expected in the course of attaining civilization and enlightenment. Recent international events indicate that the country must be prepared to fight if it expects to deal successfully with the West. He therefore criticizes the isolationism of the Edo period, maintaining that "the national

---

[12] *Heifūron*, *NAZS* 1966, pp. 18-96. It first appeared serially in *Naigai heiji shinbun*, 166-289 (Oct. 20, 1878 to Feb. 27, 1881). The first thirteen lectures in this series were included in *Nishi sensei ronshū* in 1880.
[13] Ōkubo, "Nishi Amane no gunburon," p. 7.
[14] *Heifūron*, p. 22.   [15] *Ibid*., pp. 23-24.

policies of a state are not established to suit the convenience of internal affairs in that state but according to the conditions of the entire world."[16] Neither adventurism (which he describes as "Russianism") nor the opposite extreme ("Ryukyuism") is suitable for a country of Japan's size. The events of the past thirty years demonstrate that neither international law nor treaties of amity are sufficient to protect Japan's national interests. Therefore, he concludes, "that which preserves our independence is our army and navy."[17] Without them the nation's wealth will be drained, the ports will become sites for slave auctions, and Japan will suffer the ravages which have beset Poland.

It is quite apparent that Nishi regarded nineteenth-century international relations as a struggle for survival.[18] Conditions in East Asia, he declares, resemble riding in a third-class train: "At first, when there are only a few passengers, there is freedom, but as the number of persons increases, standees cannot find seats and jostle one another. Once you stand up and lose your place, you cannot return to your previous seat. . . . This is the condition of the world at present."[19] Japan must thus build a strong army today to prepare for her expanded role in the community of nations tomorrow, so that future generations can realize the goal of eternal peace. He observes that this chain of developments is based on the "necessity of the course of events."[20] It is therefore clear, he argues, that economic development should not take precedence over establishing a powerful military force: "strengthen the army" was just as important as "enrich the country" in the *fukoku kyōhei* prescription.[21] Nishi illustrates the need to pursue both goals equally by citing the example of a government with a million yen: "It should use 500,000 to increase production and promote the people's wealth. The other 500,000 should be used to protect against aggression

[16] *Ibid.*, p. 33.   [17] *Ibid.*, p. 35.
[18] See Umetani Noboru, *Meiji zenki seijishi no kenkyū* (Tokyo, 1963), p. 59.
[19] *Heifūron*, p. 44.   [20] *Ibid.*, p. 47.
[21] *Ibid.*, pp. 51-54. Nishi's argument is an expansion of the same theme in *Jōrinpō heibi ryakuhyō*, NAZS 1966, pp. 131-132.

Civil and Military Society

and marauding . . . therefore it is our fate today to grasp the plow with the right hand and the rifle with the left . . . this is the course of events. Though we be farmers, artisans, or tradesmen, we must also be soldiers."[22]

According to Nishi, those who argue that Japan should postpone *kyōhei* until *fukoku* has been accomplished ignore the likelihood that the foreign powers would quickly siphon off the country's wealth. By the same token, military considerations should not overshadow other domestic reforms, because the ideal of eternal peace can be gained only through war, not only against aggressors but also against poverty and ignorance.[23]

The place of expansionism in Nishi's writings is not entirely clear. He suggests that because of the international struggle for land and riches Japan may need to join the Asian nations in repulsing the European challenge.[24] He stopped short of advocating Russian-style expansion for Japan, however, and he seems to have based his justification for military strength primarily on the presumption that it would prevent future trouble: "War preparations do not constitute something to be employed after blood has flowed and corpses have piled up; rather, their effect occurs before the sound of rifles is heard or the flash of gunpowder is seen."[25] Nishi's position thus encompassed the two domestic aspirations of early Meiji Japan: to establish a powerful and wealthy independent state and to join the world family of nations. But it is uncertain whether he fully anticipated or supported the late Meiji drive for expansion on the Asiatic mainland.

At first glance it may seem contradictory that such a paramount figure in the intellectually liberal *keimō* movement could so forcefully advocate a powerful military establishment and contribute to its realization. Indeed, this paradox has led at least one scholar to conclude that by the year 1880 Nishi had laid aside his *keimō* beliefs and turned conserva-

[22] *Heifūron*, p. 54. [23] *Ibid.*, pp. 59-60.
[24] Umetani, *Meiji zenki seijishi no kenkyū*, p. 189.
[25] *Heifūron*, p. 63.

197

Civil and Military Society

tive.[26] Such a view may lose sight of the fact that throughout his term of Rikugunshō service Nishi continued to lecture and write on most of the same themes expressed in such earlier works as *Hyakugaku renkan, Chichi keimō*, and *Jinsei sanpōsetsu*. Although his later academic writings added little to the theories which he had presented prior to 1878, they are firm evidence that he at no point abandoned his enlightened convictions. Nishi could continue to serve in the military bureaucracy at the height of his personal *keimō* research because he firmly believed that there was no conflict between public service and private scholarship.

Furthermore, in the case of *Heifūron* it is possible to demonstrate that Nishi's justification for a strong army, far from signifying a conversion to conservatism, in fact complemented his earlier thought. Admittedly, although he nominally gave the Enkikai lectures as a private citizen, all his military essays were prepared within the context of his position in the Ministry of War, and he never addressed himself to the issues in *Heifūron* in his purely academic writings. These considerations notwithstanding, the crucial question is whether there is any similarity between Nishi's personal philosophy and the attitudes expressed in *Heifūron*. The answer is strongly affirmative. First of all, these lectures are similar in tone and feeling to the earlier works, in that his approach is very scholarly. He examines the need for a strong army from historical and philosophical points of view, borrowing Kant's ideal of eternal peace as the goal of all nations. This was his only significant reference to Kant throughout his career, despite Tsuda's claim that in the Leiden years Nishi "was fond of the Kantian school of philosophy."[27] A second point is that he manifests the same progressive

[26] Roger F. Hackett, "Nishi Amane—A Tokugawa-Meiji Bureaucrat," *Journal of Asian Studies*, xviii, 2 (February 1959), p. 220. It is interesting that deterministic historians have mainly ignored Nishi's military writings, apparently because they have been satisfied that Nishi's earlier essays show sufficient evidence of his "absolutist" leanings.

[27] Quoted in Asō, *Kinsei Nihon tetsugakushi*, p. 66. See also Umetani, *Meiji zenki seijishi no kenkyū*, pp. 186-187.

Civil and Military Society

view of history in *Heifūron* that is apparent in *Hyakuichi shinron* and *Jinsei sanpōsetsu*. He frequently refers to the "necessary course of events" as the reason for European imperialism in nineteenth-century East Asia. He likewise believes that a strong army is justified by the processes of history. Third, there is a direct link in *Heifūron* with Nishi's ideas about civilization and enlightenment. Struggle and warfare, he maintains, are a necessary part of the civilizing process that will one day lead to perpetual peace.

Furthermore, there is considerable evidence from his Hokkaido petition of 1857 onward that Nishi, in common with most Japanese intellectuals, believed in reforming and strengthening the army. It is therefore totally consistent with his *keimō* philosophy that he advocates an effective military establishment in *Heifūron*. A fifth point is that there is no hint of exclusionism or militant isolationism in these lectures. His contention that the force of arms would speed Japan's entry into the community of nations by increasing her strength vis-à-vis the West is in full accord with the thesis expressed in "Naichi ryokō," in which he advocated free internal travel by foreigners as another means of promoting Japan's international standing. Finally, Nishi's understandable concern lest Japan be bullied by the great powers is in keeping with the sentiments contained in "Kaikanzei no setsu," in which he argued that it was the right of a sovereign nation to determine its own tariffs. His fears in *Heifūron* about Western imperialism are therefore not the result of any sudden change in his attitude toward foreign relations. In the same manner, his insistence on building a strong army to protect the national wealth is a direct outgrowth of his theory of the three treasures, in which he charged the state with the responsibility of protecting the country's health, knowledge, and wealth from both external depredation and internal decay.

There is good reason to doubt that Nishi seriously espoused the Kantian ideal of eternal peace, inasmuch as he never stressed it in his philosophical works. Nevertheless, *Heifūron* is a temperate document based on the assumption that war

Civil and Military Society

is an unpleasant but necessary means to attain nobler goals. Nishi's outlook in these lectures is perhaps best characterized as more frank and realistic, but hardly more conservative, than his thought during the *bunmei kaika* period.

ETHICS FOR THE JAPANESE ARMY

One of the most crucial problems for the architects of Japan's modern army was to lay a new basis for ethical conduct that would apply to every soldier, regardless of rank. The Conscription Act of 1873, which was as revolutionary as any early Meiji reform, had permanently destroyed the aristocratic military system of the Edo era by rendering commoners liable to armed service. Once this act had taken effect, it became increasingly apparent that the personal code of lord-samurai loyalties known as *shujū kankei,* which had functioned as the principal ethical underpinning of Japan's feudal armies, was ill-suited to the requirements of a modern mass army conscripted from all levels of society. It was natural that Yamagata turned to Nishi for counsel on this matter, for Nishi not only was well versed in Western military practice but also had written numerous essays on the larger problem of morality for Japanese society as a whole. Nishi prepared several memoranda on military ethics for Yamagata, and he also delivered a group of lectures to the Enkikai dealing with the moral responsibilities of the modern military officer. As in the case of the *Heifūron* series, these lectures constitute a more accurate reflection of Nishi's own attitudes than the official memos drafted for his departmental superiors,[28] although again it must be remembered that the invitation to lecture at Enkikai meetings came to him only nominally as a private scholar.

The series on military ethics is entitled *Heika tokkō* (The Moral Conduct of Soldiers) and first appeared in *Naigai heiji shinbun.*[29] These lectures were given between February 19 and May 21, 1878, at the Tokyo headquarters of the

[28] Ōkubo, "Nishi Amane no gunburon," p. 7.
[29] *Heika tokkō, NAZS* 1966, pp. 3-17. The series first appeared in *Naigai heiji shinbun,* 132, 136, 140, and 145.

Civil and Military Society

Kaikōsha. The first significant question in *Heika tokkō* concerns the organization of the armed forces. All modern armies, Nishi states, are based on the concept of "mechanism" (Nishi uses the English term in phonetic transcription). "Mechanism" means both mechanized equipment and "the idea of using people like instruments"—in other words, "discipline" (*sessei*).[30] Discipline is ordinarily achieved via strict regulations and drill. The idea of *sessei,* Nishi contends, never existed in Japan's feudal wars and has been adopted as a policy only since the restoration. "Although it cannot be said that our army has been altogether successful to date, in general it has attained this objective."[31]

In lieu of discipline, it was the feudal moral code which held the ancient armies together. Now that the Meiji reforms have done away with lord-samurai loyalties, "The army is disciplined and there are regulations for everything, but we cannot yet say that moral conduct on the part of the soldiers is unnecessary . . . we should not simply employ the ancient moral code as a means to use others, but we cannot call moral leadership insignificant."[32] For example, in the Satsuma Rebellion of 1877, the government troops won because of superior organization and discipline, but Nishi believes that Saigō's army offered such stiff resistance because of its moral strength: "The rebels held out for nearly a year's duration and were barely defeated in the siege of Shiroyama because the soldiers' hearts were unified and not fragmented into a hundred pieces."[33] Thus Nishi concludes that: "It goes without saying that discipline is essential for the modern army, but we must not ignore the matter of maintaining group morale through moral conduct on the part of the soldiers. In short, the point is that we should have both things complementing each other."[34]

It is well to observe that in emphasizing the importance of soldierly morality, Nishi did not seek to perpetuate the

---

[30] *Ibid.*, pp. 4-5. The term usually means "moderation," "restraint," or "abstinence."
[31] *Ibid.*, pp. 5-6. [32] *Ibid.*, p. 6.
[33] *Ibid.*, p. 7. [34] *Ibid.*, p. 7.

feudal ethical code itself; instead he proposed a set of values that was largely modern. Just as he had stressed the need for morality in society at large while condemning Neo-Confucian ethics in *Hyakuichi shinron,* Nishi argued in *Heika tokkō* that some sort of morality was essential for the post-restoration army and that the existence of discipline was not itself sufficient to guarantee success.

An integral part of military ethics, Nishi contends, is the idea of "obedience" (once again the English term is used in transcription).[35] This is the source of a fundamental distinction between civil and military society: "Although we assert that people generally have the same rights in ordinary society, no one has equal rights in military society. There are of course distinctions of rank and position, from general to private. . . . It is a fixed rule that we must always obey orders, even when we disagree."[36] Nishi offers a clear illustration to characterize the dichotomy:

"Ordinary society is like the game of go. Although there are differences between black and white, each stone has the power of only one stone. Military society is like chess. There are kings, queens, rooks, and finally pawns. Their respective powers are distinct and must not be confused. The military order, when compared with the normal social order, is much more strict, and indeed, if there is no such regulated system, we cannot have a mechanism that controls and manipulates a million men like one body."[37]

A further distinction between the two societies concerns politics. Nishi contends that the current popular trend toward parliamentarianism must be encouraged, "since it is a means to promote the wealth and strength of the country."[38] Soldiers, however, must not become involved in political movements because they are antithetical to military discipline. The ordinary public supports parliamentarianism "in order to ward off tyrannical government, but soldiers resign them-

---

[35] *Ibid.,* p. 8.   [36] *Ibid.,* p. 8.
[37] *Ibid.,* pp. 8-9.   [38] *Ibid.,* p. 14.

selves to servitude from the moment they enter the ranks—this is inevitable."[39]

Likewise, there is a clear distinction between civil and military obligations to the throne. "Of course, both commoners and soldiers have the same sovereign emperor, but there is a difference between subjecthood and servitude."[40] A spirit of liberty and self-rule should be created among the people at large, but this must not extend to men under arms. Instead, Nishi asserts that "the emperor is the supreme commander of the Japanese army and navy, and we must strengthen the hierarchical [military] order to the utmost and observe obedience."[41]

Finally, the civil and military strata differ in their positions regarding personal gain. It is essential that private citizens aspire toward wealth, but soldiers must refrain from individual profit-seeking. Their material needs are amply satisfied by the state, and the accumulation of money among the troops will only serve to disrupt discipline.[42]

Nishi differentiated between the two societies in order to reinforce his insistence on discipline and obedience in the new army. He presumed that the two realms could exist together harmoniously and envisaged no progression from one to the other.[43] The net effect of his thesis, however, was to set military society apart as a unique subculture with its own regulations, code of conduct, and organizational system. Although Nishi's outlook on modern army structure almost certainly derived from Europe,[44] where the services were generally subject to political control, his lectures represented one of the earliest instances of the drift toward establishing the armed forces as a sacrosanct unit directly beneath the

[39] *Ibid.*, p. 15.   [40] *Ibid.*, p. 15.
[41] *Ibid.*, p. 15.   [42] *Ibid.*, pp. 16-17.
[43] See Ōkubo, "Nishi Amane no gunburon," p. 9.
[44] Nishi makes no reference in any of his military writings to European books, and it is impossible to know which works served as his sources. There were no Western military books in his library in 1897. His frequent use of the English terms "mechanism," "discipline," and "obedience" leaves no doubt that his ideas on military organization were inspired by Western practice.

throne, beyond the reach of politicians. Nishi hardly intended in *Heika tokkō* to promote military supremacy; he merely wished to establish the principle that strict military discipline, a prerequisite for modern warfare, required considerable deviation from civilian morality and customs. There is no evidence that he ever foresaw the likelihood that the civil and military orders could not exist side-by-side peacefully.

On the main topic of morality for army officers, Nishi maintains in his lectures that it is important for every military leader to set a good example in his personal conduct. Only by practicing upright behavior can an officer expect to obtain the cooperation of his men in battle. Hence, Nishi argues, the proper military ethic concerns the individual's responsibilities to his troops: "It is not so much a matter of duty arising from one's station [*meibun*] as an obligation complementing obedience. In short, it is the art of winning the faith of others."[45] Just as the rank and file are morally obliged to follow orders, their commanding officers should deport themselves in such a way as to gain their troops's confidence. However, Nishi adds, the officer should never exploit his skill at obtaining the trust of his men by making them his retainers, for this was an evil of the feudal period that would hinder modern military efficiency.[46]

Nishi thus specifically denied the concept of *meibun* that had been central to Confucian morality. The term meant that each person's ethical obligations were determined by his social position without relation to the realities of his occupation or means.[47] Nishi also attacked the custom of vassalage and the notion of *shujū kankei* upon which it was founded. In place of the feudal moral code, he sought to introduce norms of conduct for soldier and officer alike that turned on the new virtue of obedience.

A question that in Nishi's opinion is intimately related to military ethics is that of the general bearing or demeanor

---

[45] *Heika tokkō*, p. 10.　　　　[46] *Ibid.*, p. 10.
[47] Carmen Blacker, *The Japanese Enlightenment: A Study of the Writings of Fukuzawa Yukichi* (Cambridge, Eng., 1964), p. 70.

Civil and Military Society

(*fūshō*) of army officers.[48] By this he means the officer's personal deportment, which affects his troops and fellow officers and thus sets the tone and character of the entire army. Because this soldierly demeanor "differs in kind from such things as scholarship, arts and crafts, and law, it is not something to be copied from the West. . . . Demeanor is an intangible existing only within character, and it cannot be learned like a science or established and regulated like law."[49] The demeanor of the Japanese army, Nishi thinks, must be "based on Japan's characteristic nature."[50] He acknowledges that it is virtually impossible to describe a nation's character, but he cites a familiar poem by Motoori Norinaga, the National Learning scholar, as "probably the best label for the character of our people":

> Shikishima no Yamatogokoro o kowaba
> Asahi ni niou yamazakura hana.
>
> If you ask about the spirit of Japan,
> It is the fragrant flower of the wild cherry
> in the morning sun.[51]

Nishi then repeats his own analysis of the Japanese character that was first stated in "Kokumin kifūron" in 1875. Its two main attributes are "faithfulness" (*chūryō*) and "compliance" (*ichoku*). Faithfulness connotes loyalty to superiors, Nishi says, while "compliance means to be cooperative and submissive."[52] In ordinary society, he argued in 1875, these qualities must be reformed in order to bring an end to autocratic government. Otherwise, "when the people desire to establish a popularly elected assembly, the greatest hindrance will be this character."[53] In *Heika tokkō*, however, he maintains that "it is most advantageous for our army officers to promote these characteristics as the demeanor

[48] The term *fūshō* ordinarily conveys the idea of noble mien or honorable character, but inasmuch as Nishi speaks of both bad and good *fūshō*, the best rendering is "demeanor."
[49] *Heika tokkō*, p. 11.   [50] *Ibid.*, p. 12.
[51] *Ibid.*, p. 13.   [52] *Ibid.*, p. 13.
[53] "Kokumin kifūron," *MRZS*, 32 (March 1875); *MBZ*, xviii, p. 209.

for soldiers generally. These should be suitable qualities for soldiers."[54]

Obedience was clearly the keystone of the ethical code which Nishi recommended for the new Japanese army. It was an absolute requirement for the organizational structure of the armed forces that he helped to institute. He thought that the modern concept of strict discipline must be substituted for the feudal warrior code if mass armies were to work smoothly. While Nishi conceded the similarities in protective function between samurai and soldier, he argued that the ancient *bushi* morality was inadequate both because of the huge size of the new army and because it might promote the evil of feudalistic personal servitude within the ranks. Another reason for his emphasis on discipline was undoubtedly that Japan's new troops were mainly commoners for whom the aristocratic military code of the feudal warriors had little meaning. The new morality based on obedience was of such paramount importance that Nishi was willing to borrow in part from the Japanese past to reinforce it. He therefore constructed a synthesis of Western concepts of obedience and the native characteristics of faithfulness and compliance, with the purpose of establishing a modern, well-disciplined force. Nishi recognized this national character as a constant but not a *donnée*, in the same fashion as he treated the *kokutai*. He saw it as desirable (or intuitively divinable, as by the National Learning scholars) but not as impervious to change and direction. It was thus to the indigenous tradition (including Motoori Norinaga), not to Confucian loyalty patterns,[55] that Nishi turned for support of his thesis. Far from seeking to reestablish the dominance of feudal military society, he attempted to instill modern, pluralistic loyalties to both the emperor as commander-in-chief and each soldier's direct superiors.[56] In short, he insisted on different

[54] *Heika tokkō*, p. 13.
[55] For a view emphasizing Confucian loyalties, see Hackett, "Nishi Amane," p. 222.
[56] See Umetani, *Meiji zenki seijishi no kenkyū*, pp. 192-193, and Umetani, "Kindai Nihon guntai no seikaku keisei to Nishi Amane," *Jinbun gakuhō*, IV (February 1954), pp. 29-30.

standards from those he espoused for the ordinary public not because he sought to perpetuate illiberal ethics *per se* but in order to build a sound force to protect the normal pursuits of civil society. His primary goal was thus not to establish military supremacy but to insure peaceful domestic development via a secure external defense.

NISHI'S DRAFTS FOR YAMAGATA

Apart from the Conscription Act itself, the two most important documents in Meiji military history were the Admonition to Soldiers (*Gunjin kunkai*) of 1878 and the Imperial Rescript to Soldiers and Sailors (*Gunjin chokuyu*), promulgated on January 4, 1882.[57] The former, issued in Yamagata's name, contained rules for proper military conduct together with a reminder that the armed forces should cultivate certain distinctive virtues not expected of ordinary civilians. The latter was a ukase from the throne enunciating the concept of absolute loyalty on the part of soldiers and sailors to the emperor as supreme commander. It also reinforced the moral basis for military behavior expressed in *Gunjin kunkai*. These proclamations contained the final, public position of the Meiji government on the questions which Nishi had discussed in *Heifūron* and *Heika tokkō*. The imperial rescript, which was the more important of the two, had a particularly great effect both in indirectly enhancing military power within the new state and in nurturing the unique character of Japan's modern armed forces.[58]

[57] *Gunjin kunkai* was first published in *Naigai heiji shinbun* 166, in the fall of 1878. An abbreviated version appears in Umetani, *Meiji zenki seijishi no kenkyū*, pp. 170-171. It is also reprinted in vol. 2 of Tokutomi's biography of Yamagata, as is *Gunjin chokuyu*. The latter has been partially translated into English in *Sources of Japanese Tradition*, ed. Wm. T. de Bary (New York, 1958), pp. 705-707, although this version omits the most important paragraph. The full translation is contained in Arthur Tiedemann, *Modern Japan, a Brief History* (Princeton, 1955), pp. 107-112.

[58] The best study of these works is to be found in Umetani, *Meiji zenki seijishi no kenkyū*, pp. 163-240. See also Roger F. Hackett, "The Meiji Leaders and Modernization: The Case of Yamagata Aritomo," *Changing Japanese Attitudes Toward Modernization*, ed. Marius B. Jansen (Princeton, 1965), pp. 259-261.

Civil and Military Society

Nishi Amane was the principal author of both of these documents. In 1878, at Yamagata's request, he prepared the first draft of *Gunjin kunkai*, which with few emendations was adopted as the final version.[59] Two years later he drew up a proposal which became the basis for *Gunjin chokuyu*.[60] Both drafts, of course, were executed in the course of Nishi's official responsibilities and constitute less reliable sources for understanding his own thought than *Heifūron* and *Heika tokkō*. There are two steps to be taken in examining his manuscripts for the Admonition to Soldiers and the imperial rescript. The first is to determine the extent to which the ideas stated in his Enkikai lectures are incorporated in his drafts, and the second is to assess the degree of Nishi's influence in creating the moral basis of Japan's new army by comparing his manuscripts with the final, official versions of these two documents.

Gunjin kunkai was promulgated in response to the general belief within the Ministry of War that a code of military ethics was urgently needed to insure the loyalty of the government army. It was widely thought that the new conscript troops could have suppressed the Satsuma Rebellion with greater dispatch had they exhibited a higher degree of discipline and motivation.[61] The ill-fated mutiny in the Imperial Guard in 1878 added weight to the demand for moral regimentation. In short, the army had a splendid new organizational structure but lacked the proper spirit. Nishi, whose *Heika tokkō* lectures show that he shared in this consensus, was given the task of drafting a memorandum to be circulated to all army units outlining those qualities of spirit befitting the modern soldier. His text, known as *Gunjin kunkai sōkō* (Draft of Admonition to Soldiers), is divided into a

[59] Nishi's version is known as *Gunjin kunkai sōkō* and appears in *NAZS* 1966, pp. 97-108.

[60] His draft, entitled *Gunjin chokuyu sōkō*, appears in Umetani, *Meiji zenki seijishi no kenkyū*, pp. 180-184. It is also included in *NAZS* 1966, pp. 109-113.

[61] Umetani, *Meiji zenki seijishi no kenkyū*, p. 170; Ōkubo Toshiaki, "'Chūsetsu' to iu kannen no seiritsu katei—'Gunjin chokuyu' o chūshin to shite," *Nihon rekishi*, 65 (October 1953), pp. 15-16.

preface, summarizing the proper martial virtues to be cultivated, and a list of seventeen specific rules for the troops.

Nishi states in his draft that the army is already well organized externally but needs a strong inner spirit as well. "To mention those things which sustain the soldierly spirit, they are none other than loyalty, bravery, and obedience [*chūjitsu, yūkan,* and *fukujū*]. . . ."[62] These qualities, he observes, are central to the spirit of all armies, not just in Japan but in the various countries of Europe and America as well. Loyalty and bravery are inborn characteristics which cannot be learned, Nishi reasons, and it is fortunate that the Japanese people have possessed them in rich abundance, in both the feudal and modern periods. He treats them as positive strengths bequeathed to the post-restoration era from centuries of clan warfare. Obedience, however, is an attribute which can and should be learned, because it is essential for building an army out of squads and companies, "just as mortar cements bricks into fine buildings."[63] Officers should demand obedience of their men, and ordinary footsoldiers should expect their superiors to teach it to them. Thus Nishi concludes that if the soldiers uphold the three virtues of loyalty, bravery, and obedience, "They will gain the trust and admiration of commoners. But if they violate these obligations, they will be rejected and the commoners will become angered."[64]

This preface to *Gunjin kunkai sōkō* reflects an outlook quite similar to that in the *Heika tokkō* series in several respects. There is strong emphasis in each on obedience as the keystone of modern military ethics, and there is considerable resemblance between the concepts of faithfulness (*chūryō*) in *Heika tokkō* and loyalty (*chūjitsu*) in the *Gunjin kunkai* draft. Furthermore, in each document Nishi stresses certain characteristics from the feudal past as desirable values for the modern soldier: faithfulness and compliance in *Heika tokkō*, loyalty and bravery in the *Sōkō*. In neither work does he urge a revival of the samurai code of values, and, indeed,

---

[62] *Gunjin kunkai sōkō,* p. 99.   [63] *Ibid.,* p. 101.
[64] *Ibid.,* p. 102.

those aspects of the feudal period ethics which he seeks to preserve are tied more closely to the national character as a whole than to the mores of the aristocratic elite. But far from advocating a peculiarly native set of values for the modern army, Nishi acknowledges in *Gunjin kunkai sōkō* that the elements of loyalty, bravery, and obedience are to be found in all good Western armies. Finally, there is the implication in both *Heika tokkō* and the *Sōkō* that the armed forces have an obligation to the public at large and that these attributes are not merely to be pursued for their own sakes. Of the principal topics in the preface to *Gunjin kunkai sōkō*, only the common martial virtue of bravery was not foreshadowed in the *Heika tokkō* lectures.

The seventeen rules of conduct in the main body of Nishi's draft establish a dichotomy between the civil and military orders and teach soldiers how to deal with ordinary society. In this respect the *Sōkō* is grounded upon the theory of separate societies expressed in *Heika tokkō*. The first few rules implement Nishi's insistence on discipline and embody his concept that the armed forces exist purely for defense. The ninth rule closely parallels his previous warning to soldiers not to join in the current parliamentary movement: "Conduct such as criticizing the imperial government or insulting and slandering the various regulations promulgated by the administration is contrary to the duty of soldiers. If one man does so, all will follow suit, and finally the spirit of scorning superiors will be born."[65]

Soldiers must not petition concerning political matters or write articles in magazines and newspapers. "In short, since soldiers accept the emperor as ruler and swear their loyalty to the court from the time they first stand in military ranks, no matter how faint their hearts they must not renounce this true purpose."[66] Unlike *Heika tokkō*, Nishi's draft does not explicitly state his belief that ordinary citizens should tenaciously cultivate the new goals of acquiring profit and protecting their individual rights, whereas soldiers should eschew these objectives. However, the contrast with the values of

[65] *Ibid.*, p. 104. [66] *Ibid.*, p. 104.

Civil and Military Society

civil society is patently implied in rule thirteen, which says that "soldiers should cherish taciturnity, calmness of demeanor, composure of action, frankness in their dealings, integrity in matters of food, drink, and wealth, and respect in handling instruments. These are all components of loyalty."[67] This moderation and restraint, so crucial for military discipline, were precisely those aspects of the national character which he had already said should be corrected among the common people.

Gunjin kunkai sōkō hence lays down regulations peculiar to military life, but it plainly renounces any suggestion that the army constitutes a special stratum superior to ordinary society. In four separate rules, Nishi takes great pains to warn the soldiers not to take an aloof or arrogant stance toward civil officials. One cautions all military personnel to show proper respect to any national or local official; another observes that since the feudal class structure has been abolished, soldiers must treat all officials, whether commoners or ex-nobles, with equal politeness. A third rule admonishes the troops to assist civil leaders in preserving peace and making investigations, within the limits of the law. A fourth instructs the soldiers to deal scrupulously with any matter pertaining to civil regulations and warns them not to scorn the business and commercial activity of normal citizens.[68]

The seventeen stipulations show that Nishi considered both civil and military societies responsible to the common imperial government administered by the Meiji oligarchy. Ordinary persons might properly question the state's policies, but soldiers must always accept its judgment. The result of Nishi's prescriptions was to establish the two orders as separate units under the government, with the military ultimately responsible to the general public interest in the sense that its main function was protective. In order to preserve the liberal climate of civil society, Nishi could justify illiberal but essentially modern modes of behavior for the military order. The key to Nishi's draft was the emphasis on obedience as he had previously formulated it in *Heika tokkō*,

[67] *Ibid.*, p. 106. [68] *Ibid.*, pp. 102-104.

which in turn was highly consistent with his earlier academic writings. Inasmuch as the final version of *Gunjin kunkai* that was published under Yamagata's name agrees fully with the ideas in Nishi's draft,[69] it is safe to credit him with the primary role in developing the code of military behavior in 1878. It is less surprising that *Gunjin kunkai sōkō* was in essential harmony with his previous scholarly thought than that a draft written by a *keimō* intellectual, rather than by a general or admiral, was incorporated with no significant change as the official code of conduct for the early Meiji army.

Nishi made a more modest contribution to the Imperial Rescript to Soldiers and Sailors, and it in turn is less representative of his personal convictions. *Gunjin chokuyu,* issued on January 4, 1882, constituted an imperial code of ethics for Japan's armed forces. Its principal feature was that for military personnel it elevated such qualities as loyalty, bravery, fidelity, and frugality to the status of sacred obligations to the throne. The main impetus to issue the rescript derived from intricate readjustments of power in the upper political echelons during 1880-1881. Ōkubo Toshimichi's assassination in May 1878 had brought about a realignment of the oligarchy, and the parliamentary movement came to a crescendo two years later with demands that an elective body be instituted without further delay. With the government experiencing considerable discomfiture at this juncture, the Rikugunshō seized the opportunity to enhance its influence in state affairs by manipulating the court into issuing the rescript, which in terms of prestige placed the military in a special position directly beneath imperial authority, beyond political control.[70]

Nishi's draft of this document, entitled *Gunjin chokuyu sōkō*, was written for Yamagata in the autumn of 1880. It was apparently the earliest of many versions of the rescript.[71] The first half of *Gunjin chokuyu sōkō* contains a summary of official court history, emphasizing the new national unity

---

[69] See Umetani, *Meiji zenki seijishi no kenkyū*, p. 176.

[70] See *ibid.*, pp. 178-179.

[71] Tokutomi, *Kōshaku Yamagata Aritomo den*, II, p. 810.

under the Meiji Emperor. The balance of the draft is devoted to a set of rules of behavior for the soldiers and sailors, divided into four sections. The first and most important stresses Nishi's familiar theme, obedience: "The first requirement of the soldierly spirit is that the hierarchy [*chitsujo*] must not be disturbed."[72] Nishi offers practically the same explanation of this concept as in *Heika tokkō* and *Gunjin kunkai sōkō*. The second rule extols fearlessness (*tan'yū*) and courage (*yūki*),[73] which are virtually synonymous with bravery (*yūkan*) as set forth in his draft of *Gunjin kunkai*. The third calls for forthrightness and frugality, admonishing military personnel not to seek private gain. This rule similarly conforms to Nishi's earlier ideas. The final stipulation asserts the importance of fidelity or loyalty (*shingi*), by which he means scrupulousness in carrying out promises.[74] It is in this sense that he used the terms faithfulness and loyalty (*chūryō* and *chūjitsu*) in all of his previous military writings. Thus there is very little difference between the ethical code proposed in *Gunjin chokuyu sōkō* and those in *Heika tokkō* and *Gunjin kunkai sōkō*. The rules for moral conduct in Nishi's draft of the rescript are novel chiefly in that they were primarily directed toward the conscript soldier, whereas his previous texts contained numerous admonitions to officers as well.[75]

However, in two respects this document differs from the *Gunjin kunkai* draft, demonstrating the tightened control of Nishi's bureaucratic superiors over his military writings by 1880 and indicating the waning effect of his personal thought on Rikugunshō policy. First, *Gunjin chokuyu sōkō* does not preserve the *Gunjin kunkai* warnings that soldiers should deal politely with civil authorities. This omission was not a result of any change in his thought, because the same attitude toward civil-military relations appears in a constitutional plan which he prepared a year after *Gunjin chokuyu sōkō* was written. Second, Nishi's draft of the rescript contains the

[72] *Gunjin chokuyu sōkō*, p. 182.   [73] *Ibid.*, pp. 182-183.
[74] *Ibid.*, p. 183.
[75] Ōkubo, " 'Chūsetsu,' " pp. 16-17.

Civil and Military Society

tendentious discourse on imperial history, for which there is no precedent in his previous writings. It seems that whereas in 1878 Nishi's formulation of *Gunjin kunkai* became the official policy of the Ministry of War, by 1880 his ideas were sufficiently discredited that he was obliged to delete the negative caveats about respecting civil authority and to insert a slanted account of court history. Whatever we may think of Nishi's willingness to make these changes, that he did so is evidence not of a transformation in his personal philosophy but of his continuing ability to separate official duties from personal convictions.

Unlike his 1878 draft, Nishi's version of the rescript underwent extensive revision and as a consequence suffered a considerable change in emphasis. According to Yamagata's biographer, the manuscript was revised ten times, and Yamagata personally inscribed his changes in each version.[76] Others who helped to rework Nishi's text included Motoda Eifu (1818-1891), Fukuchi Gen'ichirō (1841-1906), and Inoue Kowashi (1843-1895), all of whom served as unofficial advisers to the Ministry of War. Although the final form of the rescript retained the format and style of Nishi's draft, the most significant alterations have been attributed to Inoue.[77] Chief among them was the insertion of the concept of absolute loyalty (*chūsetsu*) to the emperor as the first rule of military behavior. *Chūsetsu* meant an entirely new type of undivided adherence to the throne, differing in object and intensity from such familiar ideas of loyalty as *chūryō, chūjitsu,* and *shingi.*[78] The effect of this shift in emphasis was to deflect Nishi's primary stress on obedience and military hierarchy and to subsume the other values in his draft in support of total loyalty to the emperor. It was this imperial insistence on the absolute devotion of his servants in the army that soon led to the ascent of the military above politics.

---

[76] Tokutomi, *Kōshaku Yamagata Aritomo den,* II, p. 811.

[77] Matsushita, *Meiji gunseishi ronshū,* pp. 516-517; Umetani, *Meiji zenki seijishi no kenkyū,* pp. 198-210; Umetani, "Gunjin chokuyu no seiritsu to Nishi Amane no Kenpō sōan," *Shirin,* XXXVIII, 1 (January 1955), pp. 64-65.

[78] Ōkubo, " 'Chūsetsu,' " p. 16.

Civil and Military Society

It is quite clear that Nishi took no part in instituting this new concept, nor is there any indication that he ever used the word *chūsetsu* in this sense. The term appears once in *Gunjin chokuyu sōkō*, but there he uses it in the sense of harmonious relations between military superiors and inferiors.[79] In both *Heika tokkō* and *Gunjin kunkai sōkō*, Nishi included loyalty to the emperor as one of several components of obedience, but there is no evidence that he ever espoused the idea of absolute loyalty to the crown. Indeed, much more representative of his attitudes toward imperial authority was a moderate constitutional plan which he drew up in 1881 as the Rikugunshō entry in the contest to decide what form Japan's plunge into constitutionalism would take. Nishi's lengthy proposal, known as *Kenpō sōan* (Draft Constitution),[80] had no influence on the Meiji Constitution which was proclaimed in 1889, but its specific enumeration of the limits on imperial authority indicates that he regarded the emperor as something less than absolute sovereign.[81] He assigned legislative authority jointly to the court and a bicameral assembly, forbade active military officers to serve in the parliament, and provided for the same separation and mutual respect between the civil and military realms that he had advocated in *Heika tokkō* and *Gunjin kunkai sōkō*.

Nishi's military writings demonstrate that he played a major part in supplying the Meiji army with a new moral

[79] Umetani, "Kindai Nihon guntai," p. 36.

[80] *Kenpō sōan*, *NAZS* 1961, pp. 197-237. Cf. Terajima Munenori's remark in his *Jijoden* (Autobiography) in August 1882 concerning the fate of Nishi's draft: "I called on Yamagata, to ask whether a diet would in fact be helpful or harmful to the state. . . . I said that, ideally, scholars should investigate its suitability. Yamagata agreed with this and ordered Nishi Amane to retract [his draft]. On August 24, Nishi came and received orders to study a diet, but he said that there were no reference books. I then said that some should be sent from America. The next year several hundred volumes were sent from Washington, but I never heard whether they were studied or not." Quoted in Osatake, "Nishi Amane no jiseki," p. 13. Nishi's *Kenpō sōan* was thus disregarded after August 1882, and Yamagata ordered him to continue to study Western constitutionalism, which Nishi did from time to time until his stroke in 1885.

[81] See Umetani, *Meiji zenki seijishi no kenkyū*, pp. 203-204; Umetani, "Gunjin chokuyu," p. 67.

basis that was essentially modern, rational, and temperate. That he borrowed certain elements of the feudal tradition to support his arguments is no more surprising than his use of Soraigaku as a bridge between traditional thought and modern European philosophy. Just as his *keimō* thought marked time and grew increasingly obsolete after the Meiro-kusha era, his military ideas did not evolve beyond the attitudes expressed in the *Heika tokkō* lectures in 1878. From that date onward his opinions were increasingly disregarded within the Ministry of War, until the official version of *Gunjin chokuyu* transformed the ethical standards which he had proposed into an uncompromising doctrine of imperial supremacy and military privilege.

nine

Nishi and Modern Japan

The decline of the Meirokusha after 1875 coincided with the close of the creative phase of Nishi's scholarship. He by no means ceased investigating and writing about Western knowledge, but he published few really original works on academic topics between 1876 and his illness in November 1885.[1] He gave a number of speeches as president of the Tokyo Academy and overseer of the Tokyo Normal School, but most of his free time was devoted to translating a number of Western books on philosophy, psychology, and law. In 1877, for example, his translation of Mill's *Utilitarianism* was published under the title *Rigaku*.[2] He also translated works by the Amherst psychologist Joseph Haven and the German social scientists Ihering and Zimmermann.[3] He also wrote a great deal of poetry.[4]

It is difficult to write of Nishi's later years, because of the series of crippling illnesses he suffered during the final eleven years of his life. With characteristic prescience, he told a friend in 1880: "The important business of my career has

[1] Modern research has indicated that Nishi suffered a cerebral hemorrhage on November 15, 1885. He had repeated illnesses thereafter and did not go outdoors between May 1894 and his death at age sixty-eight on January 31, 1897. See "Nishi Amane," *Kindai bungaku kenkyū sōsho*, ed. Shōwa Joshi Daigaku (Tokyo, 1956), III, p. 118; Mori Ōgai, *Nishi Amane den*, *Ōgai zenshū* (Tokyo, 1923-1927), VII, pp. 190-197.

[2] *Rigaku* was published on May 18, 1877, in two volumes. The translation is entirely in *kanbun*. It is said that the abbot of Nishi Honganji, Suzuki Keijun, encouraged Nishi to make the translation. See Gino K. Piovesana, *Recent Japanese Philosophical Thought, 1862-1962, A Survey* (Tokyo, 1963), p. 17.

[3] Haven's *Mental Philosophy* was published in 1876 as *Shinrigaku*, and Ihering's *Der Kampf um's Recht* appeared as *Gakushi Ireishi kenri sōtōron* in 1882. The latter was translated at the request of Yamagata Aritomo. It is unclear which of Zimmermann's works were translated as *Seibutsu chōkigaku* and *Unka ijin* in the 1880's.

[4] Selections from Nishi's poetry appear in *NAZS* 1966, pp. 363-398.

already ended. . . . I merely want to relax in places like Shiba and Ueno Parks."[5] As he gradually assumed the position of an elder statesman, Nishi's accomplishments as scholar and bureaucrat received due public recognition. He served for six years as president of the Tokyo Academy and was a charter member of the Philosophical Society (Tetsugakkai), founded in 1884. He was appointed to the Council of Elders (Genrōin) in 1882, to the Kizokuin (House of Peers) in 1889 and to the peerage as a baron two days before his death on January 31, 1897.[6]

The life of Nishi Amane spanned a critical period in Japan's transition from feudalism to modernism. Nishi chanced to be born in 1829, on the eve of the abortive Tenpō reforms of 1830-1843 which for many historians represent the first overt challenge to the feudal Tokugawa system. His death in 1897 came shortly after Japan's resounding military victory over China, which to many observers was the first tangible sign that the modernizing efforts of the Meiji era had borne fruit. If Nishi's life span is emblematic of the changes that took place in nineteenth-century Japan, his own career serves to confirm the personal transformation that permitted him to drift from a setting that was thoroughly traditional to a milieu which was overwhelmingly modern.

Contemporary scholars usually acclaim Nishi for introducing the positivism of Auguste Comte and the utilitarianism of John Stuart Mill, as well as the thought of such lesser figures as Alexander Bain and Joseph Haven. For this reason, he is commonly regarded as the father of modern Japanese philosophy. Because his contributions to this discipline were the transmission of European ideologies and the invention of new academic terminology, rather than original thought systems of his own, Nishi did not found any new school of

[5] Quoted in Ōgai, *Nishi Amane den*, p. 188.
[6] See Piovesana, *Recent Japanese Philosophical Thought*, pp. 26-27. An entry in Nishi's diary for Feb. 21, 1884, confirms that he attended the first meeting of the Tetsugakkai. *Nikki, NAZS* 1966, p. 464. See also Ōgai, *Nishi Amane den*, p. 194.

Nishi and Modern Japan

Japanese philosophy. However, his influence is to be found in the works of Kiyono Tsutomu, who studied at the Numazu Military Academy and subsequently became one of Japan's foremost scholars of logic, and Ōnishi Hajime (1864-1900), a leader in introducing Western thought who ranks with Nishida Kitarō (1870-1945) as one of the two greatest philosophers of the later Meiji period.[7] Nishi's scholarly approaches are also reflected in the writings of Toyama Masakazu (1848-1900), his direct heir as the major translator and critic of European philosophical works in Japan.[8]

From the vantage point of the present, even more important peaks than philosophic transmission and verbal innovation stand out in Nishi's career. The uses to which he put Sorai—first as a stepping stone to positivism, later as a link with his past—remind us of the extraordinary flexibility of pre-modern Japanese thought and yield a glimpse of the tortuous processes by which men can attempt to reconcile tradition with change. Nishi's flight from his feudal clan and study in Leiden show the strength of his curiosity and the courage of his convictions about the West in a country whose isolation had only recently been forcibly ruptured.

Why it was that Nishi favored Mill's thought over Comte's, as revealed in *Hyakugaku renkan*, further elucidates the route by which Nishi evolved from a young Neo-Confucianist to a thoroughgoing utilitarian in the 1870's. In a scholarly sense, *Hyakuichi shinron* looms as the most elaborate and elegant of his writings (despite its colloquial style), inasmuch as it is a forceful articulation of the case for destroying Shushi epistemology—a vital step forward for Japanese scholarship. Nishi's creation in *Jinsei sanpōsetsu* of a morality that was fundamentally Western in character, justifying the pursuit of knowledge and private wealth, represents a useful contribution to the rationalization of economic and social life in the new Japan. Finally, as the first person to define the nature

---

[7] Funayama Shin'ichi, *Meiji tetsugakushi kenkyū* (Tokyo, 1959), p. 18. See also Piovesana, *Recent Japanese Philosophical Thought*, p. 47.
[8] Funayama, *Meiji tetsugakushi kenkyū*, p. 37.

of modern military society and its relation to civil society, Nishi played a significant part in helping to build Japan's armed forces without stepping out of character as a *keimō* intellectual.

As a scholar of philosophy, Nishi was far more progressive and much less inhibited by traditional thought systems than most critics would allow. To say that "Nishi was never among the most progressive Westernizers"[9] is to slight his manifold contributions to philosophy as a modern discipline in Japan, based squarely on European analytical methods, terminological categories, and concepts of social relevance. That he took a less liberal position on political matters in no way diminishes his stature as Japan's leading pioneer in modern, secular academic philosophy. It was precisely his ability to relate European ideologies to certain aspects of the native tradition, and the fact that he did not undergo the alienation from Japanese thought characteristic of such intellectuals as Baba Tatsui (1850-1888),[10] that insured the success of many of his efforts as a scholar of philosophy.

None of Nishi's later scholarly writings significantly altered the philosophical or political positions expressed in his best works during the first decade of the Meiji era. He seems to have marked time after 1877, choosing to restate the themes of the *bunmei kaika* period rather than moving on to new areas of knowledge. The remarkable consistency of outlook throughout Nishi's mature essays may perhaps be explained by the fact that he was intellectually removed from public affairs and felt no need to adjust his thought to changes in current events. From his scholarly standpoint, the broad requisites for Japanese society in 1868 still held true in the 1880's. Despite his insistence on practical analyses and applications, Nishi's indifference toward political action cost him a place in the public mind beside Fukuzawa as one of the most widely revered leaders of the Japanese "enlightenment."

[9] Piovesana, *Recent Japanese Philosophical Thought*, p. 17.
[10] See Eugene Soviak, "The Case of Baba Tatsui: Western Enlightenment, Social Change and the Early Meiji Intellectual," *Monumenta Nipponica*, XVIII, 1-4 (1963), pp. 191-235.

Nishi and Modern Japan

Nishi in his maturity exhibited the irrepressible admiration of the West that was both the hallmark of *keimō* thought and the major reason why it failed to survive the 1870's. Fastidious in his appraisal of the native tradition, Nishi was often indiscriminating to the point of fantasy in borrowing ideas from the West. As Japan entered the 1880's, Nishi was no less concerned with national questions than Fukuzawa or Katō, but the answers he gave contained no real advance from the positions he took in the Meirokusha era. Whereas most of the enlighteners became Spencerians, modern Confucianists, or nationalists after the first Meiji decade, Nishi remained a syncretist in a new age of specialists, still an apostle of *bunmei kaika* long after that concept had outlived its usefulness in Japan's intellectual world. By the 1880's it was apparent to most scholars that the nation could profit from more selectivity in emulating Europe than had been the case during the massive injections of Western culture ten years before, so that the "enlightenment" of Japan became less and less obviously Western and more and more neutrally modern. Although the essence of that modernism may have been less European than men such as Nishi hoped, it is apparent that Japan managed to domesticate certain Western values as well as techniques: the bureaucratic ethos along with the modern administrative system, representative rule as well as a Diet building, the spirit of empirical investigation together with new tools and equipment. The *keimō* writers were transitional in a chronological sense, but they were essentially modern in intellectual commitment, supplying a ten-year introduction to the new Western knowledge that was a crucial foundation for the specialization of the later Meiji years.

Biographical Notes

DATE MUNENARI (1818-1892), the lord of Uwajima, a *tozama* fief in Iyo province. Ordered into retirement by the *bakufu* in 1858, he became a key plotter of the restoration. After 1868 he held various government posts, serving as a judge, an adviser on foreign affairs, and a negotiator of treaties with China.

FUKUBA YOSHISHIZU (1831-1907), National Learning scholar. Born in Tsuwano, he studied under Ōkuni Takamasa and Hirata Kanetane and in 1863 was appointed to the Gakushūin. After 1868 he served in the Jingikan and 1876 was appointed to a committee to investigate a constitution. He later became a member of the Sangiin (1881), Genrōin (1885), and Kizokuin (1890).

FUKUCHI GEN'ICHIRŌ (1841-1906), political critic and scholar. Born in Nagasaki, he studied English and Dutch as a youth. In 1868 he began publishing a short-lived newspaper. Sent to the United States by Itō Hirobumi in 1870, he also accompanied the Iwakura mission to Europe in 1871-1873. Upon his return to Japan in 1874, he became head of the Tokyo *Nichi-nichi shinbun* for fourteen years. In later life he published several novels.

FUKUZAWA YUKICHI (1835-1901), scholar and critic. The son of a lower samurai in Nakatsu *han*, he studied Dutch as a young man and subsequently became a popularizer of Western knowledge. In 1858, on orders from his fief, he opened a school of Western learning in Edo. From 1860 to 1867, he served the *bakufu* as a translator and made three trips to the West on behalf of the state. In 1868 he founded Keiō Gijuku. A charter member of the Meiji Six Society, Fukuzawa was a liberal, a utilitarian, an advocate of popular rights, and a critic of feudal thought.

HIRATA KANETANE (1801-1882), National Learning scholar. The son of a samurai family in Niiya *han* in Iyo province, he became the adopted son of the famous National Learn-

Biographical Notes

ing spokesman Hirata Atsutane (1776-1843). He taught in Kyoto before the restoration and in Tokyo thereafter.

HITOTSUBASHI KEIKI (YOSHINOBU) (1837-1913), the last shogun. The son of Tokugawa Nariaki, he was adopted by the Hitotsubashi family and became shogun in 1866. After the restoration he retired to Shizuoka, briefly plotting an abortive counter-coup. Thereafter he was occasionally consulted by the new state on foreign relations. He was made a prince in 1902.

JOHANN JOSEPH HOFFMANN (1805-1878), Dutch Sinologist. A Leiden University professor of Chinese and Japanese, he served for a time as Siebold's assistant and worked for the Dutch East India Company briefly. He wrote a number of books on East Asian subjects.

INOUE KOWASHI (1844-1895), politician and viscount. Born to a Kumamoto samurai family, he studied in Europe during 1872 and later served in the Ministry of Justice. He assisted in diplomatic talks with China and was widely consulted on foreign policy. He helped to prepare several government proposals for a constitution and assisted in writing the *Education Rescript* of 1890. In 1893 he became minister of education in the second Iwakura cabinet.

ITAGAKI TAISUKE (1837-1919), politician. A Tosa samurai, he was a disciple of Yoshida Tōyō. In 1873 he quit his position in the Meiji oligarchy over the disputed Korean expedition and a year later petitioned for a parliamentary assembly. As a leader of the Freedom and Popular Rights movement, he was Japan's chief advocate of party government. He later served in various cabinets but retired from active politics in 1900.

IWAKURA TOMOMI (1825-1883), politician and prince. He led the movement in the 1860's to unite the court and *bakufu* as a compromise solution to the political crisis. He joined the 1867 coup d'etat of the Satsuma-Chōshū clique

224

Biographical Notes

and played a leading part in the Meiji oligarchy. He led the 1871-1873 mission to Europe and the U.S.

KAMEI KOREKANE (1822-1884) lord of Tsuwano, Meiji official and count. A close ally of Chōshū leaders during the 1860's, he held a prominent position in the Jingikan after 1868.

KANDA TAKAHIRA (KŌHEI) (1830-1898), scholar of the West, bureaucrat, and baron. Born in Gifu, he first studied Confucian learning before turning to Dutch. A professor at the Foreign Books Research Institute in the 1860's, he served the Meiji government as an expert on taxation. He was a member of the Meiji Six Society and translated a number of Western books.

KATŌ HIROYUKI (1836-1916), scholar of Western politics, bureaucrat, and count. Born in a samurai family in Izushi *han*, he studied Dutch and military science under Sakuma Shōzan and entered the Foreign Books Research Institute in 1860. He turned his interests to German political thought during the 1860's and after the restoration held influential positions in the Meiji bureaucracy. A charter member of the Meiji Six Society, he later served as president of Tokyo University and the Tokyo Academy.

MATSUDAIRA SHUNGAKU (YOSHINAGA) (1828-1890), lord of Fukui. A leading supporter of Hitotsubashi Keiki's successful attempt to become shogun in 1865-1866, he advocated the union of court and *bakufu* in the late Bakumatsu political crisis. He later held numerous posts in the Meiji regime.

MATSUOKA RINJIRŌ (1820-1908), scholar of the West. The son of a samurai family in Okayama, he learned Dutch and taught military science after the restoration. He later served on the staff of the Osaka and Tokyo Normal Schools and acted as an adviser to the Ministries of the Interior and War.

MITSUKURI GENPO (1798-1863), physician and scholar of the West. A doctor in Tsuyama *han*, he took charge of

225

Biographical Notes

Dutch language instruction at the Foreign Books Research Institute from its inception in 1856. From 1861 on he taught at the *bakufu* School of Medicine.

MITSUKURI RINSHŌ (1846-1897), legal expert and scholar of the West. Born in Tsuyama *han*, he was the grandson of Mitsukuri Genpo. He learned Dutch as a youth and later taught English at the Foreign Books Research Institute. He studied in France after the restoration and acted as chief of the Civil Code Compilation Bureau in the Meiji government. A charter Meiji Six Society member, he translated many Western legal works into Japanese.

MITSUKURI SHŪHEI (1825-1886), physician, educator, and scholar of the West. Born in Okayama, he became the adopted son of Mitsukuri Genpo and studied Dutch in Osaka and Edo. He served the *bakufu* as a translator after returning from a trip to Europe in 1865 and became a school official after the restoration. He was a charter member of the Meiji Six Society and later headed a museum of natural history.

MORI ARINORI (1847-1889), educator and cabinet officer. Born in Satsuma, he served the Meiji government as acting minister in the United States during 1870-1873 and founded the Meiji Six Society upon his return to Japan. He was minister of education in the late 1880's and was assassinated by an anti-intellectual fanatic on the day the Meiji Constitution was promulgated.

MORI ŌGAI (RINTARŌ) (1862-1922), novelist, critic, and physician. Born in Tsuwano, he was the son of a court doctor to Kamei Korekane. He learned Dutch and English as a child and studied under Nishi Amane at age ten. He later became surgeon-general of the Japanese army and ranks as one of the two or three greatest novelists of the Meiji era.

MOTODA EIFU (1818-1891), Confucian educator, imperial lecturer, and baron. Born in Kumamoto, he was influenced as a youth by the thought of Yokoi Shōnan and headed a school in Kyoto during the Bakumatsu era. In 1871 he was appointed to the Imperial Household Ministry by Ōkubo Toshimichi and became a lecturer to the Meiji Emperor. He had considerable influence on Meiji educational policies, stressing Confucianism.

NAGAMI YUTAKA (1839-1907), bureaucrat and journalist. Son of a Fukui samurai, he studied Confucian learning in Kyoto until 1868, when he learned English from Nishi Amane. He attended the Numazu Military Academy and the Ikueisha and later held various public offices.

NAKAHAMA MANJIRŌ (1828-1898), fisherman and translator. Born in Tosa, he was rescued at sea by an American ship and taken to the U.S. for ten years, during which time he studied in New England. Upon his return to Japan in 1852 he was put to work translating Western books for the *bakufu*, as well as serving as an interpreter and English instructor. He was known in the U.S. as John Man and John Mung.

NAKAMURA MASANAO (KEIU) (1832-1891), bureaucrat and scholar of the West. Son of a minor *bakufu* official, he learned English and was sent to Britain in 1866. After the restoration he became an official in the Ministry of Finance and was a charter member of the Meirokusha. He later taught at Tokyo University and helped to write the Monbushō draft of the *Education Rescript*. He translated a number of important Western books into Japanese.

NISHIMURA SHIGEKI (1828-1902), moralist, educator, and bureaucrat. Born in Sakura *han*, he studied under Sakuma Shōzan as a youth and soon mastered English. He served in the Ministry of Education and lectured the Meiji Emperor. He was a charter member of the Meiji Six Society and a leading Confucian scholar. He inspired a trend toward stressing a modern version of Confucian ethics in Japanese schools and government.

OGATA KŌAN (1810-1863), physician and educator. A lower samurai of Ashimori *han*, in Bitchū, he studied Dutch medicine in Osaka, Edo, and Nagasaki and in 1838 opened a school in Osaka to teach all branches of Western learning. He headed the *bakufu* School of Medicine during 1862-1863.

ŌKUNI TAKAMASA (1793-1871), National Learning scholar. A native of Tsuwano, he studied in Nagasaki in 1821. He wrote polemics against the foreigners after Perry's visit in 1853. After 1868 he held a post in the Jingikan.

C. W. OPZOOMER (1821-1892), a Dutch philosophy professor. A disciple of Comte and Mill, he was particularly partial to the teachings of Alexander Bain. He wrote extensively on philosophical positivism.

SHIMADA SABURŌ (1852-1923), politician and journalist. Born in Shizuoka, he became editor in chief of the Yokohama *Mainichi shinbun* in 1874. He supported the Freedom and Popular Rights movement and later held a seat in the Diet.

SUGI KŌJI (1828-1917), statistician, bureaucrat, and scholar of the West. He was born in Nagasaki and studied Dutch as a young man in Osaka and Edo. After 1868 he held office in the Minbushō and became a charter member of the Meiji Six Society. In 1879 he supervised Japan's first modern census. He later opened a school specializing in statistics.

SUGITA SEIKEI (1817-1859), physician and teacher. Born in Edo, he studied medicine and astronomy, serving as a *bakufu* translator as early as 1840. He taught at the Foreign Books Research Institute beginning in 1856.

TANAKA FUJIMARŌ (1845-1909), politician and viscount. The son of a samurai family in Owari *han*, he belonged to the Sonnō faction in the Bakumatsu period and entered the Ministry of Education in 1871 as a minor official. He accompanied the Iwakura mission, inspecting American and European school systems, and later became vice-minister of education. In the 1891 Matsukata cabinet, he served as minister of justice.

Biographical Notes

TERAJIMA MUNENORI (MATSUKI KŌAN) (1832-1893), diplomat and count. Born to a Satsuma samurai family, he learned Dutch as a young man and renounced his fief in a dispute over excluding foreigners in the Bakumatsu period. After two years' study in England in the mid-1860's, he taught at the Institute of Development, held responsible diplomatic posts after the restoration, and entered the Genrōin in his later years.

TEZUKA RITSUZŌ (1807-1865), Western language instructor. Born in Chōshū, he fled to Sakura *han* under pressure from exclusionists in his native fief who opposed his teaching foreign languages. He later taught Dutch and English in Edo and was a charter member of the Foreign Books Research Institute teaching staff.

TSUDA MAMICHI (SHINDŌ) (1829-1903), bureaucrat and scholar of Western law. Born to a samurai family in Tsuyama, he studied Western learning under Mitsukuri Genpo in 1850 and Sakuma Shōzan in 1851. He accompanied Nishi to Holland in 1862-1865, translated Western works on law upon his return, and entered the Ministry of Justice after the restoration. A charter Meirokusha member, he also held a post in the Ministry of War, served as a judge, and sat in the Diet.

SIMON VISSERING (1818-1888), Dutch economist and politician. Born in Amsterdam, he became a lawyer after graduating from Leiden University but soon returned to the university as an assistant to Thorbecke. He rose to the rank of professor, advocating classic liberalism and free trade. Later he served as minister of finance in Holland.

YAMAGATA ARITOMO (1838-1922), military leader, prime minister, prince. Born to a samurai family in Chōshū, he studied under Yoshida Shōin in Kyoto during 1858 and soon joined the Sonnō-jōi movement. After the restoration he rose to a position of great prestige and power in the Meiji government, acting successively as minister of war, prime minister, and Genrō.

229

Biographical Notes

YAMAMOTO KAKUMA (1828-1892), politician and educator. As a young man, he studied Western gunnery under Sakuma Shōzan and after the restoration headed the Tokyo Metropolitan Assembly and participated in founding Dōshisha University.

YANAGAWA SHUNZŌ (1832-1870), physician and scholar of the West. Born in Nagoya, he became a doctor in Wakayama and in 1864 joined the Institute of Development as a professor of Dutch. In 1867 he published Japan's first magazine, *Seiyō zasshi*, and he served briefly after the restoration as an examiner in the school system.

YANO KUROMICHI (1823-1887), National Learning scholar. Born in Aichi, he studied Kokugaku from Hirata Kanetane and after the restoration served in the Education Office of the new government. He wrote a number of nationalistic works and held various public offices during the early Meiji period.

List of Works Cited

I. *In Japanese*

A. COLLECTIONS

MBZ   Meiji bunka zenshū, ed. Yoshino Sakuzō, 24 vols. (Tokyo, 1927-1930).

NAZS 1945   *Nishi Amane zenshū,* ed. Ōkubo Toshiaki (Tokyo, 1945).

NAZS 1960   *Nishi Amane zenshū,* cd. Ōkubo Toshiaki, I (Tokyo, 1960).

NAZS 1961   *Nishi Amane zenshū,* ed. Ōkubo Toshiaki, II (Tokyo, 1961).

NAZS 1966   *Nishi Amane zenshū,* ed. Ōkubo Toshiaki, III (Tokyo, 1966).

Nishi Amane tetsugaku chosakushū, ed. Asō Yoshiteru (Tokyo, 1933).

Nishi Masuko kankei shiryō (Tokyo, 1966).

Nishi sensei ronshū (Tokyo, 1880).

B. WRITINGS BY NISHI AMANE

A complete bibliography of Nishi's manuscripts may be found at the rear of *NAZS* 1966, pp. 115-130. The four volumes of *NAZS* contain every work of historical significance by Nishi.

The abbreviation *MRZS* is used below for *Meiroku zasshi,* the journal of the Meiji Six Society, which appears in *MBZ,* XVIII, pp. 51-267.

1. Original Works

"Aitekiron," *MRZS* 16 (September 1874), *MBZ,* XVIII, p. 136.

Bankoku kōhō (1866), *NAZS* 1961, pp. 3-102.

Chichi keimō (1874), *NAZS* 1960, pp. 390-450.

Chōsen seitō sōtoku e no chokugo sōan (1876), *NAZS* 1966, pp. 119-122.

Fukubōshisho (1870), *NAZS* 1960, pp. 291-308.

List of Works Cited

Gakumon wa engen o fukakusuru ni aru no ron (1877), *NAZS* 1960, pp. 568-573.
Gidai sōan (1867), *NAZS* 1961, pp. 167-183.
Goka gakushū kankei bunsho (1863-1865), *NAZS* 1961, pp. 134-135.
Gunjin chokuyu sōkō (1880), quoted in Umetani Noboru, *Meiji zenki seijishi no kenkyū* (Tokyo, 1963), pp. 180-184.
Gunjin kunkai sōkō (1878), *NAZS* 1966, pp. 97-108.
Gunritsu sōkō hihyō (1872), *NAZS* 1966, pp. 144-147.
"Hakkyū sōkōgi ichidai" (1874), *NAZS* 1961, pp. 238-241.
Heifūron (1878-1881), *NAZS* 1966, pp. 18-96.
Heika tokkō (1878), *NAZS* 1966, pp. 3-17.
"Higakusha shokubunron," *MRZS*, 2 (February 1874), *MBZ*, XVIII, pp. 60-61.
"Himitsu setsu," *MRZS*, 19 (October 1874), *MBZ*, XVIII, pp. 147-148.
Hyakugaku renkan (1870-1871), *NAZS* 1945, pp. 3-562.
Hyakuichi shinron (1874), *NAZS* 1960, pp. 232-289.
Ikueisha nori (1870), *NAZS* 1961, pp. 509-515.
Jinsei sanpōsetsu (1875), *NAZS* 1960, pp. 514-554.
Jōrinpō heibi ryakuhyō (1875?), *NAZS* 1966, pp. 128-143.
"Kaikanzei no setsu" (1875), *NAZS* 1961, pp. 412-419.
Kenpō sōan (1881), *NAZS* 1961, pp. 197-237.
Kihei goei no kaijo no kou jōsōbun'an (daisaku) (1873-1875), *NAZS* 1966, pp. 151-152.
Kōfuku wa seireijō to keikaijō to sōgōsurujō ni naru no ron (ca. 1873), *NAZS* 1960, pp. 555-567.
"Kokumin kifūron," *MRZS*, 32 (March 1875), *MBZ*, XVIII, pp. 207-209.
Kyōmonron (1874), *NAZS* 1960, pp. 493-513.
"Mōra giin no setsu" (1875), *NAZS* 1961, pp. 242-245.
"Naichi ryokō," *MRZS*, 23 (December 1874), *MBZ*, XVIII, pp. 166-169.
Nikki (1883-1884), *NAZS* 1966, pp. 437-488.
Oran kikō (1862), *NAZS* 1966, pp. 339-357.
Seihōsetsu. See Kanda Takahira, *Seihō ryaku*, below.
Seisei hatsuun (1873), *NAZS* 1960, pp. 29-129.

List of Works Cited

Seiyō tetsugaku ni taisuru kanshin o nobeta Matsuoka Rinji-rōate no shokan (June 12, 1862), quoted in Mori Ōgai, *Nishi Amane den, Ōgai zenshū* (Tokyo, 1923-1927), VII, p. 152.

Seiyō tetsugakushi no kōan danpen (1862), NAZS 1960, pp. 16-17.

Shakaitōron no setsu (ca. 1877), NAZS 1961, pp. 420-432.

Shiki (1867), quoted in Mori Ōgai, *Nishi Amane den, Ōgai zenshū* (Tokyo, 1923-1927), VII, p. 165.

Shōhaku sakki (1871-1872), NAZS 1960, pp. 165-172.

Soraigaku ni taisuru shikō o nobeta bun (1848), NAZS 1960, pp. 3-6.

Taisei kansei setsuryaku (1867), NAZS 1961, pp. 184-196.

Tōei mondō (1870-1871), NAZS 1961, pp. 247-277.

Tokugawake heigakkō chōsho (1868), NAZS 1961, pp. 445-469.

Tokugawake Numazu gakkō tsuika chōsho (1869), NAZS 1961, pp. 470-476.

Tōshi jūgatsu sōkō (1857), quoted in Furuta Hikaru, "Nishi Amane, keimōki no tetsugakusha," *Asahi jyānaru*, IV, 16 (Apr. 22, 1962), p. 94.

"Yōgaku o motte kokugo o shosuru no ron" (1874), NAZS 1961, pp. 569-579.

2. Correspondence

Nishi to J. J. Hoffmann, 1863, quoted in Itazawa Takeo, *Nihon to Oranda* (Tokyo, 1956), pp. 166-167.

Nishi to Matsuoka Rinjirō, June 12, 1862, quoted in Mori Ōgai, *Nishi Amane den, Ōgai zenshū* (Tokyo, 1923-1927), VII, p. 152.

Nishi to Tsuda Mamichi, May 29, 1867, quoted in Tsuda Dōji, *Tsuda Mamichi* (Tokyo, 1940), p. 101.

3. Translations

Gakushi Ireishi kenri sōtōron (1882). Translation of Ihering's *Der Kampf um's Recht.*

Rigaku (1877), 2 vols. Translation of J. S. Mill's *Utilitarianism.*

List of Works Cited

Seibutsu chōkigaku (ca. 1885). Translation of a book by Zimmermann.

Shinrigaku (1876). Translation of Joseph Haven's *Mental Philosophy.*

Unka ijin (ca. 1885). Translation of a book by Zimmermann.

C. OTHER EARLY MEIJI WORKS

Fukuzawa Yukichi, *Gakumon no susume* (Tokyo, 1872).

―――, "Naichi ryokō no setsu o hakusu," *MRZS*, 26 (January 1875), *MBZ*, xviii, pp. 179-182.

Gokoku taishō heigo jisho, ed. Rikugunshō (Tokyo, 1881).

Imperial Rescript to Soldiers and Sailors, in Arthur Tiedemann, *Modern Japan, a Brief History* (Princeton, 1955), pp. 107-112.

Kanda Takahira, *Seihō ryaku* (1871), *NAZS* 1961, pp. 103-133.

Katō Hiroyuki, "Burunchurishi kokuhō hanron tekiyaku—minsen giin fukaritsu no ron," *MRZS*, 4 (February 1874), *MBZ*, xviii, pp. 69-70.

―――, "Fukuzawa sensei no ron ni kotau," *MRZS*, 2 (February 1874), *MBZ*, xviii, p. 58.

―――, *Kokutai shinron* (1874).

―――, *Tonarigusa* (1864).

Kodanshaku Nishi Amanekun isho mokuroku (MS, 1897).

Koyama Masataka, *Nikki*, quoted in Mori Ōgai, *Nishi Amane den, Ōgai zenshū* (Tokyo, 1923-1927), vii, p. 165.

Memorial for the Establishment of a Representative Assembly, in Arthur Tiedemann, *Modern Japan, a Brief History* (Princeton, 1955), pp. 100-105.

John Stuart Mill, *Daigi seitai*, tr. Nagamine Hideki (1875). Translation of *Representative Government.*

―――, *Jiyū no ri*, tr. Nakamura Masanao (1871). Translation of *Liberty.*

―――, *Keizai ron*, tr. Hayashi Shigeru and Suzuki Jūkō (1875). Translation of *Political Economy.*

Mori Arinori, "Minsen giin setsuritsu kengensho no hyō," *MRZS*, 3 (February 1874), *MBZ*, xviii, pp. 62-63.

List of Works Cited

Nishimura Shigeki, *Ōjiroku*, quoted in Tōyama Shigeki, "Meiroku zasshi," *Shisō*, 447 (September 1961), p. 117.

Tetsugaku jii, ed. Inoue Tetsujirō (1881).

"Toka shijuku ichiran," *Shinbun zasshi* (1871, sixth month), quoted in Kumashiro Shūryō, "Meirokusha zasshi kaidai," *MBZ*, xviii, pp. 3-7.

Tsuda Mamichi, "Gakusha shokubunron no hyō," *MRZS*, 2 (February 1874), *MBZ*, xviii, pp. 59-60.

————, *Hyōki teikō* (1874).

————, introduction to Mori Ōgai, *Nishi Amane den*, *Ōgai zenshū* (Tokyo, 1923-1927), vii, pp. 125-197, quoted in *Asō Yoshiteru, Kinsei Nihon tetsugakushi* (Tokyo, 1942), p. 66.

————, "Kaika o susumeru hōhō o ronzu," *MRZS*, 3 (February 1874), *MBZ*, xviii, pp. 65-66.

————, "Naichi ryokōron," *MRZS*, 24 (January 1875), *MBZ*, xviii, pp. 171-172.

————, *Nihon kokusō seido* (1867).

————, "Seiron," *MRZS*, 9 (April 1874), *MBZ*, xviii, pp. 102-103.

————, *Taisei kokuhōron* (1868).

D. BIOGRAPHY AND CRITICISM

Asai Kiyoshi, *Meiji rikken shisō ni okeru Eikokugikai seido no eikyō* (Tokyo, 1935).

Asō Yoshiteru, *Kinsei Nihon tetsugakushi* (Tokyo, 1942).

Funayama Shin'ichi, *Meiji tetsugakushi kenkyū* (Tokyo, 1959).

————, *Nihon no kannenronsha* (Tokyo, 1956).

Furuta Hikaru, "Nishi Amane, keimōki no tetsugakusha," *Asahi jyānaru*, iv, 16 (Apr. 22, 1962), pp. 92-97.

Hattori Shisō, *Meiji no shisō, Hattori zenshū*, vi (Tokyo, 1955).

Hayase Toshio, "Meiji shoki ni okeru Nihon shakaigaku zenshi—shakaigakusha to shite no Nishi Amane to Konto no jisshōshugi," *Ōkurayama ronshū*, 1 (June 1952), pp. 84-105.

List of Works Cited

Hayashi Takeji, "Bakumatsu no kaigai ryūgakusei no sei-kaku," *Rekishi kyōiku*, xv, 1 (January 1967), pp. 8-17.

――――, "Bakumatsu no kaigai ryūgakusei—sono ichi—Nihonjin no sokuseki o tazunete," *Nichibei fuōramu*, x, 1 (January 1964), pp. 31-45.

――――, "Bakumatsu no kaigai ryūgakusei—sono ni—Nihonjin no sokuseki o tazunete," *Nichibei fuōramu*, x, 2 (February 1964), pp. 79-93.

――――, "Bakumatsu no kaigai ryūgakusei—sono san—Nihonjin no sokuseki o tazunete," *Nichibei fuōramu*, x, 4 (April 1964), pp. 90-99.

――――, "Bakumatsu no kaigai ryūgakusei—sono shi—Satsuma ryūgakusei no baai," *Nichibei fuōramu*, x, 6 (June 1964), pp. 63-80.

――――, "Mori Arinori to nashonarizumu," *Nihon* (April 1965), pp. 80-86.

Hirota Masaki, "Nihon keimōshugi no chōraku—Fukuzawa Yukichi no henbō," *Shirin*, xLVII, 6 (November 1964), pp. 1-37.

Ienaga Saburō and Ino Kenji, "Kindai shisō no tanjō to zasetsu," *Kindai Nihon shisōshi kōza*, I (Tokyo, 1959), pp. 43-125.

Inada Masatsugu, *Meiji kenpō seiritsushi*, 2 vols. (Tokyo, 1960-1961).

Iwai Chūyū, *Nihon kindai shisō no seiritsu* (Tokyo, 1959).

Kano Masanao, "Fukuzawa Yukichi to Nishi Amane," *Kokubungaku*, VI, 11 (August 1961), pp. 84-88.

――――, "Bunmei kaikaron e no ichishikaku," *Nihon rekishi*, 228 (May 1967), pp. 54-57.

Kawahara Hiroshi, *Tenkanki no shisō—Nihon kindaika o megutte* (Tokyo, 1963).

Kazue Kyōichi, "Meiji jidai no shisō," *Nihon no rinri shisō-shi*, ed. Kazue Kyōichi (Tokyo, 1963), pp. 273-372.

――――, "Nihon kindai shisō no shodankai," *Kōza kindai shisō*, ed. Kaneko Musashi and Ōtsuka Hisao (Tokyo, 1959), IX, pp. 85-112.

――――, "Nishi Amane no shōgai to sono shisō," *Tetsugaku kaishi*, 9 (1958), pp. 1-25.

List of Works Cited

———, "Nishi Amane no shūgyō jidai," *Nihon oyobi Nihonjin*, 1,428 (April 1964), pp. 42-51.

——— and Sagara Tōru, *Nihon no rinri* (Tokyo, 1959).

Kumashiro Shūryō, "Meirokusha zasshi kaidai," *MBZ*, xviii, pp. 3-7.

Kuwaki Gen'yoku, "Kaisetsu," *NAZS* 1945, pp. 65-75.

———, *Meiji no tetsugakkai* (Tokyo, 1943).

———, *Nishi Amane no Hyakuichi shinron* (Tokyo, 1940).

Maruyama Masao, *Nihon seiji shisōshi kenkyū* (Tokyo, 1952).

Masada Ken'ichirō, "Meiji shoki ni okeru kindaika no shorinen," *Shakai kagaku tōkyū*, x, 1 (September 1964), pp. 51-70.

Matsushita Yoshio, *Meiji gunsei ronshū*, 2 vols. (rev. ed., Tokyo, 1956).

Minamoto Ryōen, "Meiji ishin to jitsugaku shisō," *Meiji ishinshi no mondaiten*, ed. Sakata Yoshio (Tokyo, 1962), pp. 35-118.

Miyagawa Tōru, *Kindai Nihon no tetsugaku* (supplemental ed., Tokyo, 1962).

———, *Kindai Nihon shisō no kōzō* (Tokyo, 1956).

———, "Meiroku zasshi to minsen giin mondai," *Kindai Nihon shisōshi*, ed. Tōyama Shigeki *et al.* (Tokyo, 1956-1957), i, pp. 60-88.

———, "Nihon no keimō shisō," *Kōza kindai shisō*, ed. Kaneko Musashi and Ōtsuka Hisao (Tokyo, 1959), ix, pp. 113-147.

Miyagi Kimiko, " 'Wakon yōsai'—Nihon no kindaika ni okeru rinriteki shutai no kanōsei to genjitsu," *Nihonshi kenkyū*, 72 (May 1964), pp. 38-61.

Mori Ōgai, *Nishi Amane den, Ōgai zenshū* (Tokyo, 1923-1927), vii, pp. 125-197.

Morita Yasuo, "Meirokusha ron," *Rekishigaku kenkyū*, 254 (June 1961), pp. 39-43.

Murakami Toshiharu, "Meiji no seishinteki shichū," *Dōtoku to kyōiku*, 125 (October 1968), pp. 14-20.

———, "Nihon kindaika no katei ni okeru ten no kannen,"

List of Works Cited

Kenkyū ronbunshū, ed. Bunkakei Gakkai Rengō, XVII (1966), pp. 9-23.

——, "Nishi Amane no shisō ni taisuru Soraigaku no eikyō," *Kyōto Gakugei Daigaku kiyō*, series A, 25 (October 1964), pp. 111-117.

Nihon Gakushiin hachijūnenshi, ed. Nihon Gakushiin, 4 vols. (Tokyo, 1962).

Nihon kindaishi jiten, ed. Kyōto Daigaku Bungakubu Kokushi Kenkyūshitsu (Tokyo, 1958).

Nihon shihonshugi hattatsushi kōza, 7 vols. (Tokyo, 1932-1933).

Nihonshi jiten, ed. Kyōto Daigaku Bungakubu Kokushi Kenkyūshitsu (rev. ed., Tokyo, 1963).

Nihon shisōshi gairon, ed. Ishida Ichirō (Tokyo, 1963).

"Nishi Amane," *Kindai bungaku kenkyū sōsho*, ed. Shōwa Joshi Daigaku (Tokyo, 1956), III, pp. 107-145.

Nishida Taketoshi, "Meiroku zasshi-Hōdan zasshi," *Bungaku*, XXIII, 1 (January 1955), pp. 23-27.

Numata Jirō, *Bakumatsu yōgakushi* (Tokyo, 1952).

——, *Yōgaku denrai no rekishi* (Tokyo, 1960).

——, "Yōgaku to sono henshitsu," *Meiji ishinshi kenkyū kōza*, II (Tokyo, 1958), pp. 249-261.

Ōi Sei, *Nihon kindai shisō no ronri* (Tokyo, 1958).

Ōkubo Toshiaki, "Bunmei kaika," *Iwanami kōza Nihon rekishi* (Tokyo, 1961-1963), XV, pp. 251-286.

——, " 'Chūsetsu' to iu kannen no seiritsu—'Gunjin chokuyu' o chūshin to shite," *Nihon rekishi* 65 (October 1953), pp. 14-21.

——, "Kaisetsu," *NAZS* 1945, pp. 17-51.

——, "Kaisetsu," *NAZS* 1960, pp. 607-677.

——, "Kaisetsu," *NAZS* 1961, pp. 683-770.

——, "Kaisetsu," *NAZS* 1966, pp. 3-114.

——, "Kindai kokka no keisei," *Nihonshi* (*Sekai kakkokushi*, XIV), ed. Sakamoto Tarō (Tokyo, 1958), pp. 421-482.

——, "Meirokusha no kaisan," *Nihon rekishi*, 91 (January 1956), pp. 46-48.

238

List of Works Cited

——, "Nishi Amane no gunburon," *Nihon rekishi*, 45 (February 1952), pp. 2-10.

——, "Nishi Amane no rekishikan," *Meijishi kenkyū sōsho*, series 2, vol. 4, *Kindai shisō no keisei*, ed. Meiji shiryō kenkyū renrakukai (Tokyo, 1956), pp. 241-282.

Ōno Torao, *Numazu heigakkō fuzoku shōgakkō* (Numazu, 1943).

——, *Numazu heigakkō to sono jinsai* (Shizuoka, 1939).

Osatake Takeshi, "Ishinmae ni okeru kenpō sōan," *Teikoku Gakushiin kiji* (July 25, 1942), pp. 327-356.

——, *Ishin zengo ni okeru rippō shisō* (rev. ed., Tokyo, 1948).

——, *Nihon kenseishi no kenkyū* (Tokyo, 1943).

——, "Nishi Amane no jiseki ni oite," *Kokushi Kaikokai kiyō* 44 (Feb. 15, 1944), pp. 1-29.

——, "Nishi Amane sensei," *Shin Nihon*, II, 5 (May 1939), pp. 99-109.

Rōnō.

Sagara Tōru, "Kindai shisō juyō no gakumonteki zentei," *Kōza kindai shisō*, ed. Kaneko Musashi and Ōtsuka Hisao (Tokyo, 1959), IX, pp. 63-84.

Satō Masanosuke, *Yōgakushi kenkyū josetsu* (Tokyo, 1964).

Sekai kyōiku hōten, Nihon kyōikuhen, Yamaga Sokō-Yoshida Shōin shū, ed. Murakami Toshiharu and Kumura Toshio (Tokyo, 1965).

Sekai jinmei jiten, tōyōhen (Tokyo, 1952).

Suzuki Yasuzō, "Nishi Amane no seiji-shakai shisō kaisetsu," *Meiji bunka no shin kenkyū*, ed. Osatake Takeshi (Tokyo, 1944), pp. 255-310.

Tokutomi Iichirō, *Kōshaku Yamagata Aritomo den*, 3 vols. (Tokyo, 1933).

Tōyama Shigeki, *Meiji ishin* (Tokyo, 1951).

——, "Meiroku zasshi," *Shisō* 447 (September 1961), pp. 117-128.

Tsuda Dōji, *Tsuda Mamichi* (Tokyo, 1940).

Umetani Noboru, "Gunjin chokuyu no seiritsu to Nishi Amane no Kenpō sōan," *Shirin*, XXXVIII, 1 (January 1955), pp. 62-73.

List of Works Cited

———, "Kindai Nihon guntai no seikaku keisei to Nishi Amane," *Jinbun gakuhō* (Kyoto), IV (February 1954), pp. 19-44.

———, *Meiji zenki seijishi no kenkyū* (Tokyo, 1963).

II. *In Western Languages*

David Abosch, "Katō Hiroyuki and the Introduction of German Political Thought in Japan: 1868-1883," Ph.D. dissertation in history, University of California (Berkeley, 1964).

George Akita, *Foundations of Constitutional Government in Modern Japan, 1868-1900* (Cambridge, Mass., 1967).

William G. Beasley, *The Modern History of Japan* (London, 1963).

Robert N. Bellah, *Tokugawa Religion: The Values of Pre-Industrial Japan* (Glencoe, Ill., 1957).

Carmen Blacker, *The Japanese Enlightenment: A Study of the Writings of Fukuzawa Yukichi* (Cambridge, Eng., 1964).

Hugh Borton, *Japan's Modern Century* (New York, 1955).

———, "Modern Japanese Economic Historians," *Historians of China and Japan*, ed. William G. Beasley and E. G. Pulleyblank (London, 1961), pp. 288-306.

C. R. Boxer, *Jan Compagnie in Japan, 1600-1817* (The Hague, 1936).

Richard T. Chang, "Fujita Tōko and Sakuma Shōzan: Bakumatsu Intellectuals and the West," Ph.D. dissertation in history, University of Michigan (Ann Arbor, 1964).

D. C. Charlton, *Positivist Thought in France During the Second Empire, 1852-1870* (Oxford, 1959).

Auguste Comte, *Cours de philosophie positive*, 6 vols. (Paris, 1830-1842).

Albert Craig, *Chōshū in the Meiji Restoration* (Cambridge, Mass., 1961).

———, "Fukuzawa Yukichi: The Philosophical Foundations of Meiji Nationalism," *Political Development in Modern Japan*, ed. Robert E. Ward (Princeton, 1968), pp. 99-148.

List of Works Cited

———, "Science and Confucianism in Tokugawa Japan," *Changing Japanese Attitudes Toward Modernization*, ed. Marius B. Jansen (Princeton, 1965), pp. 133-160.

William T. de Bary, "Some Common Tendencies in Neo-Confucianism," *Confucianism in Action*, ed. David S. Nivison and Arthur F. Wright (Stanford, 1959), pp. 25-49.

Walter Dening, "The Gakushi Kaiin," *Transactions of the Asiatic Society of Japan*, series 1, xv (1887), pp. 58-71.

Ronald P. Dore, *Education in Tokugawa Japan* (Berkeley and Los Angeles, 1965).

———, "The Thought of Men: The Thought of Society— The Educational Systems and Ideologies of the Tokugawa Period," *Asian Cultural Studies* 3 (October 1962), pp. 73-86.

David M. Earl, *Emperor and Nation in Japan: Political Thinkers of the Tokugawa Period* (Seattle, 1964).

Encyclopedia of Political Science (London, 1840).

John K. Fairbank, Edwin O. Reischauer, and Albert M. Craig, *A History of East Asian Civilization*, ii: *East Asia, the Modern Transformation* (Boston, 1965).

Galen N. Fisher, "Kumazawa Banzan, his Life and Ideas," *Transactions of the Asiatic Society of Japan*, series 2, 16 (1938), pp. 221-258.

Fukuzawa Yukichi, *The Autobiography of Fukuzawa Yukichi*, tr. Eiichi Kiyooka (Tokyo, 1960).

Roger F. Hackett, "The Meiji Leaders and Modernization: The Case of Yamagata Aritomo," *Changing Japanese Attitudes Toward Modernization*, ed. Marius B. Jansen (Princeton, 1965), pp. 243-273.

———, "The Military—Japan," *Political Modernization in Japan and Turkey*, ed. Robert E. Ward and Dankwart A. Rustow (Princeton, 1964), pp. 328-351.

———, "Nishi Amane—A Tokugawa-Meiji Bureaucrat," *Journal of Asian Studies*, xviii, 2 (February 1959), pp. 213-225.

John W. Hall, "The Confucian Teacher in Tokugawa Japan,"

List of Works Cited

Confucianism in Action, ed. David S. Nivison and Arthur
F. Wright (Stanford, 1959), pp. 269-301.

————, "Feudalism in Japan—A Reassessment," *Comparative Studies in Society and History, an International Quarterly,* v, 1 (October 1962), pp. 15-51.

R. K. Hall, *Shūshin: The Ethics of a Defeated Nation* (New York, 1949).

Mikiso Hane, "English Liberalism and the Japanese Enlightenment, 1868-1890," Ph.D. dissertation in history, Yale University (New Haven, 1957).

————, "Nationalism and the Decline of Liberalism in Meiji Japan," *Studies on Asia,* ed. R. K. Sakai, IV (1963), pp. 69-80.

I. C. Y. Hsü, *China's Entrance into the Family of Nations: The Diplomatic Phase, 1858-1880* (Cambridge, Mass., 1960).

Ishida Ichirō, "Tokugawa Feudal Society and Neo-Confucian Thought," *Philosophical Studies of Japan,* v (1964), pp. 1-37.

Marius B. Jansen, "Japanese Views of China During the Meiji Period," *Approaches to Modern Chinese History,* ed. Albert Feuerwerker *et al.* (Berkeley and Los Angeles, 1967), pp. 163-189.

————, "New Materials for the Intellectual History of Nineteenth-century Japan," *Harvard Journal of Asiatic Studies,* XX, 3-4 (December 1957), pp. 569-594.

————, *Sakamoto Ryōma and the Meiji Restoration* (Princeton, 1961).

————, "Tokugawa and Modern Japan," *Japan Quarterly,* XII, 1 (January-March 1965), pp. 27-38.

Japanese Thought in the Meiji Era, ed. Kōsaka Masaaki, tr. David Abosch (Tokyo, 1958).

John Stuart Mill's Philosophy of Scientific Method, ed. Ernest Nagel (New York, 1950).

Journal of Social and Political Ideas in Japan, II, 1 (April 1964).

Kaneko Hisakazu, *Manjirō, the Man Who Discovered America* (Boston, 1956).

List of Works Cited

George Henry Lewes, *The Biographical History of Philosophy, from Its Origins in Greece Down to the Present Day* (rev. ed., New York, 1857).

——, *Comte's Philosophy of the Sciences* (London, 1845).

Maruyama Masao, "Kaikoku—Opening of the Country," tr. Isono Fujiko (mimeo., 1958).

J. R. McEwan, *The Political Writings of Ogyū Sorai* (Cambridge, Eng., 1962).

——, "Some Aspects of the Confucianism of Ogyū Sorai," *Asia Major*, new ser., VIII, part 2 (1961), pp. 199-214.

James Mackintosh, *Dissertation on the Progress of Ethical Philosophy* (London, 1830).

John Stuart Mill, *An Examination of Sir William Hamilton's Philosophy* (London, 1865).

——, *Liberty* (1859), in *Utilitarianism, Liberty, and Representative Government*, ed. A. D. Lindsay (New York, 1951).

——, *Principles of Political Economy*, ed. W. J. Ashley (London, 1909).

——, *System of Logic* (London, 1843).

——, *Utilitarianism* (1863), in *Utilitarianism, Liberty, and Representative Government*, ed. A. D. Lindsay (New York, 1951).

Setsuko Miyoshi, "The Role of Kokugoku and Yogaku During the Tokugawa Period," Ph.D. dissertation in history, Georgetown University (Washington, 1965).

Iris W. Mueller, *John Stuart Mill and French Thought* (Urbana, 1956).

Muragaki Tanso, *Kokai Nikki; The Diary of the First Japanese Embassy to the United States of America* (Tokyo, 1958).

Gotaro Ogawa, *Conscription System in Japan* (New York, 1921).

Osaragi Jirō, *Homecoming*, tr. Brewster Horowitz (Rutland, Vt. and Tokyo, 1955).

William M. Osuga, "The Establishment of State Shintō and

List of Works Cited

the Buddhist Opposition," M.A. thesis in history, University of California (Berkeley, 1949).

Herbert Passin, "Modernization and the Japanese Intellectual: Some Comparative Observations," *Changing Japanese Attitudes Toward Modernization*, ed. Marius B. Jansen (Princeton, 1965), pp. 447-487.

Gino K. Piovesana, *Recent Japanese Philosophical Thought, 1862-1962, A Survey* (Tokyo, 1963).

Joseph Pittau, *Political Thought in Early Meiji Japan, 1868-1889* (Cambridge, Mass., 1967).

John Plamenatz, *The English Utilitarians* (Oxford, 1958).

Edwin O. Reischauer, "Japanese Feudalism," *Feudalism in History*, ed. Rushton Coulborn (Princeton, 1956), pp. 26-48.

Robert A. Scalapino, *Democracy and the Party Movement in Prewar Japan: The Failure of the First Attempt* (Berkeley and Los Angeles, 1953).

Benjamin Schwartz, *In Search of Wealth and Power: Yen Fu and the West* (Cambridge, Mass., 1964).

————, "Some Polarities in Confucian Thought," *Confucianism in Action*, ed. David S. Nivison and Arthur F. Wright (Stanford, 1959), pp. 50-62.

Select Documents on Japanese Foreign Policy, 1853-1868, ed. William G. Beasley (London, 1955).

Donald H. Shively, "Nishimura Shigeki: A Confucian View of Modernization," *Changing Japanese Attitudes Toward Modernization*, ed. Marius B. Jansen (Princeton, 1965), pp. 193-241.

Bernard S. Silberman, "Elite Transformation in the Meiji Restoration: The Upper Civil Service, 1868-1873," *Modern Japanese Leadership: Transition and Change*, ed. Bernard S. Silberman and Harry D. Harootunian (Tucson, 1966), pp. 233-259.

————, *Ministers of Modernization: Elite Mobility in the Meiji Restoration, 1868-1873* (Tucson, 1964).

Thomas C. Smith, "Japan's Aristocratic Revolution," *Yale Review*, L, 3 (Spring 1961), pp. 370-383.

List of Works Cited

Warren W. Smith, Jr., *Confucianism in Modern Japan: A Study of Conservatism in Japanese Intellectual History* (Tokyo, 1959).

Sources of Japanese Tradition, ed. William T. de Bary (New York, 1958).

Eugene Soviak, "The Case of Baba Tatsui: Western Enlightenment, Social Change and the Early Meiji Intellectual," *Monumenta Nipponica*, XVIII, 1-4 (1963), pp. 191-235.

J. J. Spae, *Itō Jinsai, a Philosopher, Educator, and Sinologist of the Tokugawa Period* (Peking, 1948).

Arthur Tiedemann, *Modern Japan, a Brief History* (Princeton, 1955).

Conrad Totman, *Politics in the Tokugawa Bakufu 1600-1843* (Cambridge, Mass., 1967).

Toshio G. Tsukahira, *Feudal Control in Tokugawa Japan: The Sankin Kōtai System* (Cambridge, Mass., 1966).

H. Van Straelen, *Yoshida Shōin, Forerunner of the Meiji Restoration, a Biographical Study* (Leiden, 1952).

Emily V. Warinner, *Voyager to Destiny; The Amazing Adventures of Manjirō, the Man Who Changed Worlds Twice* (Indianapolis, 1956).

Herschel Webb, "The Development of an Orthodox Attitude Toward the Imperial Institution in the Nineteenth Century," *Changing Japanese Attitudes Toward Modernization*, ed. Marius B. Jansen (Princeton, 1965), pp. 167-191.

————, *The Japanese Imperial Institution in the Tokugawa Period* (New York, 1968).

————, "What is the *Dai Nihon Shi?*" *Journal of Asian Studies*, XIX, 2 (February 1960), pp. 135-150.

George M. Wilson, "Kita Ikki's Theory of Revolution," *Journal of Asian Studies*, XXVI, 1 (November 1966), pp. 89-99.

Index

Index

Index

Index

Index

Index

Index